AIRC

Sovereign Entrepreneurs

Critical Indigeneities

J. Kēhaulani Kauanui and Jean M. O'Brien, *series editors*

Critical Indigeneities publishes pathbreaking scholarly books that center Indigeneity as a category of critical analysis, understand Indigenous sovereignty as ongoing and historically grounded, and attend to diverse forms of Indigenous cultural and political agency and expression. The series builds on the conceptual rigor, methodological innovation, and deep relevance that characterize the best work in the growing field of critical Indigenous studies.

Sovereign Entrepreneurs

Cherokee Small-Business Owners and the
Making of Economic Sovereignty

· ·

COURTNEY LEWIS

University of North Carolina Press   Chapel Hill

This book was published with the assistance of the Fred W. Morrison Fund of the University of North Carolina Press.

© 2019 The University of North Carolina Press
All rights reserved
Set in Charis by Westchester Publishing Services
Manufactured in the United States of America

The University of North Carolina Press has been a member of the Green Press Initiative since 2003.

Library of Congress Cataloging-in-Publication Data
Names: Lewis, Courtney, author.
Title: Sovereign entrepreneurs : Cherokee small-business owners and the
    making of economic sovereignty / Courtney Lewis.
Other titles: Critical indigeneities.
Description: Chapel Hill : University of North Carolina Press, [2019] | Series:
    Critical indigeneities | Includes bibliographical references and index.
Identifiers: LCCN 2018024858 | ISBN 9781469648583 (cloth : alk. paper) |
    ISBN 9781469648590 (pbk : alk. paper) | ISBN 9781469648606 (ebook)
Subjects: LCSH: Eastern Band of Cherokee Indians—Economic conditions. |
    Cherokee business enterprises—North Carolina—Cherokee Indian
    Reservation. | Small business—North Carolina—Cherokee Indian
    Reservation. | Entrepreneurship—North Carolina—Cherokee Indian
    Reservation. | Sovereignty—Economic aspects.
Classification: LCC E99.C5 L397 2019 | DDC 975.004/97557—dc23 LC record
    available at https://lccn.loc.gov/2018024858

Cover illustration: Wampum belt by Joseph Erb; background
by Eky Chan, © Adobe Stock.

For the three who were with me every day:
Dad, Christopher, and Dart

Contents

Figures, Graphs, and Maps

Figures

Graphs

Maps

Acknowledgments

This research would not have been transformed into a completed book without the considerable support of mentors, colleagues, friends, family, and the Eastern Band of Cherokee Indians community.

My goal to work with—and for—Native Nations was honed at the University of Michigan, where I first considered focusing specifically on Native Nation economic development. This focus was galvanized in a course taught by Frank Thompson on Marxist economics that opened my eyes to alternative ways of economic being, in both theory and practice. I am also grateful to the UM Native American Student Association, where I had the rare luxury of being surrounded and supported by many other American Indian students, whether in studies, socials, or protest.

During my graduate work at the University of North Carolina, I found a true home for my research interests. The challenges, questions, and abundance of encouragement from Meg Kassabaum, Rachana Rao Umsahankar, Georgina Drew, Malena Rousseau, Joe Wiltberger, Duane Esarey, Krystal D'Costa, and Jillian Johnson—which continues today—made PhD work exciting, even at eight in the morning. I am in awe of the outstanding scholarship and generosity of spirit of those who shared my passion for American Indian studies at UNC, beginning with Jean Dennison, Julie Reed, Rose Stremlau, and Dana Powell, whose support has never wavered.

I am indebted to those whose conversations, critiques, and personal works continually inspire me, and I thank all those who took time from their own work to help improve mine. Jessica Cattelino's seminal research is foundational to my own and her extensive feedback was indispensable to this book's development. Margaret Bender's guidance on the direction of this book was crucial. Among those whose support has also guided me are Malinda Maynor Lowery, Ben Frey, Jenny Tone-Pah-Hote, Keith Richotte, Karla Martin, Mikaela Adams, Sandra Hoeflich, Megan Goodwin, Elizabeth Hoover, Clint Carroll, Honor Keeler, Geoffrey Goodwin, Anitra Grisales, Em, Margot Weiss, Sarah Croucher, Patricia Hill, Bo Taylor, Lisa Lefler, Marcie Ferris, Bill Ferris, Kay McGowan, and Faye Givens. Many thanks, GV (Wado), also to Tom Belt and Brett Riggs for their countless conversations and enduring faith in me.

Without question, my mentor and friend Valerie Lambert has had the most influence on my work. The amount of time she spent reading and rereading drafts of papers, applications, and this manuscript seems immeasurable. Her wisdom guided me—then and now—through the shifting maze of academia while bringing out the best in my work. I was also extremely fortunate to have Michael Lambert as a mentor. He never failed to provide a new, innovative perspective that always deepened my research.

Jim Peacock grounded me in the foundations of anthropology while also helping me to set my sights on its future, including what it can, and should, be. Rudi Colloredo-Mansfeld's gracious support, many hours of work, and invaluable comments continue to influence all my work. Theda Perdue's frank, essential, and much-appreciated critique of my writing helped forge me as a scholar and an academic. I deeply cherish the serious discussions as well as the social times shared in her and Michael Green's home.

I am also grateful for my colleagues at the University of South Carolina in the Anthropology Department, Institute for Southern Studies, and Lancaster Native American Studies Program. I was welcomed into the rarest of worlds where collegiality, support, and friendship meet stimulating discussions, critique, and collaboration. Because of them, I look forward to faculty meetings. Further appreciation goes to those whose time and conversations helped with this work: Jennifer Reynolds, Sherina Feliciano-Santos, Sharon Dewitte, Marco Moskowitz, Kim Simmons, David Simmons, Drucilla Barker, Mindi Spencer, Bob Brinkmeyer, Brett Burgin, Stephen Chriswell, and Brooke Bauer. My thanks to each of you.

The research and writing of this book was supported by the National Science Foundation Graduate Research Fellowship Program, the Andrew W. Mellon Postdoctoral Fellowship Program at Wesleyan University (Center for the Americas), the Royster Society of Fellows Sequoyah Dissertation Fellowship program, the Cherokee Nation Education Corporation's Nell D. Brown Memorial Award and Mission Award, David McNelis Scholars of Tomorrow, a Lynn Reyer Award for Tribal Community Development, an Archie Green Occupational Folklife Graduate Fellowship, a Special Graduate School Doctoral Merit Assistantship, a North Carolina Native American Incentive Grant, and a University of South Carolina ASPIRE grant. I appreciate beyond measure the support I have received from these programs.

I am also grateful for the love and support of my parents. I have had the fortune of knowing that I wanted to follow in the footsteps of my father,

Ronald Lewis, as a professor, working with my Cherokee people, for American Indians, and in the service of indigenous rights. His work, our regular walks and conversations, a continual stream of (prereviewed) books, and his invaluable words of wisdom are behind all my successes. My mother, Jeannine Berg, instilled in me the foundations of feminist thought, an eye for editing, and a love for new adventures. They both continue to shape who I am.

My biggest debt of gratitude is to my husband, partner, and best friend in every sense of the word, Christopher Kaminski, who could not have known the roller coaster he was stepping onto when we met. We have weathered two graduate degrees, one postdoc, six moves, six cats (and seven rats!) so far—and he is still ready for the next adventure. Without his seemingly limitless support and love, genius insights, abundance of hugs (both in celebration and comfort), exceptional business acumen, boundless encouragement, and warm cups of green tea every morning, this work would not have been written.

A heartfelt note of appreciation goes to J. Kēhaulani Kauanui and Jeani O'Brien (series editors) and Mark Simpson-Vos (editor) of UNC Press, whose many hours of work and mentorship made this book possible. Their work in, and visions for, the field of indigenous studies continues to be a tremendous source of inspiration.

Finally, I would like to thank the enormous generosity of those small-business owners (ᏣᎳᏩ ᏗᏂᎣᏍᏛᎿᎵ ᏗᏝᏨ; Tsalagi digalvwisdanedi di-yohli), government officials, and friends whom I worked with on the Qualla Boundary, especially those who took time from their lives to contribute to this work. ᏍᎩ (Sgi): TJ Holland, Russ Seagle, Jason Lambert, Hope Huskey, Russ Townsend, and Robert Queen (ᏣᏣ, Gwa Gwa). A very special thank-you to Charla, Zena, Nancy, Bruce, Bruce Jr., Ron, Teresa, Joel, Pooh, Bethany, Natalie, Alice, Abe, Ernie, and those who wish to remain anonymous, all of whom allowed their voices to be foregrounded in this work. Although I could not include every story shared with me by small-business owners in this book, their keen insights and experiences thread through each page. The credit for this book's success belongs to them; as always, any missteps are my own.

Visit the Qualla Boundary. Support these small businesses.

Abbreviations in the Text

AIM	American Indian Movement
ANC	Alaska Native Corporations
BIA	Bureau of Indian Affairs
COC	Chamber of Commerce
CPF	Cherokee Preservation Foundation
EBCI	Eastern Band of Cherokee Indians (government)
GAI	Guaranteed Annual Income
GEM	Global Entrepreneurship Monitor
GSMNP	Great Smoky Mountains National Park
IACA	Indian Arts and Crafts Act
IGRA	Indian Gaming Regulatory Act
IHS	Indian Health Service
KPEP	Kituwah Preservation and Education Program
NAGPRA	Native American Graves Protection and Repatriation Act
NLRB	National Labor Relations Board
REAL	Rural Entrepreneurship through Action Learning
TERO	Tribal Employment Rights Ordinance
UBI	Universal Basic Income

Sovereign Entrepreneurs

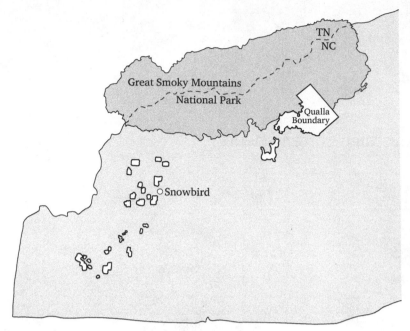

MAP 1 Map of the complete Qualla Boundary in western North Carolina. Design by Christopher Kaminski.

Introduction

· ·

The night was so cold that every breath cut into my lungs. I hustled across the parking lot, through a heavy snow flurry that signaled the very real possibility of a power outage for the weekend. Entering the crowded café (Tribal Grounds Coffee, the only coffeehouse in Cherokee, North Carolina, at that time), I shook off the snow and was immediately enveloped by the warm aroma of coffee and pastries. I had braved the weather that Friday to attend a Cherokee-language class led by a local high school student who had been working at the new children's Cherokee-language-immersion academy. He had his sights set on teaching at a college someday. This gathering was his first foray into formally teaching adults, though he had coached beginners, including me, for years.

I skimmed the café's menu, written in both English and Cherokee syllabary, and ordered an indigenously grown coffee. The beans were hand roasted by then-owner Natalie, an Eastern Band of Cherokee Indians (Eastern Band) citizen.[1] While I waited for my order, I chatted with Natalie about an open-mic night for locals that was planned for the following evening. I picked up my coffee and clung to it until my fingers regained warmth, then went into the room set aside for community events and meetings (figure I.1). The walls were covered with bright oil paintings created by a young contemporary Cherokee artist (primarily a wood sculptor), Joshua L. Adams. One piece that particularly struck me features the words "Learn or Die" above "ᎬᎤᏂᎠᏬᏯ Tsawonihisdi" in white block letters on a black background taking up two-thirds of the right-hand side; the left third is colorful, depicting a blue face with long black hair on a bright yellow background, overlooking the same syllabary laid out vertically in a graffiti style. This installment was, in the artist's words, "An attempt to establish an appealing relevance to the youth of the Eastern Band of Cherokee. . . . Our community must evolve. We must save that which makes us Cherokee."

A diverse group of students was already waiting for class to begin: one was a neighboring high school teacher who wanted to make the Cherokee language available to her students; another was a coffeehouse employee and Eastern Band citizen who was given the night off to attend class; and a

FIGURE I.1
Tribal Grounds Coffee cappuccino. Photo by author.

third was a retired woman, also Eastern Band, who wanted to become conversational in Cherokee so she could speak with her grandchild in the new language-immersion academy. "Osiyo! Osigwotsu? Osda, nihinaha?" (ᎣᏏᏲ! ᎣᏏᏊᏧ? ᎣᏍᏓ, ᏂᎯᎾ Ꭽ?)[2] could be heard throughout the coffeehouse in a repetitive chorus during our first meeting, which covered basic conversational greetings. While I sat down with everyone to practice, I considered how American Indian small businesses like this one—so vital for the economy and the exchange of language, art, and food—had yet to be fully centered in contemporary anthropological research and how much these dynamic enterprises can contribute to our understanding of political economy.[3] As this book will show, one of the most important strengths of small businesses that feeds this vitality is their collective diversity, found even in the midst of a (currently) one-industry-dominant economy.

Each reservation small-business owner specifically creates their business in response to their community, market, and personal interests, resulting in an enormous amount of variation across reservations. Small businesses also reach across the spectrum of Native Nation economic statuses, providing clear benefits in economic stability and growth for a wide variety of communities. Furthermore, owners' actions resonate beyond the economic, including participating in a range of community support activities, involvement in cultural reclamation efforts, and even shaping representations of their Native Nation. However, American Indians who want to start a small private business face unique obstacles in addition to the overall challenges of small-business ownership and, possibly, rural small-business ownership.[4] This book unpacks the layers of small-business complications specific to Native Nations and American Indian business owners while speaking to larger theoretical questions regarding the impact of small businesses in a global indigenous context. Debates regarding measures of autonomy, land status, economic identity, fluctuating relationships with settler-colonial society, and the growth of neoliberalism (along with its accompanying "structural adjustment" policies) meet with specific practices, such as the implementation of guaranteed annual incomes, cultural revitalization actions, environmental justice movements, and the potentially precarious choices of economic development—issues that are exacerbated during times of economic crisis.

It was by chance that my work on the Qualla Boundary was able to chronicle the shifting challenges small-business owners faced during the Great Recession, documenting the means by which these critical components of our worldwide economy survive as they buttress themselves against economic shocks. The contiguous core of my fieldwork took place over fourteen months of participant observation in 2009–10 (just after the initial economic crash), not including previous travels as well as subsequent years of return through the present. However, the impetus for my research topic emerged much earlier, from my own experiences as a small-business owner beginning in 2002 and as a Cherokee Nation (Oklahoma) citizen who was inspired by my Cherokee grandparents' small business in Muskogee, Oklahoma (Paul's Top Dog).

During this turbulent time on the Qualla Boundary, my research became focused on the innovative expressions of self-determination exercised by Eastern Band citizens through their small-business sector as well as this sector's delicate relationship with the EBCI's tourism industry and related gaming enterprises. This demonstration of indigenous agency through the lens of economic self-determination shows the ways in which small businesses help reduce economic precarity, thereby supporting their community's long-term economic stability. This subsequently explains how the EBCI and its citizens are able to contribute to a strengthening of their overall sovereignty through actions of what I term *economic sovereignty*.

This focus expands on much of the recent economic work done in American Indian studies. The 1987 founding of the Harvard Project on American Indian Economic Development galvanized a new wave of scholars from diverse disciplines to conduct comprehensive investigations into reservation economies. However, nearly all of this work has focused exclusively on large Native Nation–owned and operated businesses, such as factories and casinos. This book provides the research for a more complete understanding of Native Nation economies by detailing the crucial impact small businesses can have on reservations as they diversify, stimulate, and help sustain the robustness of their Native Nation's economy. I assert, as others have, that encouraging the diversity of small businesses can help support a Native Nation's long-term economic stability, but I demonstrate this uniquely through the eyes of the small-business owners themselves along with an in-depth examination of their local, national, and international contexts. In doing so, this work also addresses the ways in which Native Nations, by supporting small businesses, are responding in politically and socioeconomically meaningful ways to settler-colonial economic subjugations. Until now, lack of information about these small businesses has had a cascade effect, hindering our understanding of American Indian people as entrepreneurs and small-business owners and, thus, our overall understanding of reservation economies, which then narrows our understanding of sovereignty. I expand this knowledge by revealing how the boundaries within which Native Nations and American Indians must work—land, legal, and representational—affect these small businesses; how these boundaries are transformed; and how these transformations can truly alter the landscape of a Native Nation economically, politically, and sometimes even physically.

At its heart, *Sovereign Entrepreneurs* tells the provocative story of astute and experienced American Indian small-business owners through the personal experiences of contemporary Eastern Band citizens located on the Qualla Boundary (the reservation homeland of the EBCI, also known as "the Boundary"), challenging established conceptions of entrepreneurship and indigenous peoples as business owners.[5] This work follows the difficulties and the support networks that these "Indianpreneurs" and "Entreprenatives" encounter in their quest to remain successfully stable.[6] Their individual stories highlight the contextual distinctiveness and complexities of American Indian small-business owners. These include issues of American Indian citizenship and land ownership, including how these intersect with intergenerational business ownership. There are also the influences of Native Nation governments, which include the government's financial and business motivations as well as the support mechanisms they can offer to small-business owners located within, and even beyond, their jurisdictions.

Native Nation governments are increasingly turning their attention toward small businesses to bolster the ongoing and essential pursuit of economic stability. The issue of economic stability is inextricably linked with contestations over economic development (especially in the case of one-industry economies), the weathering of economic shocks, and the practices of economic sovereignty. As is the case for the EBCI's gaming and tourism success, a one-industry-dominant market may create wealth and economic power for a Native Nation, but it can simultaneously cause concern in terms of its inherent vulnerabilities. With or without the one-industry problem, the ability to weather economic shocks, like the Great Recession, is also of primary importance in the pursuit of sustainable economic stability. Consequently, it is this foundational issue of stability that helps to more broadly establish the importance of including small businesses in our discussions of Native Nation and indigenous sovereignty via the concept of economic sovereignty. However, while my central premise informs these larger discussions by arguing that the collective actions of small businesses reinforce indigenous economies and sovereignty, the foundation of all these broader topics remains the individual small-business owners who help empower these changes.

Many of these subjects coalesced while visiting two businesses on one afternoon midway through my fieldwork on the Qualla Boundary; both of these businesses, Cherokee by Design and Tribal Grounds, would experience many unexpected transformations in the following two years. In addition to attending occasional evening language classes at Tribal Grounds, I enjoyed stopping there in the afternoons, along with many others—the line to order was often several customers deep. As a regular, I had decided on that particular month to slowly work my way through the coffee menu, trying one new item each visit. On this day, I decided on a house-special cappuccino called the ᏎᏉᏯ,[7] or "the Sequoyah," so named after the famed creator of the Cherokee syllabary (as well as a distant relative of mine). Normally I would have lingered after picking up my order to chat with folks there, but today I took my drink to go and eagerly drove off. I weaved my way onto the crowded four-lane road in Cherokee's Cultural District to go visit Charla and Zena—Eastern Band citizens—at their store, Cherokee by Design. Their business began in 2007 as a small section of hand-painted ceramics in Charla's dad's nearby store, which was across the street and mere steps from the Harrah's Cherokee Casino and Hotel (known as "Cherokee Casino" or "the casino"). This familial arrangement of business integration and "incubating" before a separate launch is not unusual, as family-owned businesses in Cherokee are common. Frequently, the children of business owners start their own businesses using the legacy of knowledge, physical location, on-the-ground experience, and occasionally even capital to bolster the success of their own endeavors. Eventually, Charla and her business partner, Zena, were able to move into a vacant store space, also owned by Charla's dad. This location was farther down the main road and one street away from the Cherokee Casino entrance, though the lack of sidewalks severely reduced the number of walk-in customers from the casino.

For most of the Cherokee Casino's history, this area, even with its lack of sidewalks, would still have been a prime location in which to situate a small store, as most tourists would need to pass by it in order to park at the casino or to take a drive through the famous Great Smoky Mountains to Maggie Valley. The casino's overall impact on small businesses has been varied, though, with some tourist-oriented business owners relishing the increased numbers of visitors attracted to the Qualla Boundary (3.6 million in 2011). But other small businesses, such as hotels and restaurants, have been forced to compete with the casino, which has premium amenities and is the only location on the Qualla Boundary at the time of this writing that can legally sell beer, wine, and liquor.[8] Although Cherokee by Design was not directly in competition with the casino, the casino's newest phase of construction came at a price for the small store.

As I continued down Highway 19 toward the shop, my drive became a crawl—cars gridlocked, waiting to turn left into the casino's main entrance. At that time there was no traffic light in place to accommodate the steady stream of tourists coming from the now two-lane road. After finally passing the casino entrance, there was an eruption of noise and dust from jackhammers and heavy earth-moving machinery. On my left was the massive skeletal structure of a parking deck and a gaping hole beneath it; on my right was a temporary parking area in a field reserved for the construction workers. It was here that you could, if you looked hard enough, see a tidy sign, barely larger than the size of a piece of paper and nearly completely obscured by construction workers' trucks, that read "Cherokee by Design." Following the sign's arrow, I turned right down the paved but dirt-covered road and found a very small building tucked away from the highway (and, luckily, away from the rolling dust clouds), with a manicured lawn and garden. Inside, the store was no bigger than ten feet wide. Zena sat at a small table, carefully hand-painting ceramics, while Charla was nearly hidden in a curtained-off space in the back, barely wide enough for her computer and some supplies. Charla's difficulty in finding an appropriate space to lease for her business is unfortunately a typical problem for small-business owners on the Qualla Boundary who need a physical space in which to

FIGURE I.2
Cherokee by
Design—Charla
Crowe. Photo by
author.

operate. Cherokee's mountain location puts accessible land at a premium, keeping leasing prices high and affordable vacancies rare.

Charla and Zena (see figures I.2 and I.3) each had backgrounds in small-business ownership before this venture. Charla's family is famous for their Bigmeat pottery, and Zena owned a landscape design company. Both have easygoing personalities, laughing at themselves as they work long hours crafting their products, researching new designs, and taking orders from locals for the upcoming holidays. By 2009, Charla had won a Minority Enterprise Development Week Award, after working with the EBCI's Sequoyah Fund (an independent EBCI office offering business lending and training services) to prepare her business plan and taking the signature Indianpreneurship course, also offered through the EBCI government. These programs were popular throughout the Qualla Boundary, and many business owners I spoke with had used these government-sponsored services to bolster their own businesses.

Cherokee by Design was lined with shelves and packed with one of the most impressive arrays of unique and contemporary items found on the

FIGURE I.3
Cherokee by
Design—Zena
Wolfe. Photo by
author.

Qualla Boundary, including handmade and hand-painted ceramics covered in Eastern Band and Cherokee-specific designs, such as the Road to Soco basket-weave pattern, as well as the Cherokee language in phonetic and syllabary. A variety of non-ceramic items (iPhone skins, clocks, jewelry, wallets) were also covered with these patterns. All of Cherokee by Design's products, including the ceramics, are made with daily use in mind, as opposed to many of the Native-made and Eastern Band–made pottery-as-strictly-high-art items found in the upscale galleries around Cherokee. From the beginning, Charla and Zena's products were proof that these ceramics could also be contemporary pieces that anyone, especially Cherokee citizens, could own and use every day. This need was readily apparent, as Cherokee by Design quickly became a local favorite on the Qualla Boundary. Eastern Band citizens, as well as other businesses in the area that commission bulk orders, come back time and again to Charla and Zena because they sell products that are modern, inexpensive, and expressive in aspects of Eastern Band culture, especially in emphasizing the proliferation of the written language. As we discussed the choice of designs and products, Zena explained, "It just depends on what people's tastes are, because people want to preserve, and people always want a part of, the Cherokee culture. I'm flattered by that. I'm really flattered that people like our native culture, but at the same time, I'm more proud that . . . Charlie came up with this idea. Man, she's preserving. She's preserving our language, our heritage."

What makes Charla and Zena's business even more impressive is that it was launched as the Great Recession was just materializing. It then continued through those dismal economic times, changing location and participants (Zena has since branched off to start other businesses: The Flower Bug florist shop and The Hungry Wolf Deli and Fresh Market). Despite a crippling family illness, Cherokee by Design is still open today—accomplishing in staying power what many larger businesses globally could not. This resiliency in the face of adversity is reflected in many small businesses, whose numbers can grow in times of economic turmoil. The efforts of Charla and Zena in creating and sustaining Cherokee by Design illustrate many of the issues that American Indian business owners may face—from infrastructure to citizenship—in their quest to remain viable. The fate of Tribal Grounds coffeehouse would be much different, succumbing to financial collapse and loan default following the personal separation of the co-owners. The story of the shuttering of Tribal Grounds will later highlight the potential fragilities of even highly successful small-business ownership. It will also help illustrate the role of a Native Nation government as an economic-hybrid structure deeply involved in this sector—in this case, through small-business assistantship programs.

While the specific issues that these two visits highlight may be unique to the EBCI and its citizens, the overall challenges they represent exist on many reservations and in many indigenous communities, especially in relation to *economic precarity*—here defined as potential instability that can hamper a community's capacity to recover from economic shocks.[9] In this ethnography, I aim not just to expose various causes of this precarity but also to document the political and economic ramifications of this instability and the ways in which the EBCI has attempted to mitigate these issues. One proposal for reducing this precarity is to support small-business development and encouragement efforts, often enacted through Native Nation governments, as the EBCI has done. In examining these efforts, I use the cumulative economic successes achieved by the EBCI—in both private small businesses and EBCI enterprises—to address the larger geopolitical challenges that they and other Native Nations continue to face in the context of the federal government's economic and legal policies. I claim that small businesses help reduce this precarity, contributing to the sustainability of a community's long-term economy as they also support economic sovereignty. Small businesses accomplish this not only by providing economic diversity, enabled by their numbers and potential nimbleness of form, but also through their private ownership, relieving Native Nation governments from the possible burden of owning and managing multiple enterprises in addition to carrying out their political bureaucratic responsibilities.

The Resilience of Small Businesses

The Great Recession was in full swing by the time I moved to the mountains of western North Carolina in 2009. Although the core of my fieldwork spanned roughly fourteen months, I had been commuting to the Qualla Boundary intermittently for the years preceding (and since) that time, allowing me to see the changes that were taking place there and in the southern Appalachian region as a whole. Gas prices had soared to well over four dollars a gallon, and unemployment had grown to its highest rate since the Great Depression,[10] causing visitors to the mountains to slow to a trickle. The freeways became nearly empty, even on major travel holidays like Memorial Day and the Fourth of July. But poverty has never been a stranger to those living in the Appalachian Mountains,[11] and small-business owners had faced times like these before, either personally or through close family members who had carried their own businesses through similar periods, such as the 1973 OPEC oil crisis.

After the initial 2008 Lehman Brothers' corporate crash that accompanied the Great Recession, companies across the country began laying off their employees; U.S. employment plummeted from a 1999 high of nearly 65 percent to a 2009 low of almost 58 percent.[12] In Cherokee, however, one small-business owner, Abe, chose instead to go without a salary himself, sinking thousands of dollars into debt in order to keep his staff employed. He continued to buy artists' work, albeit in lesser quantities, so their families could eat. And he kept his stores open. This was no easy feat, and the decision was not made without anguish or anger, as he related to me.[13] To add salt to the wound, in 2009, two landslides blocked both major freeway access routes to North Carolina from the west, and a series of snowstorms blocked the section of the 441 Highway that traverses Great Smoky Mountains National Park into Tennessee (see map 2).[14] Even if travelers could bypass the landslides to reach Cherokee, the threat of unpredictable ice storms meant that there was no guarantee they would be able to return home that weekend. And in the midst of all of this, banks began refusing to loan money

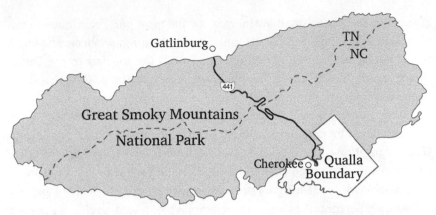

MAP 2 Regional map with central Qualla Boundary. Design by Christopher Kaminski.

to small businesses. Bank of America was one of the worst offenders, having taken "relief" money from the federal government but then refusing to make loans for under $50,000 to small businesses. Their behavior may have earned them class-action lawsuits, but that did nothing to help the small-business owners struggling to come out on the other side of a dismal year.[15]

Time and again, I heard stories from small-business owners concerning their trials trying to stay afloat through these years. Nancy Martin of the Long House Funeral Home relayed, "The problem with the economic stimulus package and everything is that none of that filtered down to us, not a dime."[16] Carl, a restaurant manager on Qualla Boundary, observed, "It is a tougher year because people aren't spending as much money as they have been. . . . Our customer loyalty—you might say, they're still here. It's just people are not spending as much money. . . . They're not buying the higher ticket items. They're splitting plates."[17] Darlene Waycaster, then head of the Cherokee Chamber of Commerce, reported, "Everybody's doing good this month, but the hotels have been down about 10 percent. . . . That, and the shopping. The shops, they're down. . . . And the restaurants are down. And that's the reason the cabins and the campgrounds are up, because you can cook out, or cook your meals in your cabin." And, finally, Joel Queen, a prominent Eastern Band artist, commented, "People think that we're becoming millionaires out here. We're not becoming millionaires. We struggle just like everybody else. Artwork is a very volatile market to be in because if the economy goes down, people don't have the money to invest much. If the economy's up, people will buy. It hit us last October, a year ago in October. [But] we made it a year in this economy."[18] This book chronicles how these small businesses, for the most part, continued to survive during this time, providing employment, training, services, and goods to the people within their communities and to the tourists to the Qualla Boundary, their collective actions helping to provide the EBCI with a stable base in a shaky economic world.

Although much academic and popular media attention has been given to the trends in monopolization, homogenization, and globalization of large U.S. corporations, small businesses (those with fewer than five hundred employees) represent 99.7 percent of U.S. employer firms—27.9 million in 2010 alone—while creating 64 percent of net new private-sector jobs, providing 49.2 percent of private-sector employment, and paying 44 percent of total U.S. private payroll.[19] In 2008, small businesses also created 46 percent of the nonfarm private gross domestic product (GDP). By 2012, 29 percent of businesses were majority-owned by minorities, representing 8 million businesses contributing $1.38 trillion in revenue and 7.2 million jobs to the U.S. economy. As reported by the Small Business Administration (SBA), between 2007 and 2012 (the years encompassing the Great Recession), "a net 2 million minority-owned businesses were created, while a net 1 million non-minority-owned businesses closed."[20] American Indian and Alaska Native peoples owned 272,919 small businesses, representing 1 percent of all U.S. businesses. This number represents an increasing trend, as seen in the ratio of population per business during that period, which decreased from 7.2 to 6.8 (i.e., one Native-owned business per every 6.8 Native people).[21]

Entrepreneurship is often studied separately from small-business activity, commonly defined as "any attempt at new business or new venture creation, such as self-employment, a new business organization, or the expansion of an existing business, by an individual, a team of individuals, or an established business," as measured by "total entrepreneurial activity."[22] In 2010, entrepreneurship was at 12 percent among working-age Americans (eighteen to sixty-four years of age) according to studies by the Global Entrepreneurship Monitor (GEM).[23] Although GEM has no American Indians represented in its studies, the SBA data regarding the increase in new American Indian business ownership is an indicator that their entrepreneurship is also on the rise.[24]

Research on American Indian citizen entrepreneurship, and specifically on small businesses, is critical not only because we have so little in-depth contemporary ethnographic research available but also because the collective action of these businesses helps to counter many of the pressing economic and related social issues facing Native Nations, such as inadequate tax revenues and high unemployment rates. Small businesses generate many direct economic benefits, including the multiplier effect,[25] increases in the tax base for the tribe, job creation and talent retention, and reservation-economy diversification that supports economic stability—an especially important factor for Native Nations whose economies are largely based on one industry. This *economic stability* means that the economy consistently and reliably has enough resources to provide for its citizenry, which, in turn, helps protect Native Nations from both cyclical and unpredictable exoge-nous, negative shocks. In addition to these economic contributions, a robust small-business sector can have many sociocultural benefits, such as quality-of-life increases (access to goods and a variety of jobs), the dismantling of economic stereotypes, and increased self-representation (in and beyond the tourism industry). Politically, small businesses also help strengthen prac-tices of Native Nation sovereignty.

Economic Sovereignty

Current discourses on Native Nation political sovereignty generally con-ceive of it as a form of autonomy that is enacted through a bundle of rights, directed by a central government authority, which at times lies in a "third space" of potential political ambiguity.[26] Comparatively, economic sov-ereignty, as I consider it throughout this book, is the ability of Native Nations to exercise their inherent authority through actions of economic self-determination. While economic self-determination is a more general concept referring to an individual's or a state's capacity for economic decision-making, *economic sovereignty* is a specific form of economic self-determination that focuses on state-level autonomy in crafting and implementing economic systems and directions.

The goals of economic sovereignty are (1) to establish and support a sus-tainably stable economy (i.e., an economy that is robust and resilient enough to consistently and reliably serve the needs of its citizenry) and (2) to pro-tect economic bases.[27] Economic sovereignty for Native Nations is expressed through actions such as the *management of funds*: who holds these funds (including debt), who manages and distributes them, who determines how—and how much—they are managed and distributed; choices in *economic development* efforts: what kinds of development are allowed, who makes these determinations, how these restrictions are implemented and by whom; choices in *economy management*: such as who and what is taxed, and who receives those funds; and *overlapping issues* of economic sovereignty and political sovereignty, as with negotiations of reduced sovereign immunity in order to attract certain businesses or investments to a reservation. In these considerations, we also see how the actions that federal and state governments take through policy and legislation to limit Native Nations' economic sovereignty are enacted in various forms (debt creation, fund mismanagement, taxation, finance regulation). Engaging theoretically with economic sovereignty, as distinct from political sovereignty, gives us a heuristic device that allows us to better expose the linkages in practices of political and economic structures at the state level.

Economic sovereignty also allows us to analyze the methods that Native Nations have used to mitigate the impact of strategic economic attacks levied by settler-colonial society both historically and contemporarily, specifically through acts of economic violence and economic hegemony.[28] While *economic violence* focuses on the destruction of a primary economic element, such as agricultural fields, water supplies, or factories, *economic hegemony* refers to actions and manipulations by the state (country or body of countries) that use economic means—such as the accumulation of debt and the manipulation of resources—to subjugate a country or people. One example of this economic hegemony is the U.S. government's mismanagement of Native Nation and American Indian funds. This mismanagement has been the target of multiple lawsuits, many successfully found in favor of Native Nations (e.g., *Cobell v. Salazar* and the Ramah Navajo Chapter Settlement, a class-action lawsuit in which the EBCI was included).[29] Together, these settler-colonial economic strategies attempt to suppress overall practices of Native Nation sovereignty and the associated development of a strong political presence in order to ultimately access Native Nation resources. They do so by creating numerous socioeconomic obstacles that then divert valuable human and financial resources away from Native Nations' political advocacy and practices at the state and federal levels. This book explores these strategies as they relate to practices of economic sovereignty both at a national level, such as through the Indian Gaming Regulatory Act (IGRA), and at a local level in regulation decisions, such as taxation rates.

Important to the conceptualization of economic sovereignty is that it can be vastly different from economic power. While economic sovereignty focuses on the ability to exercise autonomy in economic decision-making, economic power refers to a level of prosperity measured by the flow of profits and earnings, in addition to the overall economic impact a Native Nation's economy has on its surrounding state(s) and the United States as a whole.[30]

As Jessica Cattelino states, a certain amount of economic resources are necessary for exercising overall sovereignty.[31] With enough resources, a Native Nation can begin to exert some influence using this economic power, gaining leverage regionally, statewide, and federally. Cattelino warns of possible repercussions for those Native Nations whose economies grow to the point that they hold such economic power; this success can instigate an increase in the number and severity of attacks that settler-colonial society levies on them. As she notes, "Once [Native Nations] exercise economic power, the legitimacy of tribal sovereignty and citizenship is challenged in law, public culture, and everyday interactions within settler society."[32] These attacks aim to limit Native Nation sovereignty and reduce economic power, potentially exacerbating vulnerabilities leading to economic precarity. Economies in which one enterprise is dominant, as is the EBCI's current position, find themselves in an especially (although not singularly) precarious position. These types of economies are more likely to face challenges if they establish economic power and may also be more vulnerable to possible negative shocks due to their economy's lack of economic diversity.

These issues reveal that holding economic power does not equal exercising economic sovereignty; subsequently, Native Nations can hold a great amount of economic power while also being challenged in their ability to practice economic sovereignty. However, as this book will demonstrate, economic sovereignty can be supported not only by the Native Nation government but also individually. The economic stability that a robust small-business sector provides serves as a protective foundation, enabling Native Nations to expand their ability to exercise economic sovereignty. In other words, when a Native Nation government is not single-handedly shouldering the responsibility of creating revenue and adjusting to economic shocks, it has more resources and flexibility to practice its economic sovereignty in meaningful ways. This can include engaging in external financial negotiations with local, state, and federal entities, or strengthening internal financial structures by, for example, creating its own credit union or bank.

Through *Sovereign Entrepreneurs'* focus on small businesses, I endeavor to expand our conceptions of economic development. Within the field of contemporary American Indian studies, many leading-edge scholars—including Jessica Cattelino, Kirk Dombrowski, Valerie Lambert, and Stephen Cornell and Joseph Kalt—have focused specifically on the government-level efforts made by Native Nations to stabilize their economies. Although this has produced excellent work on Native Nation–owned enterprises in the areas of gaming and natural resource utilization, scholars examining contemporary transformations in Native Nation economies have not yet fully explored the importance of the long history and present-day practices of American Indian entrepreneurship and its role in creating and sustaining the political economy of these nations. Scholarship discussing general Native American business practices actively emerged in the late 2000s from the fields of business, leadership/management, and education;[33] because my research is ethnographically grounded, it complicates these discussions by revealing the key differences between, and nuances of, individual entrepreneurship practices by American Indians, specifically those of Eastern Band citizens. Although recent research trends have begun focusing on the individual's economic and political impact on Native Nations via wage labor and labor unions,[34] even the most contemporary works in indigenous studies have not fully addressed the central question of alternatives to, and nongovernmental support structures of, potentially problematic domination by single large enterprises. More specifically, the role of small businesses as a force to counter Native Nation economic precarity, and thus bolster practices of sovereignty, has not yet been given sole attention. Particularly in anthropology, there is little to no dedicated literature on the impact of small businesses on the economic development and practices of sovereignty on reservations, even though the broader social science literature emphasizes the importance of entrepreneurial activities to both of these endeavors. I demonstrate that our lack of information about small businesses has impeded understanding not only of American Indian people as entrepreneurs but also of the overall workings of reservation economies in times of crisis. Without this knowledge, we are left with an incomplete analysis, which ultimately contributes to ill-informed economic and political policy decisions at Native Nation and federal levels. This, in turn, continues the cycle of economic instability, monetary drain, and restricted expression of sovereignty for Native Nations. Focusing on small businesses allows us to engage with these issues while developing a more complete understanding of Native Nation economic and political systems.

Internationally, the timing of this project was especially relevant, as the continuing effects of the Great Recession took their toll on the stability of economic systems worldwide (see Graph 1)—the lingering effects of which are now compounded by more economic turmoil that erupted in 2016, making economic development and economic resiliency pressing global issues. Scholars across fields and disciplines have addressed the question of economic instability for indigenous peoples and other small communities,

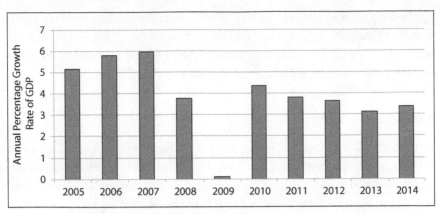

GRAPH 1 The World Bank Data Catalog. Annual percentage growth rate of GDP at market prices based on constant local currency. Aggregates are based on constant 2005 U.S. dollars. GDP is the sum of gross value added by all resident producers in the economy plus any product taxes and minus any subsidies not included in the value of the products. It is calculated without making deductions for depreciation of fabricated assets or for depletion and degradation of natural resources. Source: World Bank national accounts data and OECD National Accounts data files.

debating the merits of both globalized and local economic development projects. In *Sovereign Entrepreneurs*, I focus on Native Nations in the United States, but I do so using critical global-economic anthropological work (and, more specifically, entrepreneurial anthropological work) that encompasses the Americas more broadly. These works all address, to varying degrees, issues of border theory, authenticity, modernity, and the place of indigenous people in a globalized market.[35] In wider academic works, as the role of the local and individual in statewide economic development is addressed, the role of the private business in community development is also being explored internationally.[36] This global dialogue often seeks a means of stabilization with a focus on locally based solutions; *Sovereign Entrepreneurs* furthers this discussion with experiences and actions of Native Nations who have engaged these very issues—extensive unemployment, poverty, instability—throughout periods of their histories on reservations. My research, which demonstrates the stability that small businesses can provide for economies, may be applied directly to other communities in which one industry dominates the economy, leaving that community vulnerable and potentially powerless if that industry fails. These results, which foreground the importance of economic-sovereignty protections and practices, can be applied even more broadly, as they have extensive implications for small communities globally, providing these communities with another tool to use when planning the best means to support their citizens in creating a vibrant economy that can also sustain their community's goals.

The Road to Stability

This economic-development research joins the experiences of small-business owners, existing economic anthropology and related interdisciplinary literatures, and data on U.S. small businesses to build, throughout each chapter, a case for the importance of small businesses to the growth, stability, and sustainability of an economy. The EBCI nation boasts an unusually long history of incorporated, citizen-owned businesses on their reservation, with the rate of locally owned small business surpassing those of other communities in the region.[37] Ethnographically exploring the variety of small businesses on the Qualla Boundary through the lived experiences of generations of small-business owners thus provides a unique opportunity to study the recursive impact of small businesses on governance and economy. This includes the ways in which the small-business sector supports the Qualla Boundary, but it also contextualizes these small-business owners' experiences with discussions regarding the interventions of the EBCI government, as well as the effects of the EBCI's large governmental corporations (especially focusing on the casinos) on the small-business sector.

I begin this book by first framing the conceptual and logistic complexities of defining and understanding the attributes of indigenous and American Indian entrepreneurship, following this discourse as it unfolds in academia, in popular media, and within indigenous communities themselves. The presence—and even abundance, as is the case on the Qualla Boundary—of American Indian and indigenous small-business owners raises questions about the distinctiveness of their economic identity in relation to capitalism and neoliberalism, the essential characteristics of their entrepreneurial practices, their virtual absence in media (outside of gaming), and the lack of primacy they are given in discussions of economic development in the context of the United States. From the larger questions of defining indigenous entrepreneurship, I introduce the topics that will thread throughout this book, asking who the entrepreneurs on the Qualla Boundary are and what markets they are serving. This begins by focusing on family-business ownership, which features prominently in Cherokee, a town that has seen many generations of small-business owners. While there is much to be said regarding gender and business ownership in this context (discussed further in subsequent publications), it is interesting to note that, in Cherokee, family ownership concerns usually surpass those of gender. In other words, it is more important for a business to stay within a family than who (genderwise) owns the business. Consequently, it was relatively easy to find women small-business owners to speak with.[38] For Cherokee, the businesses here are also heavily shaped—both internally and externally— by the tourism market.

The Qualla Boundary economy has been built on this robust tourist industry, the focus of chapter 2, for much of its federally recognized history. Although there are many varieties of businesses on the Qualla Boundary, tourism has been a mainstay, exerting both subtle and overt influences on EBCI economic sovereignty. Recently, the local industry has gone through many changes, instigated by politicians, tourists, and Eastern Band citizens. These changes have raised important questions about who determines the nature of representation (e.g., of cultures or identities), especially in a tourist-oriented economy; who demands this representation; how it is strategically performed; and what happens when this boundary is transgressed. In other words, what are these tourists looking for when they come to Cherokee (the epicenter of tourism for the Qualla Boundary)? Who is "the Indian" that tourists ask for? Who answers these expectations and how? Small businesses on the Qualla Boundary have historically been at the forefront of crafting representations in and of Cherokee (with the EBCI initially hosting three main enterprises: a museum, a theater, and a cooperative shop). The draw of the Cherokee Casino heralded a new representational transformation on an EBCI governmental level, but still, it is the small businesses that line the streets and small-business owners who personally interact with visitors. It is here that tensions arise between small businesses and the EBCI (and within the small-business sector itself) over representation and autonomy in creating this national representation.

Chapter 3 reviews the business history of the EBCI as a nation and its citizens before examining the unique structural boundaries that Native Nations and American Indians face, building on current border-theory work.[39] I begin by discussing the two structural (and controversial) limits associated with Qualla Boundary small businesses: geography and citizenship. I demonstrate how the case of small businesses makes evident the specific ways in which the EBCI has chosen to exert its sovereignty within these boundaries in order to stabilize its economy. I begin with land and the various issues of its scarcity on the Qualla Boundary. I then examine the intricacies of citizenship delineations (e.g., who can own a business on the Qualla Boundary), including the recent citizenship audit. Following this, I consider the effects of citizenship boundaries, such as economic drain and scarcity, as well as its intertwining of federal laws, like the Indian Arts and Crafts Act with the bounding of artistry.

These boundary examinations serve as the foundation for chapter 4's discussion of sovereignty. As Cattelino, Cornell and Kalt, and Miller, among others, discuss, Native Nations need stable economies to strengthen their practices of political sovereignty. One foundational method for accomplishing this is through diversification. For the EBCI, which owns two casinos, a significant question arose in relation to the benefits of small-business ownership: What (if anything) do these small-business owners and their businesses contribute to their nation that their successful Native Nation–owned enterprises alone do not—or cannot? The EBCI's first casino has been very successful in increasing economic power, but it has brought new challenges common to one-industry markets, which the small-business sector has been able to offset in many ways. Although one-industry-dominant economies can be precarious, allowing for increased political vulnerability, this precarity can be significantly reduced if they are buoyed by a diverse network of small businesses that contribute not only to economic and community structures but also to the support of national practices of sovereignty.

Finally, having established the importance of small businesses to the economy and sovereignty of indigenous peoples, I address in chapter 5 the question of how Native Nations can support and encourage this small-business growth, potentially mitigating some of the challenges that these entrepreneurs face as businesspeople—specifically as American Indian businesspeople—on reservations. This support spans issues of land ownership and capital building, financial relationships (from loans to taxes), education, and challenges faced by small rural businesses generally. All of these discussions, however, start with one question: Who are these small-business owners?

1 Economic Identities

Conceptions and Practices

· ·

Cherokee has been well known as a primary tourist destination in western North Carolina for nearly one hundred years. A short drive through the main streets of this town reveals strips of small back-to-back buildings and stores that seem to be dedicated to the tourist market. Behind these dominant facades, however, lies a rich world of small businesses. In fact, as reported by the EBCI's Office of Budget and Finance's Revenue Office, less than half of the businesses on the Qualla Boundary are strictly tourist oriented. There are many construction and landscaping businesses (some of which have won small-business awards, such as those given at the yearly National Minority Enterprise Development Week Conference), as well as other community-oriented businesses—including a funeral home, mechanics, craft-supply stores (wood, beads, leather), a cab service, accounting services, hair salons, office supplies, legal services, hardware supplies, website services, pest control, video-production, photography services, day care, a children's clothing shop, signmaking, local convenience stores, painting services, and DJ services—with more emerging every year. This overall small-business diversity is crucial in serving the local community, tourists, and the EBCI's national economic sovereignty.

The physical spaces of these businesses vary: some have their own offices or building storefronts, while others are run from a vehicle (the Sound of Music DJ service's van uses only biodiesel that the owner produces in-house)[1]—and then there are those that operate out of the owner's home or out of a building on the owner's family's land. Many of the local-oriented businesses would be quite challenging to find if you did not know the area well as they may have little to no web presence for promotion or mapping. In fact, for some homes with small farms tucked into the back roads of the mountains, the practice of leaving produce or cornmeal out in the front yard with the expectation that payment will be left in return is common. As I was told, you "just know" that they will have it, so you drive by to check to see if they have any ready for sale. Getting more coveted produce, such as the delicious and difficult-to-find wishi mushroom (wild-harvested in the fall), requires knowing how to contact the owner to get on a waiting list.

Sorting out this diversity of small businesses and small-business practices begins with two seemingly simple but central questions: Who owns these businesses, and what markets do they serve? To delve into these questions, we must begin by examining the contextual distinctiveness of American Indians' economic identities and their related experiences. Addressing these constructions helps refine our theoretical understandings of what has been termed indigenous entrepreneurship by following how the external shaping of indigenous economic identity has hindered its representation as well as its expression.

The Absent Indigenous Entrepreneurs

> These are the *dying breed* stories that we try to capture whenever we are on the road with our cameras.
>
> —The Travel Channel's *Bizarre Foods* on Eastern Band citizen Johnnie Sue Myers's cooking (emphasis added)

As I sat down in the crowded little diner in the midst of the Great Smoky Mountains, the waitress asked me, "Siyo, doiyusdi tsaditasdi tsaduli?" (ᏏᏲ, ᏙᎢᏳᏍᏗ ᏣᏗᏔᏍᏗ ᏣᏚᎵ? "Hi, what would you like to drink?"). Still skimming the menu, I answered, "Siyo, kowi agwaduli" (ᏏᏲ, ᎪᏫ ᎠᏆᏚᎵᏍᎩ; "Hi, I'd like a coffee"). I had learned from Bo Taylor's summer language-immersion course (taken at the Museum of the Cherokee Indian, well before I started my fieldwork) that this was one of a handful of restaurants you could go to on the Qualla Boundary where, if the wait staff recognized you, you could speak Cherokee. During this language course, we would eat lunch every day at a different restaurant. Some, like the Little Princess restaurant (which features "Indian dinner" nights, including items such as bean bread and grease, as does Paul's Diner and the Newfound Restaurant), have a few staff members who spoke Cherokee. The servers at other restaurants, such as a local Chinese buffet, now speak remedial Cherokee as a result of Bo's persistent attempts to teach them a bit of the language each time he goes in (making this, quite possibly, the only place where you can enjoy lo mein while ordering hot green tea in the Cherokee language). For me, these restaurants—ranging from local to tourist oriented, franchise to home cooking, and buffet to diner—reflect the diversity and community of small businesses on the Qualla Boundary.

Considering this diversity, watching the above-mentioned episode of *Bizarre Foods* reinforced the absurdity of the non-Native world's continued perception of American Indians as a "dying breed." This claim was made even as the show creators were watching American Indians writing cookbooks about "Cherokee feasts," providing guided tours of reservation waterways, serving meals, and promoting local American Indian artists, all in front of a television crew. Even when people like Andrew Zimmern are surrounded by Cherokee people and their many businesses all day, they still see them as "vanishing." Philip Deloria began to trace this contradiction by examining how indigenous anomalies, as interpreted through the settler-colonial gaze, were necessarily rendered invisible in order to continue settler-colonial agendas (e.g., land procurement).[2] One of these anomalies discussed by Daniel Usner is the "Indian work" that settler-colonial society deems inauthentic for American Indians (conveyed in media and pop culture but also given legitimacy through academic and government officials).[3] The tactic—and necessity—of applied invisibility by settler-colonial society continues today.

Throughout their histories, American Indians have practiced what has been termed entrepreneurialism.[4] Indigenous peoples throughout the Americas had extensive trade routes established well before Europeans arrived. Following European arrival, American Indians were the driving force supporting international business networks and trade, supplying European countries with goods that eventually contributed to the development of (by European standards) a "native elite,"[5] in addition to the wealth created for European businesses and individuals. According to Cherokee Nation citizen Gary "Litefoot" Davis, president and CEO of the National Center for American Indian Enterprise Development, former rapper, and self-described entrepreneur, "I think that business and being entrepreneurs is probably one of the most traditional things that Native people have ever done. For me, being an entrepreneur is a very traditional activity."[6]

However, it has long been argued that as a "pan-" whole, American Indians, historically and contemporarily, are "culturally" unable to accept or practice entrepreneurship due to its supposed inherent focus on the primacy of the individual over community—an argument that is also paralleled internationally in regard to indigenous peoples.[7] This cultural mismatch fallacy has, until recently, caused indigenous entrepreneurialism to remain under-acknowledged. Rudi Colloredo-Mansfeld astutely describes this problem and its impact in his descriptions of Otavolo history:

Given the ancient history of long-distance commerce in the region, its reemergence within the context of a global market for ethnic arts does not signal the corruption of a more "authentic" native Andean way of life. In fact, the absence of merchant Indians, long-distance exchange, and complex deals for "foreign goods" represents a diminishing of indigenous society. [Studies neglecting Andean's interest in business] reflect not the natural economy, but *the repression of rural peoples* by hacienda owners and urban business interests. *Such simplistic descriptions obscure the histories, careers, and aspirations of commercially minded indigenous peoples.*[8]

Susan Sleeper-Smith also supports these ideas, saying, "U.S. people were, for Indians, another stage in *a continuous process of encounter with foreigners. The struggle to maintain or improve their position in relation to others, less or more powerful than themselves, invoked a well-established repertoire of responses.*"[9] Duane Esarey states this even more succinctly with regard to the Americas: "Interaction, not isolation, defines social groups."[10] Indeed, the individuals who forged and honed early Amerindian trade routes embody many of our conceptions of entrepreneurial practices. These endeavors could be long, arduous journeys easily resulting in multiple failures, with more serious consequences than many contemporary concerns, such as lack of appropriate focus group testing for a new product. Beyond distant markets and trade, there are also records of private property leasing activities between American Indians, such as a Cheyenne practice of renting horses.[11]

In examining the logic of the cultural mismatch between American Indians and entrepreneurship, two primary faults become apparent. The first is that this is a pan-Indian concept that necessarily undercuts the vast differences among American Indians; the second is that this notion of an entrepreneur as a strictly individualistic, (selfishly) profit-driven person fails to acknowledge the wide spectrum of entrepreneurial activities.[12] In practice, as will be shown with Eastern Band citizens, entrepreneurs have been very active members of their larger communities, redistributing wealth and supporting community endeavors and thereby contributing to overall community wellness. This is now generally recognized as social entrepreneurship (and its various incarnations of green entrepreneurship, sustainopreneurship, and so on), which uses private business as one vehicle to mitigate social problems.[13]

Focusing on the Menominees and Metlakatlans (1870–1920), Brian Hosmer highlights the idea of socially focused American Indian business practices while arguing that historically American Indians did have a complex understanding of the overall market. They understood the ramifications of the new European-inclusive economic system on their culture, which thereby enabled them to try to minimize the damage it inflicted. Hosmer first foregrounds this indigenous economic agency when he asks, "More ambitiously, can we proceed so far as to suggest that those Menominees and Metlakatlans who *embraced* these new economic relationships did so in order to maintain a degree of independence through economic modernization? If so, what can that tell us about Menominee and Tshimtsian cultures, or about the complex dance between change and continuity that all peoples undertake, but that is, seemingly, beyond the grasp of historical Indians?"[14] In my own work, I do not conceptualize these types of actions as economic modernization as much as economic syncretism and appropriation. Additionally, I, and others, further Hosmer's argument to include contemporary American Indians, whose identities as American Indians are called into question as their bank-account balances rise.[15]

Hosmer then addresses indigenous social entrepreneurship directly by saying, "After all, Menominee entrepreneurs still took into consideration the needs of the broader community, cultural values shaped accommodations with the market, and interactions with others, and the overall objective of economic change (so far as one can be discerned) remained not assimilation, but, ultimately, a bolstering of Menominee ethnic identity. *Economic modernization does not equal assimilation*, nor should scholars confuse the two."[16] Hosmer illustrates this point when describing how white agents viewed logging as a powerful engine for cultural change, but Old OshKosh (the Menominee chief from 1795 to 1858) reversed this idea by viewing the larger American need for lumber as leverage for retaining the Menominees' land and reducing their dependence on annuities, thereby supporting the community on several fronts. He emphasizes, "To an important degree, both societies found in economic development a way to preserve unity, independence, and indeed survival."[17] Hosmer's closing statements are applicable today to Native Nations struggling with economic development issues: "The fact that both groups wrestled with changes and attempted *to incorporate the market into existing, albeit evolving, structures* indicates both the importance of heritage and their real concern that they not abandon their pasts."[18] For indigenous peoples today, I would reimagine this sentiment with less emphasis on "not abandoning their past," focusing more heavily on their abilities to combat the forced acculturation and assimilation that accompanies this economic violence and economic hegemony. As Cattelino states in regard to her work with the Seminole's gaming industry, "Casinos are not a 'new buffalo' that has descended magically on American Indian tribes. Casinos represent a new stage in the long and complex history of American Indians' economic, political, and cultural struggles."[19] As a religious leader and local businessperson told Cattelino, "Changes? I don't see changes. Things basically have stayed the same, just taken new forms."[20]

These transformations of economic sovereignty practices as seen through entrepreneurship choices also characterize the history of the EBCI. Successful Eastern Band small-business owners (including artists) have had an established, significant presence on the Qualla Boundary for many generations. As such, an internal stigma of a cultural mismatch is not as pervasive within this space as it is throughout the United States at large. However, the Qualla Boundary sits in a national and international context and cannot entirely escape this influence. According to Finger,[21] the EBCI's historically recorded tourism industry has been active since 1940, with individual entrepreneurship and small-business existence beginning even earlier that century, dating back to 1902. Finger, along with a handful of Eastern Band citizens I spoke with, has claimed that these early businesses were owned by "white Indian" Eastern Band citizens.[22] The underlying subtext of this racial qualifier is that either non-"white" Eastern Band citizens were incapable of business ownership at the same level as their white counterparts (cultural mismatch) or—a more likely cause—non–phenotypically white individuals were pushed out of the sector due to racism (especially given the continued post-Reconstruction attacks on people of color in the South at that time) and continuing racist associations of whiteness with general economic competency.[23] Today, these entrenched stereotypes of both race and racialized business acumen are readily seen in one simple question often posited directly to Eastern Band citizen business owners, "Where are the Indians?" The question reveals underlying assumptions about who is American Indian and who can be a business owner. Despite these racial qualifiers, however, it is apparent that Eastern Band citizens have had a long-standing and thriving business community throughout their history, which has greatly supported their government. This is seen not only through the long-term sustainable small businesses owned by Eastern Band entrepreneurs that support the overall robustness of the EBCI economy—some businesses in operation today are decades old—but also in the collective knowledge of business practices on the Qualla Boundary that enables the EBCI to more easily manage government-owned businesses.

Indigenous Entrepreneurship and Conceptions of Capitalism

Conceptually, discussions about indigenous entrepreneurs in the United States have focused on American-Indians-as-entrepreneurs—that is to say, an individual or Native Nation case-level activities. The shift in focus from individual case studies to the categorical study of "American Indian entrepreneurship" and "indigenous entrepreneurship" writ large has recently emerged as a topic in small-business studies.[24] In 2005, the *Journal of Small Business and Entrepreneurship* (*JSBE*) dedicated an entire issue to indigenous entrepreneurship.[25] It was during this time that we also saw the mainstream emergence (thanks to increased web presences and promotion by popular blogs, such as Adrienne Keen's *Native Appropriations*) of American Indian businesses, like Beyond Buckskin and the comedy troupe the 1491s.[26] During this time, the categorization in academic literature of a business as "indigenous" began to coalesce around several key foci. The first and requisite element is indigenous ownership (setting aside, for now, the complications of determining who is "indigenous"). From here, the second focus is on the businesses' products. They can be produced specifically for indigenous consumption (e.g., local foods) or can be culturally relevant to the indigenous owner's community but produced for both indigenous and nonindigenous consumption (many products in the fashion genre would fit here).[27] The third consideration is business knowledge and practices, as in the *JSBE* special issue, which specified "self-employment based on indigenous knowledge"; defining an indigenous business in this way usually examines both the owner's *motivation* for starting a business and the way the owner *operates* the business.[28] For example, in many instances, a primary foundation for defining an "indigenous entrepreneur" rests on the intent of the business to contribute, or "give back," to the indigenous community in some form. Essentially, this marks indigenous entrepreneurship as a subset of social entrepreneurship.

Herein lies an insidious danger. As we strive to find what is distinctive about indigenous entrepreneurship, we must also be very cognizant of the possibility that we are contributing to the creation of a new type of "noble savage"—the Noble Entrepreneur.[29] A question Hindle poses in the *JSBE* special issue illustrates these problematics on several levels: "How does deep attachment to the land and the harmonies of nature fit with the drive for profit and success?"[30] First, the assumption that all indigenous people's lives operate within the constraints of harmony with nature draws us back to the problematic "ecological Indian" stereotype. And yet it would be equally faulty to deny that an awareness of environmental impact and a deep attachment to land exist—and indeed they do, as American land *is* Indian land. Therefore, when we discuss indigenous entrepreneurs, we must give leeway for many expressions and practices of entrepreneurship, whether reactionary entrepreneurship,[31] radical entrepreneurship,[32] social entrepreneurship, or Western (capitalistic) entrepreneurship undertaken by indigenous peoples.[33] My work with Eastern Band small-business owners disrupts the easy narrative of the existence of a singular set of American Indian business practices as well as concepts of indigenous entrepreneurs as somehow "non-traditional." I instead argue that indigenous entrepreneurship is distinctive *not* because of community service or product design but because of the indigenous entrepreneur's *context*. This contextual distinctiveness is the amalgamation of uniquely indigenous experiences, including their individual and national legal, political, and historical factors as well as representational factors (economic identity) that shape and bound the experience of indigenous entrepreneurship.

For example, in the United States, American Indian entrepreneurs operate within the physical, legal, and representational realms of the settler-colonial state. This situation necessitates any one of many numerous negotiations, decisions, and practices that may differ from those required of non–American Indian entrepreneurs. This construction of entrepreneurship follows in the vein of Sylvia Yanagisako's arguments:

> Capitalism [is] a complex and uneven historical process that entails heterogeneous capitalistic practices shaped by diverse meanings, sentiments, and representations. I argue for a model of culture and capitalism that posits neither the existence of a singular homogeneous capitalist mode of production nor culturally specific capitalist modes of production that are enacted by culturally distinct groups located in different national or regional spaces. I am not interested in salvaging the concept of culture as a distinctive system of symbols and meanings in the hope of discovering the distinctive characteristics of "Asian capitalism" and "European capitalism" or "Italian capitalism" and "Japanese capitalism." Instead, I leave open

the possibility of the coexistence in any geopolitical space—whether local or translocal, national or global—of heterogeneous capitalistic practices, all of which are culturally mediated. In other words, the model I propose is not one of distinctive "cultures of capitalism" or "capitalist cultures," but one in which diverse capitalist practices coexist in the same geopolitical spaces and flow across their boundaries. The forms that these diverse capitalist practices take and their articulation with each other must be empirically investigated, rather than assumed.[34]

Yanagisako's insistence on foregrounding a diversity of practices speaks directly to the necessity of the term *indigenous entrepreneur* to be flexible enough to accommodate the tremendous amount of variability in indigenous entrepreneurial experiences. As Joel Pfister reiterates, the binary opposition of resistance to assimilation and submission to assimilation, which is so often employed in the context of American Indian economic identity, "does not capture the complexity, multiplicity, or intellectual fluidity of the range of responses to White American capitalist power. There is no single authentic way of being 'Indian.'"[35] Or, I would add, of being an Indian entrepreneur.

Yanagisako's construction, especially as related to the concept of capitalism, therefore works to strengthen the focus on the variety of entrepreneurs, businesses, and business practices of American Indian economic identity while also speaking to the external shaping of American Indian economic identity that can work against these owners. This exogenous economic identity—as seen in the "politics of perception" in the form of popular media, U.S. political statements and actions, and so on—primarily portrays one of two extremes: the poverty-stricken American Indian or the wealthy American Indian.[36] The trope of the Indian-as-poor is reinforced regularly in pop culture, as seen in shows like *The Unbreakable Kimmy Schmidt*. In this Netflix comedy, the character Jacqueline Voorhees (played by white actor Jane Krakowski) was born an Indian (Lakota) in Bear Creek, South Dakota, but decides to move to Manhattan as a teenager. She chooses to literally become white in order to pursue her dream of becoming wealthy—financial success that is achievable only after abandoning all associations with her Indianness. The rich-gaming Indian trope is especially prevalent in comedy animations, ranging from *The Simpsons* to *South Park*. In addition to rendering American Indians in the middle of this poor–rich spectrum invisible (which encompasses most small-business owners and entrepreneurs), these portrayals have serious consequences for American Indians and Native Nations in that they serve the logic of elimination.[37] If American Indians are poor, they are "incompetent" or incapable of economically succeeding and, thus, should be assimilated, removed, or, as in Elizabeth Povinelli's terms, abandoned and allowed to "disappear."[38] If American Indians are rich, settler-colonial society considers them assimilated and then attempts to remove their (now deemed unnecessary) "special privileges,"[39] thus demonstrating a "rich Indian racism" in action while building on the idea that "money whitens" and "poverty darkens."[40] As Randel Hanson summarizes in his discussion of neoliberalism in relation to Native Nation lands and policy,

> "Neo-liberalism" has been an important ideological vehicle for the institution of a particular form of economic globalization since the 1980s. Going beyond 19th-century ideas of economic liberalism as embodied in Adam Smith's *The Wealth of Nations* (i.e., that government intervention in economic affairs is to be minimized), neo-liberalism refers to an ideological position that understands the market as the central component of society (as opposed to one aspect of society). In addition, neoliberalism typically projects a deep-seated hostility toward all forms of collectivity (Bourdieu, 1998). Indeed, for many neo-liberals, the notion of "the public good" should give way to "individual responsibility," all commons (such as Indian reservations, for example) should be privatized, and peoples of the world should be "liberated" from the various forms of social protections built up by 20th-century democracies, since these are framed as having the effect of limiting the freedom of others by thwarting unfettered "free trade."[41]

The hegemonic neoliberal capitalism that has enabled the current plutocracy (or "Economic-Elite Domination" oligarchy, as Gilens and Page posit) experienced today in the United States also allows for a new type of economic termination policy, one that comes in the guise of "structural adjustment" plans.[42] Hanson points to Reagan's 1983 "Statement on Indian Policy," in which Reagan states that the free market will provide for Native Nations economic development foundations.[43] This, of course, allowed for federal government justification in severely cutting Native Nation–owed funds from education through job training, essentially attempting to (1) terminate the federal government's fiscal debt owed to Native Nations while

(2) potentially destabilizing Native Nation economic powers and further entrenching them in poverty, thus creating easier access to Native resources.

As Wendy Brown stresses, although discussions of neoliberalism have tended to focus on economic policies that have "inadvertent political and social consequences," neoliberalism has a "political rationality that both organizes these policies and reaches beyond the market."[44] This manifests for American Indians in very specific forms, becoming another facet of the economic identity "double bind" that American Indians face.[45] Much like the issue of Native Nation wealth accumulation, American Indians who choose not to engage in the "social" form of entrepreneurship are targeted as being non- or less Indian based on the cultural-mismatch fallacy. In other words, implied "pan-" Indians do not participate in capitalistic entrepreneurship because they should, by cultural definition, participate only in social entrepreneurship. The corollary to this is that if American Indian entrepreneurs choose not to take the path of capitalism, they can be accused (as in the previously described poverty example) of doing so because they would be incapable of succeeding within a capitalist framework. Colleen O'Neill addresses this capitalist version of the pan-Indian cultural-mismatch notion in her research with the Diné, in which she "counters the classic modernization tale that assumes that as soon as indigenous people encounter the capitalist market, their cultural traditions erode."[46] She does this by examining the period between 1930 and 1970, when many Navajo people initially left to find wage work, with wage work eventually emerging on their reservation midcentury. She reminds readers, as she has in other works, of "the role of indigenous peoples in the history of capitalism, as well as . . . the nature of that economic system itself."[47] In her research, she finds that Diné practices creatively engaged the capitalist market, which allowed them to diversify their household-based strategies in order to accommodate enormous economic transitions.[48]

This flexibility can also be seen in the case of the EBCI economy, as small businesses on the Qualla Boundary were the primary support for the EBCI economy for decades, helping it to weather enormous political and economic shifts well before the casinos became central figures. My examination of how current entrepreneurship manifests on the Qualla Boundary, both personally and conceptually, began by asking who owned the small businesses that have succeeded for decades. As my fieldwork began, it quickly became apparent that family involvement played a central role for these small-business owners.

Family Business Ownership

Ron Blankenship's store, Talking Leaves, is the only dedicated bookstore in Cherokee. What makes the store even more remarkable is that it is solely dedicated to American Indian topics and authors. Each wall and shelf is well stocked and immaculately organized with the latest books, movies, and music spanning topics from children's books written in Cherokee syllabary (such as ᎣᎹᎦ ᎣᏃᏓ ᏔᏏ, *Udohiyu Unole Iga* [A very "Wendy" day] to the latest academic offerings on topics such as the Native American Graves Protection and Repatriation Act (NAGPRA).[49] These are interspersed with other items, such as clothing (Cherokee High School T-shirts), Pendleton steering-wheel covers, locally made Eastern Band pottery, American Indian–centric bumper stickers (e.g., "rez diva" [reservation diva]), and American Indian–made jewelry—nearly all supplied from American Indian–owned sources. As you wander through the shelves, music is always playing, ranging from live powwow CDs to contemporary American Indian rock artists, and the staff will play any CD the store carries, so you can decide if you want to buy it. The store itself is located at the intersection of Highways 441 and 19, flanked by the new movie theater on one side and the Oconaluftee Islands Park (home of the enormously popular Children's Trout Derby) on the other, so most tourists and locals drive past it at some point on their travels through the town of Cherokee. Like many physical buildings in the mountains, the location is a bit awkward, sitting below the level of the road. The store is overshadowed by a Kentucky Fried Chicken, with one entrance to its plaza at a far end that feels like a forty-five-degree-angle climb, and the other entrance congested with constant traffic going by the park.

I found that I had to plan for significantly more time to browse Talking Leaves than I did for other stores I visited. Not only did I always find someone to talk to, but I also spent quite a bit of time just making sure that I was abreast of the newest books; often, I would find ones I did not realize had been released. Many of these items were not available to Ron (an Eastern Band citizen) at wholesale prices. As he said, "Sometimes, my problem is [that] I'm not getting a discount on some books, but I carry them anyway. Sometimes I don't make a dime, but I just call it customer service. Now, I can't afford to sell 1,000 copies of it, but one or two [won't] kill me; it's just customer service."[50] You might imagine that this kind of dedication would come from someone who has a deep and abiding interest in books, but Ron claims not to be a "reader," although his extensive traveling (more than two hundred nights per year to sell and research new products) complements

FIGURE 1.1 Talking Leaves. Photo by author.

his significant appetite for educational magazines, which travel lightly. This, combined with the information he receives from his customers about the books he sells, keeps him far more informed than most about the latest in American Indian works.

So how did a self-described nonreader come to own such a comprehensive American Indian bookstore? In this case, it was Ron's mother who encouraged him year after year (specifically 1992 through 1994) to open the bookstore. Ron recalled that he had always been "business minded," "born and bred into it"—a characteristic that he attributes to his father, a prominent Cherokee citizen. Additionally, his family owns the building that houses Talking Leaves.[51] It was not until a trip back to Oklahoma for Cherokee National Holiday that I would come across his brother, who also owns a small store, selling books and crafts in Tahlequah. As Ron's experience demonstrates, having a family with business experience can be one key factor in starting and sustaining a new business.

In examining these linkages between family, business, and cultural practices (both EBCI and settler-colonial), it can be easy to stumble into the trap of essentializing these experiences. Yanagisako's conceptions of "family capitalism" complicate these linkages and are especially fitting for thinking through family businesses on the Qualla Boundary.[52] Using this framework, we can apply the concept of "Eastern Band family business" (in Yanagisako's terms, Eastern Band family capitalism) only if we "eschew cultural essentialist formulations that deem it the product of a 'traditional [Eastern Band]' family system or an enduring, stable '[Eastern Band] culture.'" Instead, we see that Eastern Band family businesses are constantly changing in response to the ebb and flow of "broader cultural, economic, and political transformations"; it is not Eastern Band culture that produces this type of family capitalism; "people produce capitalism through culturally meaningful actions that at the same time produce families and selves with particular desires, sentiments, and identities."[53] In other words, it is the cumulative actions of owners, like Ron and Charla, who are drawing from family (knowledge, capital, or labor) while continuously innovating and adapting that construct and reconstruct what constitutes an Eastern Band family business. Thus, the diversity of Eastern Band family businesses comes not just from their choice of markets or products or practices (as in the above constructs of indigenous entrepreneurship) but from the ever-changing amalgamation of their endogenous and exogenous experiences.[54]

The impact of family on the Qualla Boundary business landscape is not easily overestimated. Nearly every business owner I spoke with came from a family that had also owned a business. And every owner I spoke with, barring one non–Eastern Band citizen, had an extended family member that also owned a business. As an owner of several small businesses, Pooh Lancaster's entrée into the business world began in childhood; her father, Jim Cooper, was a well-known business figure in Cherokee. He began his business ventures on the Qualla Boundary in 1972 when he joined with his brother, already a successful restaurant owner, to open a hotel and restaurant.[55] Pooh began helping in family stores in elementary school and loved working in the gift shop, talking with customers, and selling gifts. As an adult, she pursued her degree, returned to Cherokee, and ran her father's Hampton Inn before starting her own business in 1997. Although Pooh's family remained fairly hands-off regarding her personal business decisions, letting her successes and mistakes be her own, Pooh's intimate family business knowledge, experience through her family with business ownership, and access to a small amount of family capital were all critical factors in her ability to start up her own ventures.[56]

This abundance of family-owned businesses may give the impression that small-business ownership is extraordinarily common for Eastern Band citizens. However, unlike non-Native businesses, Native-owned businesses may need to stay within families because of structural boundaries, including those imposed by federal laws that can, in turn, reify issues of generational wealth and class status. Specifically, there are complicated reservation leasing and possessory landholding laws (discussed in chapter 3), combined with the scarcity of usable land, that result in businesses typically staying within a family for generations in one form or another—as the intact business, the business's building, or the underlying land. Familial groups also often own and pass down businesses, thus giving the impression that many individual EBCI citizens are business owners.

Currently, there are several families that control many of the most successful (financially and by length of time in operation) tourist businesses in Cherokee, ranging from hotels to craft stores to restaurants.[57] Most of these owners have relatives staffing and managing them to different degrees; their children commonly start their own businesses. As such, it was not unusual for these small-business owners to rely on extended family to play a wide variety of roles, ranging from occasional emergency substitutions to full-time employment. When looking for a specific person, I had two encounters during which I was told to go into any one of "those stores on 441" and ask where they were, as family workers are often transferred between businesses as needed ("floaters"). This was not a cost-saving measure, since the businesses generally pay their family members as employees. Rather, as I was told, family is more predictable than new and unknown employees; plus, family peer pressure tends to keep these workers on task.

Some stores extend their family-business atmosphere to their employees, deliberately cultivating a family-type environment in the workplace. This practice is not a function of the number of employees a business has, as I found that it occurred in businesses with just one employee all the way up to forty. Teresa, from Granny's Kitchen, employs a high number of workers during the summer season and has many younger people on staff. Additionally, Teresa knew from her Tribal Employment Rights Office (TERO) reports that 75 to 80 percent of her employees at any given time are either enrolled members, parents of enrolled minor children, or married to enrolled members. She said, "I have a lot of what I call babies, a lot of the fourteen- and fifteen-year-olds that are just entering the workforce, bussing tables or rolling silverware or something." Her "babies," whom she trains and coaches, generally move on to other opportunities and often do well. She told me that her former "baby" employees have gone on to become doctors, lawyers, police chiefs, teachers, and PhDs. Small businesses with this familial atmosphere tend to have dedicated employees that even self-police, as Teresa explained:

> They're family. They just are. . . . That's all I can tell you. It's just family.
>
> If you can't pull your weight and if you don't work, you won't be here because [the rest of the waitstaff] will weed you out at some point. They'll either make it so hard on you that you can't stand it or they'll just flat tell you. This business, especially the buffet type, there's three sections out here and each person's got about forty people to wait on at one time. . . . It's got to be a well-oiled, cohesive unit because if it's not, it doesn't work. They police themselves.

Growing up in, working in, and managing a small business before starting one of your own has a dramatic effect on the long-term survival of your business. Children of small-business owners may have access to financial and intellectual resources that many others may not. The issue of property ownership/leases is also directly related, as these families have land leases that commonly span twenty-five years at a time (although they can be even longer), giving them access to the physical space necessary to open businesses. The power of capital in its many forms—whether business knowledge and networking or landholding, land leasing, and subleasing—provides a very strong advantage in business ownership on the Qualla Boundary.

Consequently, for a person without family ties interested in starting a business on the Qualla Boundary, the lack of an established family-business network has several ramifications. The person may not have access to the same start-up capital, to the knowledge and expertise of owning a business, or even to a physical space. Because the leases on the Qualla Boundary are expensive *and* tend to be decades long, a potential owner must have the leasing monies available (liquid) and wait for another business's lease or sublease to expire without renewal. Some families have possessory holding over their business land, which means that unless they lease or sublease it out, it will not be available to anyone else. In light of these challenges, it is not surprising that there are few business owners in Cherokee who do not come from business-owning families to some degree, an effect also noted in other literature regarding American Indian reservation-based private business.[58]

This was the case for Natalie Smith from Tribal Grounds Coffee, who initially needed to receive financial help from the Cherokee Preservation Foundation to help launch her business. She then undertook the lengthy, expensive, and complicated process of securing a rental location through the EBCI government,[59] all of which added precious time and money to the effort of starting up a new business compared to those who may have locations and capital secured through family. The impact of established family ownership on those without family-business experience is mixed. On the one hand, we might expect that seeing community members' success would inspire potential business owners to follow in their footsteps. On the other hand, this family entrenchment may intimidate future business owners, potentially crowding out anyone hoping to get into this sector and possibly suppressing these endeavors. This problem is especially prevalent in the substantial tourism industry. However, although this industry dominates Cherokee visibly and at the government-enterprise level, I questioned whether this tourism-industry dominance held true for the small-business sector across the Qualla Boundary.

Shaping Small-Business Markets

I was the kid who didn't play house; I played store.

—Pooh Lancaster

Tourism is Cherokee's largest industry, flourishing for the better part of a century at the edge of the Great Smoky Mountains National Park (GSMNP). Pooh Lancaster, along with her husband, Todd, owned three businesses that served tourists and locals when we first met. Her businesses have grown in and around the town of Cherokee for nearly two decades. Two were located on the Qualla Boundary, and one is in the neighboring town of Bryson City. Her first store (opened in 1997) was the three-room Great Smokies Fine Arts Gallery.[60] Here, she showcased work by nationally known American Indian artists, occasionally bringing in artists such as Donald Vann to release their newest works. The Native American Craft Shop is her most prominent store, located near the GSMNP entrance, adjacent to the Atse Kituwah Academy (DⱱꓸＹＳＧ ꓒＯＳＧꞬＯ.Ꭻ, New Kituwah Academy) and the Cherokee Fun Park. This gift store is somewhat of an anomaly in Cherokee. It sits by itself on a roomy parcel of land, unattached to any other strip of stores, which sets it apart from the other businesses on 441. Inside, it is spacious and uncluttered, with American Indian–centric products that range from Pendleton clothing and herbal remedies to handmade Eastern Band baskets and jewelry from around the country. Her latest store, Madison's on Main, deviates from her others as it is off-Boundary and meant to cater primarily to local gift-giving needs. It features many upscale baby gifts, jewelry, and treats. Its location on Main Street in Bryson City (known for its train excursions through the mountains) also brings many tourists in. As Pooh's quote illustrates, owning these stores was a lifelong goal. And although the Great Recession took a heavy toll on tourism in the mountains, Pooh managed to keep all her businesses afloat and her employees at work throughout my time there. By July and August 2014, visitors were returning, post-peak recession, to the GSMNP at an increasing rate. That October (peak season for mountain "leaf peepers"—visitors who come for the brilliant leaf colors) showed the highest visitation for that month in twenty-seven years. By 2015, record park attendance reached 351,670 visitors in January alone,[61] a welcome recovery for the many tourist businesses in Cherokee.

Tourist enterprises are, by design, the most immediately visible businesses in Cherokee. Unfortunately, this gives the impression that most of the businesses that exist on the Qualla Boundary, or that are owned by EBCI citizens, are aimed solely at tourists. It also gives the impression that these businesses are the most successful because they are not only the flashiest in terms of size and appearance but also generally crowded during the high seasons. In reality, there are many successful non-tourism-based businesses that, while they have not existed for as long as some of the tourist businesses, are stable and doing very well. However, even these small businesses that were not created to serve the tourist market are heavily affected by its presence. This is most readily seen in the physical location of these businesses with relation to buffering and access, as well as in the methods of marketing a business on the Qualla Boundary—especially in Cherokee.

Buffering and Privacy

The largest streets—the ones you are diverted to if you do not know your way around Cherokee—are lined with tourist shops. However, if you do know the back streets, you can bypass the blocks of tourist paraphernalia and drive down streets that are lined instead with government agencies and, further away, residential housing. This central location of tourist-oriented businesses serves two purposes. First, in a town whose income is primarily generated from tourists, visitors must be able to find stores quickly and easily. Second, this segmentation gives locals a reprieve from the onslaught of tourist traffic and places the stores *they* need to access off the tourists' path.[62]

Invasion of privacy is a very common issue in tourist-heavy economies (ranging from invasive questioning to literally "exploring" residents' private property—seen especially in tourists searching for the most authentic experience), and this is certainly experienced in the town of Cherokee.[63] Having thematic areas to present to tourists and distinct locations for tourists to congregate has enabled the EBCI and Eastern Band citizens to construct a buffer within which to go to school, practice their various religions, and, in general, live their lives mostly separate from the inquiries of the tourists. This concept, a common topic in tourist-industry literature, is known as buffering. In essence, this is the action that tourism-based communities and residents take to separate the tourism spaces from those of their private lives. In communities that choose cultural tourism as an economic foundation (as opposed to locations that have marginal tourism offerings), each citizen becomes a representative of that industry in the eyes of tourists, whether they are directly involved in the industry or not, making this type of privacy separation necessary, not just for those individuals directly in the industry but for all residents.

The very layout of Cherokee is set up for tourists to drive down the main thoroughfares, funneling them through the middle of Cherokee directly to the entrance of the GSMNP.[64] As you drive down these main roads—Highways 19 and 441—you will see almost all the big attractions and event locations for tourists: the casino, the museum, Qualla Arts & Crafts Mutual (more commonly known as the Co-Op),[65] the visitor's center and its newly installed River Walk, Oconaluftee Islands Park, the fairgrounds, and the road leading to the mountaintop Unto These Hills theater, along with many stores and accommodation options. The storefronts present a wide range of visuals, from the heavy wooden pillars and stonework of the stores in the new Cultural District to older, sun-bleached wooden stores, with their outsides covered in bright yellow inner tubes rented out for float trips on the river. Most of the buildings on this stretch focus on souvenir and craft sales, powwow dancer exhibitions, live demonstrations by craftspeople, lodging, and diners that proudly offer "NC Mountain Trout Dinners" or "The Best Breakfast in Town."

The working areas of the Cherokee government are located primarily off of these paths—on secondary roads that run parallel to the main roads—and the buildings that are close to the main roads are set back such that they are nearly invisible. These roads are less traveled, and tourist stores, hotels, and the like are nonexistent until the road joins with the highway again near the entrance to the GSMNP. The homes and living spaces of the Eastern Band citizens are even less noticeable, as they are mainly (barring some subsidized housing) scattered throughout the mountains and forests on the Qualla Boundary. They are located on back roads that may not be labeled, paved, or even visible from certain angles (such as the case of one prominent public road, which leads to a certain quiet, and prime, fishing hole in the forest that is nearly entirely hidden behind a small building and thus invisible if not carefully pointed out). These residential areas are a maze of perpetually winding and twisting roads that follow the shape of the mountains. Even having a GPS will not help you on these roads, as the official road names (which could be something along the lines of BIA 4923) may not be the same as the local road names. This unlabeled maze covertly and subtly serves as a deterrent to those who may be considering wandering off the tourist path.

In addition to the prevalence of place-based buffering, there are also temporal and seasonal buffers. Time-based buffering could be seen at the open-mic nights in the Tribal Grounds coffeehouse, which were held only in the tourist-barren winter months, making them accessible primarily to locals. These open-mic nights, generally hosted after hours, drew a wide variety of locals from both the Eastern Band citizenry and neighboring towns. The crowd ranged in number from about fifteen to a full house, depending on the weather and the publicity. The atmosphere was warm and friendly, as nearly everyone knew each other. There was a good amount of chatting before the event started. After grabbing a hot drink, people mingled and caught up on that week's news or gossip and then eventually settled in if there were any free seats that night. The stage would be set up at the back of the store next to some soft couches and in front of the window that faces the river (although it was pitch black by 6 P.M. in the winter), with temporary chairs surrounding it. Natalie would announce each artist and speaker, who ranged wildly in scope and medium. A typical night might include Natalie reading an excerpt from 1491, followed by a young man from Bryson City playing his own songs on acoustic guitar, the children's language class singing carols, poetry readings, an elder Eastern Band citizen relating a family story, and an Eastern Band flute player. One night, Johnny Cash's cousin, traveling through town on his way to another gig, kicked off the night—outfitted in sequins and a pompadour.

Thus, winters, especially in the evenings, serve as a prime time for business owners to court local patrons and set up areas for community gathering. These kinds of events are considered a high priority for many businesses, even those that are primarily tourist oriented, because the locals are present year round. Many other businesses offer discounts to encourage locals to come to their stores and use their services. At Myrtles, your EBCI citizenship card or a driver's license showing your residency in either Swain or Jackson

County will earn you a discount—a common practice throughout Cherokee. In wintertime, these efforts are promoted even more heavily through other advertised discounts and additional services. Although courting people to buy local was of primary importance to small businesses in the winter months, during the tourist season, this sentiment could become problematic.

Balancing the Market: "Buy Local" and Community

As the Great Recession marched on, the burgeoning "Buy Local" movement grew across the United States. American Express even began sponsoring Small Business Saturday (designated as the day after Black Friday, which is the day after Thanksgiving and one of the biggest shopping/consumerist days of the year) by crediting anyone who registered their card with $25 if they spent $25 or more at a local business that day. This offer would later be extended throughout the month of December and has continued to occur each year since. In my various travels outside Cherokee, small businesses had 8½″ × 11″ signs (some collaged in elaborate displays), either given to them by the local Chamber of Commerce or printed from websites, proudly reminding consumers of the benefits of shopping locally.

At first glance, you might expect the EBCI to support such an endeavor on behalf of their small businesses. However, the "Buy Local" rhetoric and the discourse surrounding it can be problematic for some Eastern Band small businesses in this tourism-heavy economy. The problem here lies in the definition of *local*. The "Buy Local" movement began with an emphasis on the geographical location of the "local." It was aimed at encouraging consumers to spend their dollars in their own neighborhoods and towns in order to grow their local economies. While the "Buy Local" campaign could affect Qualla Boundary business owners positively, the reality is that the most visible small businesses, especially those in Cherokee, are geared primarily toward tourists and are concentrated together in tourist-centric locations. A tourist, by definition, is someone who is away from their local community, precisely where the "Buy Local" movement encourages people to spend their money. Displaying signs in the front window of a tourist store prominently suggesting that tourists "Buy Local!" could appear counterproductive at best. Alternative suggestions have included "Buy Cherokee," which was deemed untenable as it could imply that items in the stores are all Cherokee-made (even though "Cherokee" here is referring to the town rather than the product makers), and "Buy Qualla," which was also not accepted as it was not as publicly recognizable and could be seen as referring solely to the popular Qualla Arts & Crafts Mutual. As a result, the EBCI and many businesses on the Qualla Boundary were, for the most part, left out of the "Buy Local" commercial discourse—and its benefits.

Yet buying from within the community does have a strong meaning for the store owners on the Qualla Boundary. For Pooh, who estimates that over 50 percent of her store is strictly sourced from Eastern Band citizens, it was about buying from local artists (often more expensive than those she could buy from out west) even if it meant going into debt, "because it also hurts when you can't buy things and help a family." For the same reason, Pooh also buys the crafts for her store outright from artists, rather than selling them on consignment. This sentiment was repeated to me many times by store owners: Bethany,[66] whose store is bursting at the seams with locally made trinkets (often bought from a family in need even when the store already has many of the same product) as well as expensive goods; Ron, who says, "I always encourage or buy from the locals because I know they need it for income, too"; Teresa, who hires mainly Eastern Band citizens (and often the youngest and least experienced); and Joel, who used his own materials to supply the new art school when it was getting on its feet. Russ Seagle (EBCI Sequoyah Fund, non-Native), who has taught many of the new Eastern Band citizen business owners through the Indianpreneurship class and other training courses, summed it up by saying, "We've got some clients here and when you talk to them, what is their motivation? Their motivation is not all about making money. It's about surviving and making enough, but it's about creating jobs for Indians. It's about creating jobs for the Cherokee. Keeping their people employed and growing their economy, this economy, and I admire that."[67]

The question was how to translate this community-focused attitude, held by so many local business owners, into a larger discourse reaching all the consumers that come to the Qualla Boundary, which could produce more substantial benefits. One initiative that addressed this issue shifts the focus of the "Buy Local" movement away from just physical location to the concept of "independent" ownership. The Project 3/50 "Big Things Come from Small Boxes" campaign began running during the holidays in 2010. This project started with a blog post written on March 11, 2009, by Cinda Baxter, a former small-business owner,[68] asking consumers to spend $50 total at any three independently owned businesses each month.[69] In this project, the focus is on the independent ownership, not just the locale, eliminating the issue of having a customer base composed of tourists or a mixture of locals and tourists. Interpreting the notion of buying local as buying from independently owned businesses is one key to EBCI inclusion in the nationally promoted "Buy Local" discourse. If the results from the "Buy Local" movement are any indication, a more honed focus on "buying from small, independent businesses" may increase spending of both tourist dollars *and* local dollars on the Qualla Boundary. Furthermore, at the government level, supporting an effort such as this could offer encouragement to existing and potential small-business owners who serve the Qualla Boundary by showing that the EBCI does indeed advocate for them, while also reducing dependence on outside chains. The final complicating factor lies in the following question, which will continue to be asked throughout this book: How can the EBCI promote the importance of patronizing Eastern Band small businesses without seemingly undermining its own large enterprises?

Although neither the Cherokee Chamber of Commerce nor the other EBCI business-support departments had engaged in this effort while I was conducting primary fieldwork, these ideas were partially realized within the following year.[70] In November 2010, I read in the *Cherokee One Feather* (the EBCI's official government-supported newspaper) about the participation of the Sequoyah Fund and the Cherokee Business Development Center (a separate EBCI business-support office) in the new Small Business Saturday campaign:

> Support Small Business Saturday: Ensuring that we have a vibrant economy—one that creates good-paying jobs for our families and brings prosperity to our cities and towns across the country—is a responsibility we all share. I'm proud to announce that Cherokee is joining a nationwide movement to help revive one of the most important engines of our economy, independently owned small businesses. We are teaming up with dozens of partners to launch the first-ever Small Business Saturday. Department stores and large retailers have Black Friday. Online retailers have Cyber Monday. And now, starting on Nov. 27 of this year, small-business owners will have Small Business Saturday. We envision Small Business Saturday as a day when everyone, across the country, comes together to show their support for the independently owned, local merchants they love in their own hometowns. Over time, we hope that Small Business Saturday will be known as the day when everyone makes a special effort to "shop small." Small businesses were among the hardest hit sectors during the recession, and they need our support to get back on their feet. The stakes are high. Over the past two

decades, small businesses have created more than 65 percent of the new jobs in this country. For every $100 spent in locally-owned, independent stores, $68 returns to the community through taxes, payroll and other expenditures. When small businesses succeed we all benefit. More than anything else, owners of these businesses say they need more people coming into their shops and buying their goods and services. To drive foot traffic, we are supporting a major social media and advertising campaign that we hope will put Small Business Saturday on the map. . . . We're working with some terrific partners, including American Express Company, Facebook, the National Trust for Historic Preservation's Main Streets Center, and the National Association of Women Business Owners, to make the upcoming holiday season a success for small-business owners across America. Shining a light on the local businesses that contribute so much to our communities is something we can all get behind. Please join the movement and spread the word to make the first Small Business Saturday a success. Submitted by, Cherokee Business Development Ctr. and The Sequoyah Fund.[71]

The next year, the Handmade, Homemade, Homegrown market was held at the Cherokee Indian Fairgrounds each Saturday from 9 A.M. to 3 P.M. through the month of September.[72] This event was begun specifically to raise awareness of local offerings, although the word *local* in particular, as expected, was not used. While it may seem easy to parse out differing small-business markets, examining issues like "Buy Local" and even the very shape of the land help uncover the intersections of these markets and the extent of the tourism industry's influence.

· · · · · ·

Although there have been long-standing indigenous entrepreneurship practices, the perceptions of what constitutes "indigenous entrepreneurship," and even whether such a thing can exist, have been the subject of much debate. Like Yanagisako, I recognize that creating stagnant characteristics essentializes and, therefore, cannot capture the heterogeneous experiences of these business owners. This is especially true when discussing indigenous participation within market capitalism. The cultural-mismatch theory presupposes that capitalism is incompatible or necessarily destroys indigenous culture, but it ignores (1) that capitalism is always practiced on a spectrum and is therefore malleable, and (2) that many practices under the guise of capitalism have already been shaped and repurposed by indigenous peoples and peoples globally (as in the way family ownership may constitute an alteration of Western capitalism).[73] The lived experiences of indigenous people demonstrate that they have chosen a variety of paths, including being entrepreneurs within a capitalistic system, fashioning their own practices in altering a capitalistic system to their needs and requirements, and (as Wendy Brown has suggested for the U.S. Left), rejecting *homo œconomicus* entirely.[74] Due to the "mismatch" perceptions, however, American Indian entrepreneurs have been rendered publicly invisible, being dismissed in favor of brandishing the extremes of Native Nation poverty and wealth and therein exposing settler-colonial anxieties over Native Nations gaining economic power. Thus, these "politics of perception" put American Indian economic identity into a double bind in which being poor in a neoliberal context is scorned and viewed as reflective of presumed incompetence, while being wealthy renders one no longer Indian, furthering centuries-old settler-colonial ideologies about whiteness, wealth, and "competency."

While this stigma of cultural mismatch exists on the Qualla Boundary, albeit to a lesser extent than in other Native Nations, two other forces hold more sway over the small-business sector there: multigenerational ownership and the tourism industry. Due to the structural forces that constrain American Indian businesspeople as well as those specific to the Qualla Boundary, family-business ownership is prevalent. The preponderance of these intergenerational businesses makes them self-perpetuating, as each family passes down physical capital and intellectual knowledge that is not readily accessible to nonfamily members, thus enabling an easier and less risky entry into business ownership. Many of these family businesses concentrate their efforts on the EBCI's lively tourism industry. This industry has dominated the economy on the Qualla Boundary since the early twentieth century, but with the advent of the first casino—and the three to four million visitors it receives annually—this market has only become more influential for small businesses. As the tourism industry has expanded, complex and sometimes difficult questions have materialized for small-business owners—including those not directly involved in the tourism industry—such as how to market businesses, goods, and services on the Qualla Boundary to customers focused on "buying local." Because of tourism's influence on the Qualla Boundary, it is important to gain a deeper understanding of the tourism industry's developmental context, its future direction, and the ramifications of issues such as representation—not just for small-business owners but for all Eastern Band citizens.

2 Tourism

"Where Are the Indians?"

· ·

I worked right there [at the visitors center] and people would come in
and ask us the same questions that they're asking now: Where are the
Indians? Do they live in teepees? . . . I don't care how the tribe spins
their advertising budget and how they market the area, just so they
get it right. That's all I care about. It's authenticity.

—Teresa, Granny's Kitchen

Pulling up to Granny's Kitchen that day, I saw an unusual sight. Normally
the spacious parking lot was packed with tourists (some driving in from
states away for seasonal specials like fried squash blossoms) as well as locals who regularly enjoyed meals there. Today it was bare save for two lone
cars. Granny's is a buffet restaurant with a large open dining area surrounded by windows and speckled with EBCI crafts, including woven plant
baskets and carved masks. Opposite the dining area is the sprawling buffet
table, with additional private event space located nearby. The buffet menu
changes daily but almost always offers individually hand-carved meats. The
food is southern country in style, with fried chicken, mashed potatoes, green
beans, macaroni and cheese, chicken and dumplings, gravy, vegetable
soup, and many more homemade comfort foods that rotate depending on
the day and season. The year 2009 marked the restaurant's twenty-fifth
anniversary—quite an accomplishment considering an estimated three in
five restaurants close or change ownership within their first three years.[1]
Through the decades, the owners—Ray and Teresa Williamson—have actively courted the local community, going against the advice of the previous
owner, who had recommended that they concentrate only on the tourist market. By doing so, the Williamsons have weathered many changes in their clientele. As Teresa explained, "During the years, everything's kind of changed.
When we first opened, we were getting the tourist people. We were getting
the families from the mill towns in South Carolina and Georgia and [nearby],
and then after they shut all those down, our clientele changed. We still had

some of the same people. We have some of the kids that used to come in bringing their kids now. Of course, that's not as common as it used to be."[2]

After knocking at Granny's door, Ray, Teresa's husband and business partner, let me in; once inside, I realized that Granny's had recently closed for the season, like many businesses on the Qualla Boundary. The seasonal reprieve can actually be a boon for business owners in many ways, as they take this time to remodel, restock inventory, and travel in search of new products. Today Teresa and her family were setting Granny's up for an indoor community yard sale—an event that could otherwise not occur during the winter. The normal hustle and bustle of the waitstaff, clatter of plates, and gregarious conversations of customers were replaced by piles of baby clothes and Teresa's daughter as she quietly rearranged the dining space. Teresa is a vibrant woman who has a smile for everyone; her and Ray's dedication to the business and her employees has held Granny's together for over twenty-five years. As we gathered around one of the supper tables, Ray sat back quietly, deep in thought, occasionally interjecting comments about Cherokee, the economy, and what he has learned from his decades of award-winning participation in the service industry. Teresa talked about the changes that the Cherokee Casino has instigated in the tourist base: "[Our season is] spread out more. When we first got up here, we opened from about the middle of May till the end of October. Now we open about the middle of March and stay open through the end of November, Thanksgiving weekend. . . . In order to make as much money as we used to make, we have to do that because it's just not the same people coming through anymore—it's people coming to the casino or people driving through to somewhere else." The people "coming to the casino" are generally more affluent and couples, rather than the big families that used to flock to Cherokee for a family weekend. This shift in the visitor base was just one of many changes brought about by the casino's installment on the Qualla Boundary that has affected local business practices—an issue that the EBCI government is now beginning to address.

One of my primary goals is to highlight the many small businesses on the Qualla Boundary that are not featured as prominently in research and publicity as the tourist-centric businesses. However, to ignore the obvious proliferation of tourism-based small businesses on the Qualla Boundary is to ignore a principal element of the EBCI's economy and its rich history of business ownership. Furthermore, the importance of the tourism industry for Native Nations across the United States has been growing in recent years,

FIGURE 2.1
Granny's Kitchen.
Photo by author.

as seen, for example, in the institution of the 2016 Native American Tourism and Improving Visitor Experience (NATIVE) Act. It is for this reason that I dedicate an entire chapter to this topic. Here, the differences between the town of Cherokee and the rest of the Qualla Boundary are clearest, as almost all of the tourism that takes place on the Qualla Boundary is concentrated in Cherokee proper.

Economic sovereignty is founded on Native Nations' practices in choosing the economic development paths that they determine are most advantageous (economically, politically, societally, and representationally) for their nation. The tourism market exerts very specific pressures on Native Nation economic sovereignty practices. Tourism, if successful, can easily grow into a one-industry-dominant economy. Additionally, for Native Nations and American Indians who invest in the tourism industry, this economic development choice comes with the issue of how to craft this market. The EBCI and its small-business owners have chosen to transform their vibrant tourism industry in various ways during their history, but they have also been publicly criticized for some of their choices. Many of these criticisms are waged over the issue of authenticity. Today, tourist businesses on the Qualla Boundary are transforming rapidly, partially in response to both external and internal criticisms, and partly in response to their increased economic power, which now enables the EBCI and Eastern Band citizens to finance these transformations. The EBCI and Eastern Band small-business owners are not alone, as many Native Nations that have tourist-based economies are also beginning to reinvent their overall business identities toward a new "heritage tourism" or "cultural tourism" model.

Academically, heritage tourism emphasizes visiting a place with a focus on its historical context (for example, battlefield tourism), whereas cultural tourism focuses primarily on living peoples, usually emphasizing the presentation of an "authentic" cultural image. The EBCI defines its focus by stating, "Heritage tourism [is] a concerted community-wide effort to attract more visitors interested in a cultural experience to the Qualla Boundary."[3] I would also add a third type of tourism relevant to Native Nations: dark tourism. This is tourism focused on people and places linked with death or suffering (such as World War II concentration camps). American Indians are often linked to images of death, suffering, and disappearance (as in James Earle Fraser's iconic sculpture *The End of the Trail*), and tourists often bring this narrative with them, visiting reservations to see the "disappearing" Indians, as they have for generations (e.g., Buffalo Bill's Wild West show, featuring Sitting Bull in 1885).[4] This purported ceaseless disappearing is driven by misperceptions of, and misinformation regarding, reductions in both population and cultural practices (and, therefore, identity, as in the case of "rich Indian" racism). For the Cherokee Nations, this is reinforced further through their particular association in popular culture with the Trail Where They Cried (also known as the Trail of Tears), permanent and traveling exhibits about which are included in the EBCI's Museum of the Cherokee Indian. In essence, these tourists come to mourn. They mourn for the "treatment" of American Indians in the past and for the "plight" of American Indians today (both sentiments and words commonly used by tourists in my experience).

The recent developments in heritage tourism have had a dramatic effect on local small businesses, requiring them, tacitly and overtly, to remodel their identities as they remodel their businesses' physical manifestations into a "distinctly Cherokee" look. More than merely a cyclical business update, this reinvention has considerable implications not only for how business identities are constructed but also for the construction of the Native

Nation's identity as it is perceived by those visiting from outside the Nation's boundaries. Collectively as well as independently, individuals who own businesses on reservations make significant contributions not just to the overall Native Nation economy but also to the representation of the Native Nation itself. They do this via the formation of space, the distribution of knowledge, and the community support structures they offer. Yet throughout these changes, small businesses on the Qualla Boundary continue to demonstrate what many see as the most difficult accomplishment in a tourist economy: longevity and sustainability.

Growing a Tourist Industry

The presence of a tourism industry on the Qualla Boundary has been recorded since 1902, with individual entrepreneurship efforts beginning even earlier.[5] Eastern Band citizens have long been selling baskets, pottery, and goods to those from outside the Qualla Boundary.[6] Early written reports describe Eastern Band women walking to Asheville to sell baskets, and visitors coming to Cherokee to buy blowguns in 1907.[7] The town of Cherokee became firmly entrenched as the primary tourist destination in the mountains of North Carolina with the increasing popularity of its Cherokee Indian Fair (est. 1914), combined with the institution of the Great Smoky Mountains National Park (chartered in 1934) and the subsequent construction of the Blue Ridge Parkway (begun in 1935) and Highway 441, which leads visitors directly through Cherokee and onto the mountain pass to Tennessee. In the midcentury days of the tourism trade, visitors became interested in what is now termed "nostalgia tourism."[8] The Western movie genre, which nearly exclusively portrayed images of pseudo pan-Plains Indians to represent all American Indians, peaked in the early 1950s, with an estimated 501 releases between the years of 1950 and 1954 alone.[9] This translated into a surge of interest in American Indians by non-Natives. Visitors to Cherokee wanted to see a (nostalgic) version of American Indians that matched what they saw in movies that depicted fictional Plains Indians of the past.[10] In this sense, *Fictional tourism*, a term referring to the visiting of physical sites associated with works of fiction, could also be applied to Cherokee. Far from being a form of tourism seen only historically, however, tourists still flock to reservations in response to popular fictional movies. *Last of the Mohicans* (1992) was filmed in the NC Blue Ridge Mountains and still draws fans of the film to the area, and to the Qualla Boundary. More dramatically, the Quileute nation of Washington State experienced the effects of fictional tourism firsthand in the late 2000s, finding themselves in the midst of a deluge of 73,000 *Twilight* fans who came to their (then) one-square-mile La Push reservation in response to the book series and subsequent films featuring the Quileute's name.[11]

By the early 1960s, the EBCI and small-business owners provided nostalgia tourism offerings through souvenir shops, shows, and restaurants, such as the popular TeePee Restaurant.[12] This restaurant was a particularly good example of a tourist–local crossover business, as it was loved by both tourists (who still regularly ask nearby businesses what happened to it) and the Eastern Band citizens who frequented it and lament its passing. During this time, it was common to see individuals dressed up in pan-Plains regalia sitting in teepees for tourists to take pictures with, an activity known as chiefing. At that time, *chiefing* was a term given to a person who wore pan–Plains Indian regalia or costumes reflecting those portrayed in movies, answered tourist questions, and charged a fee for having their picture taken with the tourists. Often these chiefers were Eastern Band citizens,[13] but they also included other American Indians and non–American Indians. During this time, the Cherokee Crafts and Moccasin Factory was opened by a local (non-Native) man. It produced and sold tourist tomahawks and moccasins and employed many Eastern Band citizens in order to label its products "Cherokee Made." Nostalgia and fictional tourism items like tomahawks constituted the primary quantity of products sold to tourists in Cherokee. Much of the tourist goods sold in the various downtown stores were the same products, as they were sourced from the same factories. There were fewer Eastern Band–made arts and crafts readily available at these stores, although tourists (primarily collectors) could hire a guide to take them to an artist's home to buy their crafts. This emphasis on nostalgia tourism in particular as a business model served many purposes for the EBCI, the primary being the economic stability of this robust market for over four decades, as described to me by the business owners themselves and as reflected in many public EBCI discussions today.[14] This nostalgia market also augmented buffering efforts, not just in terms of physical privacy but also culturally and, potentially, politically.

The Politics of Nostalgia

It has been widely argued that tourists primarily seek the authentic in their travels.[15] In particular, the periods following the world wars signaled a point at which Americans sought cultural difference, along with authenticity in that difference, and, in so doing, created a new relationship with multiculturalism. This supports the generous amount of anthropological study regarding the deeply embedded concept of authenticity itself, the foundation of which begins with the recognition that, as Richard Handler observes, authenticity is a "cultural construct of the modern Western world. That it has been a central, though implicit, idea in much anthropological enquiry is a function of a Western ontology rather than of anything in the non-Western cultures we study. Our search for authentic cultural experience—for the unspoiled, pristine, genuine, untouched and traditional—says more about us than about others."[16] That this concept of authenticity innately plays heavily into nationalist ideologies is also foundational to understanding the constructions of authenticity; this aspect of authenticity has been extensively examined in relation to the constructions, assertions, requirements, and protections of nationalism in an indigenous context. This can be seen in the continuous couching of authenticity as an implied prerequisite for the acknowledgment of sovereignty, as happens with the racialization of Native Nations. The long history of racializing Native Nations in order to question their authenticity and, therefore, their inherent rights as polities—especially with regard to control and ownership of resources—has been supported (intentionally and unintentionally) by anthropologists, from early "scratch-test" blood-quantum measures on the White Earth reservation for land allotment determinations (1906–1915) to the 1996 "Kennewick Man" lawsuit, which argued in part that the "Ancient One" was not phenotypically Native American (a claim later disproved by DNA evidence).[17] As Handler states, "Thus nationalist ideologies, as well as anthropological thought, attach authenticity to cultures just as the larger 'consumer culture' that we live in attaches it to individual human beings. . . . Now it is precisely anxiety about existence that characterizes nationalist ideologies, whose fundamental premise is always that 'a' nation, bounded and distinctive, exists. Such anxiety is particularly apparent where national or ethnic groups find themselves in a struggle for recognition, seeking either national sovereignty or equal rights within a larger polity."[18] During the time of the Red Power movement, a public influx of indigenous voices—including a new wave of academics such as Vine Deloria Jr. and Robert Thomas—began speaking directly to the field of anthropology, questioning these conceptions of authenticity from an indigenous perspective and breaking ground for the new generation of indigenous scholars to come. Even with these academic advances, though, we continue to see these same controversies echoed on a federal level. One recent example of this is Donald Trump's 1993 testimony to the Congressional Subcommittee on Native American Affairs regarding implementation of the Indian Gaming Regulatory Act. In attempting to block potential Native Nation gaming competition, and with it Native Nation's rights to economic sovereignty, Trump directly questioned the authenticity of American Indians based on phenotype, saying repeatedly, "They don't look like Indians to me and they don't look like Indians to Indians."[19]

In my study of tourism and authenticity, I argue that for the EBCI during the mid- to late twentieth century, in contrast to Dean MacCannell's concept of "staged authenticity," there was little pretense of representing their "authentic" culture.[20] Instead, as Edward Bruner observes, midcentury tourists were far more interested in seeing their existing expectations realized (here, of stereotyped American Indians as portrayed in film) than in experiencing the "authentic" per se.[21] The settler-colonial expectation and insistence on American Indians as embodied nostalgia in a tourism context also reflects O'Brien's critique (building on Latour) that "Indians can never be modern," as settler-colonial society (still) needs this "past" juxtaposition in order to assert its own modernity.[22] The EBCI accommodated this tourist expectation with attractions like the popular Frontier Land (since closed), which had, among other attractions, a tourist train ride that was "attacked" by real Indians (which, based on the conversations I had with those who lived on the Qualla Boundary at that time, were commonly played by Eastern Band citizens).

Because the EBCI served this nostalgia market through the 1980s (and, to a lesser extent, still does), the EBCI has been publicly accused of selling out to pan-Indian stereotypes and undermining its own heritage, as mentioned by other scholars.[23] While individual attractions, such as the Museum of the Cherokee Indian (opened in 1948), had a specifically educational purpose, many of these early small-business and EBCI tourism enterprises included far from accurate representations of EBCI, Cherokee, or American Indian life.[24] But it would be erroneous to compare the purpose of this former nostalgia market model to that of modern heritage tourism, with its primary focus on education. In essence, the EBCI's former market promoted the town of Cherokee as you would an entertainment theme park based on the immensely popular Western movies of the day (versions of this theme, this time from the cowboys' perspectives, are still popular in states like Arizona; see, for example, Rawhide Wild West Town). Tourists came specifically to see a depiction of the American Indians that reflected the movies they watched in their hometown theaters and on television—their most readily accessible sources of information about American Indians. When these people came to Cherokee, the images they had in their minds shaped what they expected—and demanded—to experience. For nearly fifty years, the EBCI was very successful at fulfilling these expectations. The nostalgia tourism market was a successful business model that supported the EBCI's levy and, thus, the EBCI's national economy while keeping food on the tables of many Eastern Band citizens by providing steady incomes for many decades.

Beyond the business model, there is another possible underlying motivation for the portrayal of these images by the EBCI. The Termination era spanned roughly from 1953 to 1968, overlapping with the peak years of EBCI nostalgia tourism. While profitable, the portrayal of an "Indianness" that was immediately recognizable to settler-colonial society could have also served as a type of defense against federal government aggressions. As authors like Kirk Dombrowski (citing Gerald Sider) have illustrated, people are simultaneously "within and against" culture.[25] American Indians in particular, however, have very different pressures than other people of color in the United States to produce and represent their cultures in specific ways. This includes issues of "competency" and ranges of "civilization," political constructions and structures, economic status (both in class and system), and even the abstraction of their literal blood. These representational pressures have very real consequences, ranging from physical violence to political termination. The choices that Dombrowski presents in the context of the Tlingit and Haida reflect these contradictions and tensions within American Indian cultures (which, as he says, others are fond of pointing out) in times of difficult decision-making. That he highlights decisions based on issues of economic sovereignty is no coincidence for indigenous peoples, who may not have the economic power to choose among multiple pathways; for example, should a Native Nation conserve its environment, use it as a community, or develop it to support the community financially?[26] For the EBCI, the decision to focus on nostalgia tourism may have had the (un)intentional effect of buffering against settler-colonial government accusations that they were no longer "Indian enough" to warrant recognition. In this light, the question is not whether the EBCI could have been even more successful with other approaches to tourism (as they have chosen today) but what the impacts, both economically and politically, would have been if they had chosen other development options during that time.

However, this does not mean that these choices were not problematic or without consequence. Like the situation facing many American Indian actors even today, Eastern Band citizens at that time had to make the choice of either working in nostalgia tourism—with this income going primarily into the hands of American Indians rather than non-Natives playing Indian—or not reproducing the stereotypes and images demanded by settler-colonial society but, in doing so, relinquishing their economically foundational industry.[27] Eastern Band citizens on the Qualla Boundary tested this conflict and found that tourists visiting Cherokee during this time soundly rejected non-stereotypical portrayals of American Indians. One example of this is "Chief" Henry Lambert (a chiefer often labeled "the World's Most Photographed Indian"), who, according to Finger, tried an experiment with various modes of dress. On days that he wore either a war bonnet or pan-Plains regalia, he earned about $80 per day. But on the day he wore Cherokee clothing and beadwork, his grand total was $3.[28] In the tourists' reality, pan-Plains regalia *was* the accurate representation of all American Indians. Essentially, these tourists positioned themselves as the authority on what an authentic Indian was (continuing settler-colonial society's historic trends, seen in competency determinations, termination efforts, and so on). However, the decision for American Indians—often a very difficult one—to partake in the continuation of stereotypical portrayals has consequences for all American Indians, whether it is seen today in American Indian actors taking stereotypical and pan-Indian roles or in more complex issues, such as the Florida State mascot, Osceola, and its ties to the Seminole Tribe of Florida. But the market is an ever-shifting, productive site where social and cultural life are constantly generated, reproduced, and challenged. Tourism markets are especially susceptible to change, whether through external shocks, tourist whims, or internal calls for change.

Shifting Politics, Perceptions, Power: World War II

Internationally, global tourism began to increase significantly post–World War II due to three primary factors: travel technologies improved physical access and reduced travel costs, the postwar economic boom allowed for more travel, and the surge of international travel experience necessitated by both world wars (reflected in songs such as "How Ya Gonna Keep 'Em Down on the Farm [After They've Seen Paree?]"). United States heritage tourism, as seen in National Park Service visitor use statistics, also followed this upward trend through 1975 before beginning to level out around 1987.[29] Several changes occurring at this time contributed to this leveling off. One, reflected in the concurrent change in tourism to Cherokee, was the establishment of the commercial-jet era. The more public commercialization of jet flight made flying more accessible, which, combined with the declining price of airline tickets, caused a shift away from family road trips to airline-based vacations. This increase in flying and reduction in road trips, later compounded by the OPEC gas crisis, meant that the number of tourists coming to Cherokee for family vacations began to dwindle, especially since the closest airport is a small regional facility in Asheville, an hour and a half away.

Another significant change after the initial postwar boom in tourism for the Cherokee tourist market occurred during the late 1960s as the civil rights movement began to galvanize many American Indians into collective action. The Red Power movement began in the late 1960s and then continued through the late 1970s as part of the civil rights era. The group most associated in the public imagination with Red Power was the American Indian Movement (AIM), a collective founded by urban American Indians inspired by the Black Power movement. The psychological impact of the Red Power movement was profound—not just for American Indians but for all Americans. Assumed by most non-Natives to be "vanishing," American Indians, suddenly and surprisingly, appeared to be flourishing, modern, and politically active due to media images of Red Power movement participants. This surprise manifested itself in the non-Native public along a spectrum of support and fear.

As the Red Power movement reached its apex, images of AIM members filled American television screens. These were not the fake headband wearing, painted-skin, support-cast American Indians of the silver screen, portrayed as saying little beyond gibberish or "Tonto-speak" (or even English played backward).[30] These American Indians wore jeans, button-down shirts, and sunglasses, speaking both perfect English and their native languages as they articulated their demands. The impact of this change in the American imaginary was profound. Although there was much resistance to the AIM movement for many reasons, as described in other literature,[31] the movement did, for a time, check the non-Native-created mythology of the vanished American Indian. Where blatant and, not uncommonly, violent racist aggressions against American Indians were once the norm,[32] non-Natives began reconsidering their actions when faced with the (imagined at times) possibility that AIM could be called in for support.[33] The public actions of AIM along with the concerted and momentous efforts of many more American Indians, from elders to scholars to lawyers, culminated in the subsequent passage of various federal acts during that time (Indian

Child Welfare Act, Indian Religious Freedom Act, and so on) as well as successful court cases, and with the actions of these individuals, it became safer—or at least somewhat more legally protected—to be "out" as an American Indian.[34]

The Red Power movement demanded that the larger public see American Indians for what they really were at that moment—not what they were five hundred years ago or what they would be in another five hundred years (i.e., the implication of being vanished)—and the public began, bit by bit, to respond.[35] However, once this "cowboys and Indians" nostalgia was altered by widely broadcast images, such as those of the Wounded Knee Occupation and the Alcatraz Occupation, a void was created. The public began to realize that there was more to American Indians than movie nostalgia, but they had no information with which to fill this newly discovered gap in their knowledge. The public was left with a desire for "authenticity" and no real way, outside of the images created for mass consumption, to conceptualize individual Native Nations. The majority of popular literature, movies, and television shows produced by non-Natives did not provide the general public with enough information and were woefully lacking in self-authored portrayals of modern American Indians, while nationally impactful American Indian–authored critiques were just emerging in the mainstream.[36] This period saw another increase in Western films with the rise of spaghetti westerns, but this time the effect on nostalgia tourism for American Indians was mitigated by the emergence of contemporary American Indian portrayals, such as Billy Jack, and, more importantly, contemporary American Indian roles played by American Indians, such as Will Sampson (Muscogee [Creek] Nation) in One Flew over the Cuckoo's Nest. It is during these collective moments that we see how the Red Power movement, with its widely documented varying impacts, would have specific repercussions for the EBCI and its economy.[37]

Echoing Bruner, I have argued that prior to this moment instigated by the Red Power movement, most midcentury tourists pursuing particularly indigenous American spaces did *not* truly seek authenticity. In seeking American Indian cultural difference, tourists wanted a sanitized, safe, recognizable, and palatable difference, supporting a belief in multiculturalism based on the melting pot myth that promised all difference would eventually be dissolved to the benefit of all. Most of these tourists had no desire to experience the authentic lives of American Indians, which could remind them of their own complicity in the continuous oppression of indigenous peoples; instead, they wanted the fun family destination that nostalgia tourism provided. The high number of visitors to Cherokee during this time, along with the personal experiences of men like Henry Lambert, support this claim.

It was only after the impact of the Red Power movement had been felt, including federal legislation and the national attention it garnered, that tourists' interests visibly began to shift from nostalgia tourism to heritage and cultural tourism. After this shift occurred, tourists to Cherokee began to vocally and publicly complain about the lack of "authenticity." Phrases such as "tacky," "old timey," and "not real" were thrown around. These shifts in the tourism market contributed to nearly two difficult decades for the EBCI. Travel books would publish reviews such as, "Cherokee is the last gasp of commercialism at the edge of the national park, a traffic-clogged gauntlet of places where you can See Live Bears, Eat Boiled Peanuts, Pan for Gold, or ride the Rudicoster. . . . The upscale casino, the region's biggest draw, looms over a fading roadside lined by tacky old-time souvenir stands like the 'Big Chief.'"[38]

This issue of a location becoming "too touristy" or "too popular" and thereby invalidating its perceived authenticity is not an uncommon problem in tourist markets and is cited often in tourism studies. In such cases, a location is first promoted as authentic (read: undisturbed by the "modern" tourist world), then becomes popular, then is deemed too popular (i.e., "mainstream"), and finally is abandoned by tourists in search of the next "authentic" location.[39] It was this emerging issue, as seen in such scathing reviews as the one just quoted, that coincided with the EBCI's initial forays into the heritage tourism model. In the 1970s, the average income of an Eastern Band citizen was down to 60 percent of the national average.[40] By 1982, Frontier Land had closed.[41] Clearly, the draw of nostalgia tourism had faded, and without a financially viable alternative, tourism in Cherokee during the 1980s continued to decline.

Authenticity and Representation in the Gaming Era

The post–Red Power era, which witnessed these market changes, accompanied the non-Native realization that American Indians were still very much here. This acknowledgment of contemporary American Indian existence sparked the interest of those people who supported, or were inspired by, American Indians' contemporary political actions. This interest then manifested itself as a belief by some that, tucked away in their genealogy, they, too, could possibly have American Indian ancestry.[42] Thus, as the overt racism of decades preceding the civil rights movement transformed into more subdued and subtle aversive racism,[43] the next white trend of claiming Indianness emerged. Tourists no longer just wanted the American Indians of the big screen; they also wanted "real" American Indians—the ones who were part of what they believed to be their own heritage.[44] These tourists did not simply want to experience the heritage of the EBCI; some tourists, who had been told stories of a mysterious Cherokee great-grandmother, sought their own heritage in Cherokee. In many ways, these types of tourists, who wanted the "authentic" experience, come to Cherokee *to be Cherokee*.[45] This desire persists today—and it makes sense; during a time in which illegal immigration is being heavily persecuted and Berlin-style walls are being proposed for U.S. borders through Native Nation territories (such as the Tohono O'odham Nation), laying claim to being one of the "original Americans" seems almost a necessity.[46] These politics remind me of something Pooh told me: "I do remember after 9/11 hit, that was when I took my biggest leap at the gallery; I doubled my business."[47] I do not believe it was a coincidence that in a time of attack on U.S. soil, people would clamor for what is deemed to be the most true, authentic symbol (and I use the word "symbol" deliberately) of Americanness: the American Indian. Yet many of these tourists did not, and still do not, know how to conceptualize this new "authenticity" that they desired. As the earlier tourist critiques indicate, they did not believe it was the "tacky" pan-Indian tomahawks, but they did not know what "it" was. The concept of authenticity is, in and of itself, complicated and contested, shifting in meaning based on who is deploying it and in what context.[48] Some items, like the headdresses for sale on the Qualla Boundary, rejected by some tourists as inauthentic, are actually made by Eastern Band citizens. Are these authentic American Indian crafts, or are they historically inauthentic "junk"? And who has the authority to determine these differentiations?

During my time in Cherokee, tourists regularly asked small-business owners to be the authority on authenticity. Ron sometimes deflected these inquires: "One time this guy came in my store [and asked,] 'Which one is your most accurate book?'—I guess he thought I was going to go sell him a book [like,] 'Oh, you need this.' I said, 'Sir, I don't know. These are from different people's perspectives. I don't know what's true or not.' Even if I've read it, I can disagree with it. I said, 'You got to decide on your own.' I don't know which one might [be accurate]—none of them may be accurate. We can [sell ten people one book and] ten people are going to have a different story. That's all I'm saying." This dilemma of determining and negotiating

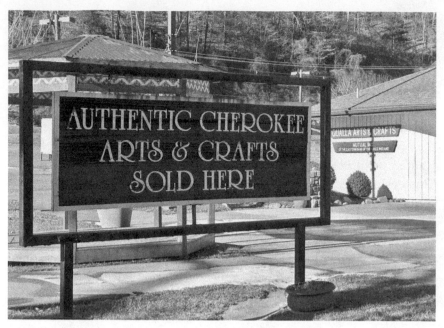

FIGURE 2.2 Qualla Arts & Crafts Mutual, Inc. Photo by author.

product authenticity with tourists is also contingent on the customer's preconceptions.

One June day, I was visiting a gift store called Medicine Man and enjoying the springtime combination of plentiful sunshine and a cool breeze on the store's porch overlooking the Oconaluftee River. As I made my way back inside, I noticed a man in his thirties, wearing jeans and a T-shirt, squatting in front of one of the glass display cases filled from top to bottom with pipes that had wooden stems and carved stone pipe bowls. He had an intent look on his face, and when the cashier asked if she could help him, he said, "Which of these is your most authentic?" The cashier told him that they were all made by American Indian citizens and pointed out the ones made by artists from the Qualla Boundary. This was not what he was looking for, although he was having trouble describing exactly what he was envisioning. He then rephrased his question to, "But which is the most traditional?" He further specified that the more ornate ones did not seem like they were "traditional" and that *he* believed the ones used "before" would have been more functional looking (he stopped short of using the word "primitive," but that seemed to be the concept that he was trying to convey). The cashier attempted to reassure him that decorations have always been a part of even the most functional of items but soon gave up after explaining that she could not be sure that any of them were exact historical replicas. She eventually directed him to "the Co-Op," which is the Qualla Arts & Crafts Mutual.

The Co-Op is an organization formed in 1946 by Eastern Band artisans and the EBCI government to promote and sell Eastern Band citizen-made crafts.[49] Today it also includes a small selection of other southeastern American Indian–made goods. The cashier directed the man to the Co-Op because of its extensive inventory and because its employees are specifically trained to work with first-time tourists and complicated tourist requests. Here we see the contestation and confusion over authenticity, and who is the authority on this authenticity, play out as the tourist struggles with his own conceptions of what is authentically Cherokee (pre-historic, simple, pragmatic) while the employee shows him products made by contemporary Eastern Band artists (these particular ones being composed of some modern materials, ornate, and intricate). I would see these kinds of exchanges about authenticity repeated in various forms again and again.

The demand for authentic representations of American Indians has not been limited to tourists, however. During the emergence of the Red Power movement, American Indians from across the country again demanded action to address the issue of stereotypes. This call led to the subsequent emergence of Native studies programs in universities across the country and a bolstering of Native filmmakers and authors. This shift in representation also emerged on the Qualla Boundary, as some Eastern Band citizens and officials made internal calls for change. Even the famous chiefers, a major tourist draw for the Qualla Boundary, were transformed, both internally by the chiefers themselves and by EBCI legislation. Today, chiefing primarily entails entertainers who dress in historical Cherokee or powwow regalia, play music, tell stories, perform powwow dances, and have their picture taken with the tourists for a fee or tips. They generally stand in covered areas ("summer huts") outside the shops lining the main tourist drags and are extremely popular with the tourists who come to Cherokee. Performers must pass a licensing program and reference check and are "required to incorporate Cherokee culture into their presentation, including their regalia, songs, dances and stories."[50] A *One Feather* poll reflected the community's concern for the chiefers'—and thereby its own—representation. The poll asked, "What is your opinion of Chiefing?" Responses showed 21 percent opposed, 18 percent in favor, 11 percent "Just don't care," and 50 percent "Ok with it as long as they wear traditional Cherokee clothing."[51] The creation of the Warriors of AniKituhwa (the official EBCI ambassadors), the (former) Cherokee Ambassadors program, and the Cherokee Friends (DhGWY ᏗᏎᏆ, AniTsalagi Digali) program are all forms of official "live" representational assertions, authored by the EBCI and grounded in historical research, meant to educate tourists while training Eastern Band citizens in historical practices spanning dress (e.g., the Cherokee Friends dress in the Cherokee style of the 1700s), dance, storytelling, carving, and games (like chunkey).[52]

As Ron related previously, this growing representational change heavily influenced his choice of products when opening his own store. He asserted, "There's a lot of shirts at the other stores, I call them junk, I call them tourists shirts. I won't carry it. . . . I carry more shirts that Natives buy than tourists," and "the crafts have got to be Indian [made]."[53] Instead of being forced to provide the public with a movie version of American Indians, Eastern Band citizens—small-business owners in this instance—wanted to be the authors of their own story about the Qualla Boundary, but not just for the tourists or to educate the wider public. They wanted their children to be surrounded by their own language, in documents and on signs, and to have access to a historical grounding not authored by Hollywood.[54] Eastern Band citizens criticized the lack of EBCI resources for themselves and their children to learn about their past and immerse themselves (if not already in artist families) in EBCI-based crafts and practices.[55] This desire for more EBCI resources extended, as in Ron's case, to the desire to buy products for *themselves* that they believed represented the EBCI. For Eastern Band citizens, in the larger discussions of representation (as opposed to individual perspectives, which vary widely), "authenticity" was reflected in the identity of the authors and creators of these histories, arts, buildings, and so on. Authenticity in this case is located in Eastern Band agency.

Unfortunately, the EBCI nation faced a significant lack of tribal funding and a rapidly shrinking tourism industry at this time, leaving them without means to address this issue. Thus, the call for change would be left unanswered until the 1990s. We can clearly see here the link between an arrested economy and a lack of power to effect wide and sweeping change even within your own nation. Without capital and reliable revenue, a museum cannot be updated, teachers cannot be hired, and business owners cannot update their stock. Beginning in the late 1990s, the Cherokee Casino's success changed all this. Suddenly generating a new influx of funds, EBCI leaders were able to update, design, and build new structures; start educational programs for citizens, ranging from Cherokee language to

"18th Century Cherokee Clothing Workshops";[56] and develop grants for their schools' Cherokee-specific courses, such as the basketmaking and pottery program, which brings in a master artist each month to help teach.[57] They assumed the power to re-create their representations themselves. They could, and did, reinvent the Qualla Boundary from the ground up, demonstrating their power to create and disseminate representations of themselves in their own words.

The EBCI's new emphasis on historical and cultural accuracy from an EBCI perspective (rather than from settler-colonial perspectives) and concepts of authenticity had many consequences. EBCI leaders began buying and clearing out old remnants of the Qualla Boundary's past—including buying and shutting down generically pan-Indian businesses. They began rebuilding a state-of-the-art Museum of the Cherokee Indian in 1998 (complete with a holographic Cherokee), which would add on an 8,500-square-foot research wing in 2010 (see Figure 2.3). EBCI leaders also renovated the Oconaluftee Village. Its original opening in 1952 followed on the heels of popular living-history villages begun in the 1920s and 1930s, such as Greenfield Village in Detroit and Colonial Williamsburg in Virginia, and led the adoption of living-history events in national parks and re-enactments across the country that would emerge and become popularized in the 1960s.[58] Despite their long presence, however, Native Nation living-history museums are not formally recognized in popular culture as living-history sites: they are noticeably and completely absent at this time from Wikipedia lists, blogs, and websites that advertise and review such places.[59] In the Oconaluftee Village today, you can walk around a replica of a historic EBCI village, circa 1759; see artists working at their crafts (which you can buy in the gift shop) and ask them questions; hear lectures in the replica council house about the EBCI political system; and watch Cherokee social dances in the small square pavilion, all for, as the advertising says, "a more authentic and historical experience."[60] Additionally, EBCI leaders updated two more attractions: the Unto These Hills outdoor historical drama (updated both technologically and in content) and the Qualla Co-Operative art market.[61] Eastern Band citizens then took up the governing boards of the Cherokee Historical Association, which had long been managed by outside entities, and a new Greater Cherokee Tourism Council was formed.[62] Finally, these groups began providing funding to businesses to update their storefronts, created a new marketing campaign, and started planning new attractions for tourist families vacationing on the Qualla Boundary. The heritage-tourism change

FIGURE 2.3 Museum of the Cherokee Indian with Sequoyah Bear. Photo by author.

in attractions combined with the casino revenue thus allowed EBCI leaders to exercise a high degree of control over the content of their image, culture, and history on the Qualla Boundary.

This is not to imply that all Eastern Band citizens agreed on the new representations, or that all even cared about them. Like all nations, Native Nations are composed of individuals who each have their own ideas about how their nation should function. Some Eastern Band citizens did *not* want to change their representations. After all, the nostalgia representations had served as a privacy barrier between themselves and the waves of tourists that descended on Cherokee—and they still fueled part of the tourist market. Furthermore, some citizens and government employees could not agree on what they should be portraying—or how. As noted in regard to the Southeast Tribes Festival hosted by the Museum of the Cherokee Indian, "What's unique about this festival is that only enrolled tribal members are included. This means that all the traditions are authentic."[63] While citizenry is one basis for a claim to authenticity (as we will see in the discussion of the Indian Arts and Crafts Act), citizens are not bound to dictates of authenticity in their art or representations. Crafting a representation that people can (hopefully mostly) agree on is a common conundrum for any nation creating a museum. This comes down to choosing what to include and what *not* to include. A museum has a finite amount of space. Decisions must be made on what elements of this portrayal will be shown to the public and what will not. But regardless of these points of contention, changes on the Qualla Boundary in representations of the Eastern Band, from their museum to their drama, were indeed enacted.

When I give talks about these transformations, I am regularly asked whether it was tourists or the EBCI and Eastern Band citizens who initiated these representational changes. My answer to this question is that both had a hand in instigating them. There was a kind of synchronicity between tourists who wanted to experience new representations but lacked a vision of what the new representations should be, and the EBCI and its citizens, who wanted to reformulate their own representations and were able to empower themselves to do so. The EBCI's choice to change these representations demonstrates the community's desire not to be preserved in a bottle of cultural formaldehyde, evincing that American Indian societies (as with all societies) have always adapted to ever-changing environments, and they are no different today. Many tourists may have wanted this change and demanded an "authentic" experience, but it was EBCI leaders, citizens, and businesspeople who were the agents of this change. It came from within, and the economic power and autonomy that the gaming revenue produced fueled it. Transformation in this case occurred at the juncture of economic sovereignty and representational control via the tourism market. And this boundary of representation is still in the process of being transformed, as seen in the ongoing public dialogue concerning small businesses. A July 2017 *One Feather* Facebook poll asked, "Should stores, located on the Qualla Boundary, be required to use Cherokee cultural guidelines in the selection of their products?" The top "liked" comment, out of forty-nine total, questioned what these guidelines would be and who they would apply to.[64] Regardless of the internal conflicts that inevitably occur, the fact is that EBCI leaders and citizens were empowered to re-create their representation during a time when the visiting public was ready to see, hear, and experience it.

The EBCI has many more short- and long-term plans for construction and reconstruction both physically and in representation. As mentioned, one of the calls from almost all tourist-oriented small-business owners is for the EBCI government to help re-create Cherokee as a more family-friendly destination, which they believe it was before the casino became the EBCI's primary focus. Teresa, of Granny's Kitchen, noted, "In the summer, we still get the summer visitors and stuff—Fourth of July, for example. Fifteen years ago or twenty-five years ago when we first started out, Fourth of July was hell week. It was. You couldn't keep enough people working. You couldn't keep enough food cooked. The traffic would be backed up almost to the foot of the mountain down here and coming in from all directions." Another business owner (anonymous) echoed these sentiments:

> The target market has changed here in Cherokee since that casino. In my opinion it used to be like family oriented. Family would come and they would do family activities and then part of those activities involved the shopping downtown. It can be completely dead here and it used to be bumper-to-bumper here in the summer. We still have some families coming through but everything is just down in the last twenty years. We've talked to business owners that have been here thirty years and they say, "We don't know if we can make the mortgage."

EBCI officials, such as Gary Ledford and Patrick Lambert, admitted that "Cherokee no longer meets that requirement of a family destination" and noted, "What we have to do is re-create the family environment."[65] Chief Hicks backed this in his 2011 Comprehensive Plan for Progress by including the goal to continue seeking family-oriented attractions in line with the vision for responsible tourism expansion. To this end, the EBCI government reopened the Cherokee Fun Park in 2011. The EBCI had bought the park from a private owner a few years earlier after a consulting firm had commented that it needed to be updated and retooled into a more culturally appropriate venue.[66] At that time, it was a generic fun park that included mini-golf, go-carts, and an arcade that had become increasingly worn down over the years. It was also in a prime location as one of the first attractions tourists see on the Qualla Boundary coming out of the GSMNP. The EBCI bought the fun park, but then it languished, abandoned, for at least two years while neighboring business owners tended to the weeds and landscaping so that their stores would not look deserted, too. In May 2011, the park reopened after renovations, although its long-term viability remains in question.[67] It is interesting that despite multiple efforts on the part of the EBCI to address the inclusion of Cherokee-specific imagery on the Qualla Boundary instead of pan-Indian representations, the mini-golf course still retained one lone teepee.

Immediate plans for larger projects are also being enacted, including a study of how a proposed adventure park could physically integrate with other approved EBCI business ventures in renovated tourism districts. Specifically, an outdoors-brought-indoors adventure park solves several issues that have challenged EBCI tourism, including the winter off-season slump and the lack of larger family-based attractions that extend the time spent on the Qualla Boundary; as William Ledford further stated in his *One Feather* commentary: "We could and would attract more people to the Rez if we had facilities that could attract families. Not everyone enjoys gambling. Not everyone enjoys fishing. People enjoy a good adventure park. Ain't no skeeters in the adventure park."[68]

Small Business Crafting Representation

The reopened Cherokee Fun Park's single teepee is a unique exception to the increasingly standardized representations in the town of Cherokee. These representations are beginning to be physically established and enforced in order to project a new, more structured image to the tourist marketplace. The EBCI government has recently offered encouraging incentives, created guidelines, and passed laws requiring businesses to change their appearance to one that is more "mountain" and "Cherokee" themed. The EBCI encouraged small-business owners to promote the new representational strategy by offering loans and grants (see appendix A) to refurbish business facades. The new style, of stone and heavy lumber, was required for a more authentic, "distinctly Cherokee" (in this case, historically Cherokee) look, as specified in the EBCI's Downtown Business Master Plan, which the EBCI government and small-business owners designed jointly over the span of a few years. The *Downtown Cherokee Revitalization Design Guidelines* state: "Traditionally Cherokee structures were covered with plated mats of cane and sticks and then covered with mud. As interaction with settlers increased, the Cherokees occupied log homes similar to those of their neighbors; this provides us with an example of *identifiable Cherokee architecture*. Buildings in the business district should be sided with cedar sita, lap siding, board and batten, or log construction. Plaster or exterior insulation finish systems may be used to create the *historical texture*."[69]

Later, new regulations were enacted that required business signs to be culturally appropriate to the EBCI.[70] Stricter guidelines began to be enforced by law on November 5, 2012, with the passage of Ordinance Number 310 into the Cherokee Code of the Eastern Band. This ordinance includes Article III: Streetscapes and Display of Merchandise, Sec. 136-31, which specifies, among other terms, exactly what merchandise can and cannot be displayed outdoors (see appendix B); permitted items include authentic, handmade Native American products, art, or crafts; art, crafts, or products indigenous to the Appalachian region; and items that are respectful of traditional Cherokee culture. This leaves pan-Indian and pan–Plains

FIGURE 2.4
Tribal Grounds
Coffee, 2010.
Photo by author.

FIGURE 2.5 Qualla Java coffeehouse, 2017. Photo by author.

Indian items, such as headdresses and teepees, in a gray area, as they are not specifically banned in the "Items that are not permitted" list but are generally not compatible with the permitted-items list. All businesses were required to be in compliance with the ordinance by May 1, 2014. According to the *One Feather* notification, "Fines for non-compliance, which result in revocation of a business license, will be issued on May 2. Again, no exceptions!"[71]

For the near future, in order to re-envision the physical context of these tourist businesses, Resolution No. 717 authorized the Cherokee Department of Transportation (CDOT) to seek $500,000 in funding from the Cherokee Preservation Foundation for the completion of phase two of the Cultural District Streetscape.[72] Phase three, which began in October 2011, "includes culturally themed streetlights, underground utility wires, new and wider sidewalks, crosswalks stamped with cultural symbols, improved landscaping and signage, and the addition of benches, bike racks and recycling bins" on the major thoroughfare through Cherokee, Highway 441.[73] Another renovation, enacted in 2016, is the "Artisan and Craftsman" District, which will encourage walking traffic and promote "cultural integrity."[74]

Signage laws like these are ubiquitous in the United States, running the gamut from federal laws that specifically focus on enhancing appearances, such as the Highway Beautification Act, to local zoning restrictions aimed at safety issues (e.g., banning signs that mimic traffic control signs). Cherokee's nearby tourism competitor, Gatlinburg, Tennessee, is also concerned with signage, stating in section 411.1 of their ordinance, "It is recognized that the City of Gatlinburg is a Premier Resort City with its only industry being tourism. . . . Therefore, the purpose of this ordinance is to . . . preserve, promote, and protect: (1) the unique character of the city by the orderly display of signs," further stating in section 706 on the zoning of their C-1 tourist district: "The requirements are designed to protect the essential characteristics of the district by promotion of business and public uses which serve the general public" and, consequently, prohibits all outdoor display and sale of merchandise (within the specified front-yard setback).

What is interesting here are the differences in regulations. While Cherokee allows for outdoor merchandise displays, the EBCI has found it necessary to regulate this content in order to form a more cohesive tourism narrative for their town. Gatlinburg, equally concerned with its own "unique character," avoids this issue by the outright prohibition of outdoor displays. Both of these locations' concern with uniqueness is not a surprise given that they are the bookend towns of Highway 441 running across the GSMNP, only a mere hour away from each other. Downtown Gatlinburg has taken the path of more generic family fun and attractions that are not necessarily tied to "place" (e.g., a Ripley's Aquarium, featuring sharks, stingrays, and penguins) and that provide standard, predictable entertainment—a plus for families with finicky children—with an undercurrent of mountain flair. However, Cherokee's tourism uniqueness, whether it is in nostalgia or heritage form, has long been tied to its difference—a point noted by many government officials, consultants, and small-business owners on the Qualla Boundary when discussing the concerns of signage and outdoor merchandise displays that appear to "Gatlinburgize" Cherokee. Thus, while these regulations may seem to constrain small-business owners' agency, and they do prompt questions (who gets to determine what is "respectful of traditional Cherokee culture"?), the response has been generally positive within the business and larger Cherokee community. Many consider it to be an answer to the internal call to have Cherokee's representation focus more on the uniqueness of Cherokees (thus differentiating itself from other tourist sites), whether that is in the form of rewriting the Unto These Hills play or rewriting the laws governing the face of Cherokee—its businesses.[75] It is important to remember as well that many internal calls for representational change preceded the new laws being implemented. Thus, these formal policies are augmenting the market changes that individual business owners had already begun to respond to and, in so doing, are continuing a historical and economic trajectory that was already being defined by those individuals.

One clear manifestation of these changes taking place for tourism in Cherokee can be seen in the products that small-business owners choose to sell. Many businesses that serve tourists are battling with two competing interests. First is the new heritage tourist, who primarily wants locally made, hand-crafted, "authentic" Eastern Band items. Second are the more regional and locally based tourists who come to Cherokee regularly for day-trips. Many of these visitors are either not able to afford—or simply do not want any (or any more)—artisan crafts; rather, they are looking for items that are more generic, fun, and cheaper (a plastic Cherokee snow globe, colored headdresses, cheap T-shirts).[76] Every season, store owners struggle with how best to serve the needs of the tourist market as a whole. In addition to customer desires, there is another aspect to consider when choosing inventory: cost to the owner. Stocking a store with foreign-made, pan-Indian nostalgia goods is far cheaper for the store owner than keeping local, hand-made crafts in stock (especially when the store owner buys the items, as Pooh does, instead of selling them on consignment), leading to lower start-up costs and lower overall inventory costs.[77]

As a result of these factors, the products sold by the privately owned stores on the Qualla Boundary fall into three primary categories. First, while there are fewer of the nostalgia tourist items than in the past, these items are still very much a part of the product line for tourist-centric stores—and are often highly visible. After all, it is much easier (physically), more eye-catching, and less risky to hang an inexpensive hot-pink dreamcatcher outside your store (rain or shine) than it is to hang a five-foot-wide, $1,500 hand-carved set of Cherokee clan masks. These are the products that stir up the most controversy on the Qualla Boundary. As business owners struggle to provide consumers with the products they want and can afford, some Eastern Band citizens object to being represented by pan-Indian, and even blatantly offensive, products. Patrick Lambert addressed this during his run for principal chief in 2011, when he emphasized that the Cherokee tourist industry needs to try to get away from the "rubber tomahawk-type shops."[78] More controversially, while I was in the midst of my summertime business visits during the height of the tourist season, the One Feather printed a picture of a new T-shirt being sold in several stores on the Qualla Boundary. It read, "My Indian Name is 'Runs with Beer'—Cherokee, NC." The One Feather asked its readers to weigh in on this topic: funny joke or offensive? It was not surprising that those who took the time to write in did not support the T-shirt. Some even called for temporarily closing the stores over this item, which pushed the town of Cherokee past merely appearing to promote a pan-Indian stereotype to blatant mockery of American Indians as (falsely) associated with drunkenness,[79] on a reservation that has consistently voted to be dry, partially in order to combat this perception.[80] These types of goods are increasingly dwindling, but given the ease of stocking and selling these low-priced products, they continue to have a place in the market.

The second category of goods sold by stores on the Qualla Boundary includes Cherokee handmade arts and crafts. Historically, a tourist might have had to go to an artist's home in order to buy an Eastern Band craft; today, nearly every store carries some items that fit into the broad category of arts and crafts made specifically by local Eastern Band (and even Cherokee Nation or United Kituwah Band) artists—baskets, masks, beaded jewelry, and so on. The One Feather described the changes in these goods: "Traditionally, the Cherokee used wood carving for creating things of necessity, such as: bowls, utensils, tools, furniture and ceremonial masks. After the opening of the Great Smoky Mountains National Park, wood carving transformed into a more decorative art to appeal to more to visitors."[81] As previously mentioned, one set of items representing a curious crossover between these first two categories of goods for sale is the pan-Indian items—such as headdresses and bows and arrows—handcrafted by Eastern Band artists in Cherokee. The overall products in this handmade category range widely in price, scale, and materials—from simple woven friendship bracelets to enormous stone carvings—and are the foundation product category for Cherokee. Most stores carry items from both of these categories, stocking more or fewer of them depending on their location on the downtown strip and the store owner's personal preference.

The third and final category of goods sold on the Qualla Boundary stores comprises the non-Cherokee, American Indian–made arts and crafts. These are stocked by individual store owners who travel throughout the country during the winter season lull to find new American Indian artists and products. The Indian Arts and Crafts Act (IACA) has made this category much more prominent, as has the relative ease of travel that increases store owners' access to these products. Many local owners have stated that people inquire about the artists who make the items stocked in their store and whether they are American Indian; the post-IACA laws have made the answer to this question a much more clear-cut one for store owners. Having said that, some owners handle this question of citizenship (with its many subtle and not-so-subtle complexities) in their own way. For Ron, the answer with regard to Eastern Band artists is simple, "A lot of the local [artists], [I] grew up with them, I know them. I know they're locals. [So if a tourist] asked me, 'How do you know this is Indian made?' I said I grew up with them, went to school with them. That's all."[82]

Another interesting distinction is the difference between products made by an artist for general sale and those that are available only by request—custom-made products that one has to know about to ask for. Sometimes these are plain, utilitarian items that would be useful only to Eastern Band citizens, other Cherokee, and possibly other American Indians. One example is a talking stick (usually a simply decorated piece of carved wood), which is used to indicate who has the floor in a group setting and assures that everyone who would like to speak gets an opportunity to do so as it is passed around the group (be it a council or a gathering of family members). I never saw these for sale in any store, but I did see Eastern Band citizens approach artists to request them. Generally, these items are not showy and do not garner a large price for the work put into them and therefore would not be worth the effort to produce on a large (read: tourist) scale. Another example of this is Granny's catering menu. Due to this issue of scale, Granny's cannot offer many "Cherokee foods" in the restaurant, but when people began requesting them for smaller, privately catered events, it gladly obliged. In fact, it has now become expected that when certain Eastern Band citizen-focused events take place—at the new language-immersion academy or at the ceremonial grounds, for example—Granny's will be there with plenty of bean bread and grease. Teresa gave another reason why the restaurant does not offer these foods publicly (though other restaurants do): "If [visitors] are looking for Cherokee food, they're all going to be disappointed because it's just beans and potatoes and corn bread like everybody else has eaten forever. The Cherokee food's very bland. Most of these people with this educated palate [are] not going to like it. Of course, if you grew up eating it, it's really, really good."[83]

Intertwined with the question of what products to stock in this new market is the question of how to price the goods. After the EBCI-sponsored Indianpreneurship class ended, several classmates were kind enough to join me for a follow-up discussion about the class, their (potential) businesses, and their past experiences with businesses on the Qualla Boundary. We met at Myrtle's, located in what was then a Best Western hotel. Myrtle's is one large room made in the style of a log cabin, with heavy timber, a stone fireplace, a smattering of EBCI and local mountain crafts on the walls, and one large front window that faces the mountains. Myrtle's also gave discounts to local residents, especially in the winter, and judging by the empty wooden tables and seats that night, we were well past tourist season. One part of the conversation that particularly struck me was led by Alice and concerned the difficulty of pricing IACA crafts. Alice, an Eastern Band citizen, had years of experience working for a tourist business and was looking to start her own party-planning operation for locals. Robert, an expert Eastern Band craftsperson and fluent Cherokee speaker and teacher, and Daniel, who was researching opening a laundromat, briefly joined in as well.

Alice: And they're wanting more Native Americans to open their own businesses. That's what they're gearing toward, which I think is a good idea because this is our town.

Moderator: Do you think a lot of people would want to start businesses?

A: I think a lot of them got burned out when they did the Native American crafts. They got burned out because, excuse me, the white people came in here and just started taking over, and they were selling them just here and there, putting us out of business, so we're like, "Why go into business?"

Robert: [They should] buy from the natives.

A: "Oh, that's too much." They don't want to pay for it, but then they come into the shops, "Oh, this is from China," "Oh, this is from here." . . . Well, they don't want to pay the price either. Do they? They don't want to pay the price for Native American–made necklaces or they want them to still be the prices of the Chinese [products].

Daniel: You're right. I've seen that when I was helping out Marian in her [herb] shop. That was the case most of the time.

M: So what do you do at that point?

A: Exactly. A lot of people have quit doing it. They go to powwows and the same things are happening. . . . What are you going to do? It's like you're being squeezed out all the way around.

In tourist markets overall, there are always trinkets (small items created for tourists) that are inexpensive—making it easy to take a family into a store, buy a few fifty-cent items for the kids, and come out without breaking the bank. If a tourist is looking for Eastern Band–made items, they can find a few of these lower-priced items, like small earrings or bracelets sold for under $5. However, Eastern Band–made crafts range widely in price, as intricately carved masks or sculptures can be sold for thousands of dollars. The non-Cherokee, American Indian–made items also have a wide range in price, but they are rarely as cheap as either the nostalgia tourist goods or local small items due to the transportation costs for the owners in acquiring them and the local availability of cheaper items. On the lower end, you can find bumper stickers for under $10, while on the higher end, there is jewelry for over $1,000. The problem of pricing goods was a topic that came up again and again in my talks with store owners. Many stressed that in order to survive, they had to stock a wide variety of products to have something available for any given tourist.

One store owner, Bethany (non-Native), who has lived on and around the Qualla Boundary for over five decades, described to me how she ended up changing her entire business model after one incident. When she first took over ownership of her store, she had decided to stock it nearly entirely with "local handmade crafts," many of high quality. One day, a woman with four little girls came into the store. As Bethany said, "They had just spent a night in a motel and they wanted a doll and the only dolls we had were a hundred bucks because they were all handmade. I said [to myself,] 'No. This is not going to work. We've got to have something for everybody.' We don't want them to feel like . . ."[84] Her sentence trailed off as she recounted how those girls and their mother left disappointed that day. From that moment on, Bethany decided that her store would carry products for every budget, so that no one would be turned away if they wanted a souvenir. Today, her store's incredibly dense stock and wide range of items attest to this philosophy. As you walk in, you are overwhelmed by the sheer volume of products covering every surface, a result of over three decades of accumulation since the incident with the woman and her girls: jewelry, pottery, tobacco, pipes, books, CDs, salves, coats, T-shirts, bows and arrows, sculptures, and more, appear the more you look. At first glance, it may read as a nondescript tourist store (especially in the children's section, which carries the usual inexpensive plastic tom-toms and neon headdresses), but it only takes a moment to see that most of the store is filled with craft items made by Eastern Band artists, natural medicines made by neighboring locals, and supplies for local artists (especially beads and other art supplies). Although she stocks some items worth just a bit of change, Bethany also carries intricately carved wooden sculptures worth thousands of dollars that cannot be found at other stores, as well as jewelry made by young artists who are just learning the trade. The density and variety of the products cultivated by Bethany over her years in business would be difficult to match.

In a neighboring district to Bethany's, another longtime business owner, in an attempt to modernize his store, decided to use an offer from the Sequoyah Fund to have a consultant come and evaluate his store's image.[85] The consultant suggested a series of changes to make the store look "less cheap." The owner made the changes, only to have customers become so intimidated that they stopped purchasing items that had not changed price at all. As he told me, he had to sell the fancy shelves that he had bought to display his T-shirts and place the shirts back in plastic bins on collapsible tables in order to move the product again. In the end, he relayed, you need to have customers in order to survive as a business.[86] Natalie, of Tribal Grounds, knows this balance well, as her business was on the cutting edge in Cherokee. Her store emphasized waste reduction (with compostable materials) and even offered vegan options (an option nearly unheard of west of Asheville). She said, "But the fact is, a business is a fine balance between structuring yourself for your community and you structuring your community."[87] In other words, as a business owner, when you choose to make deliberate changes such as these, you may eventually change the community because you *are* the community.

As we have seen, businesses have been functionally affected on several levels as a result of the rise of the new type of heritage tourism and concurrent increase in the EBCI government's constraints on business practices through its larger "cultural revitalization" efforts. But as Natalie pointed out, these small businesses are not merely the passive receivers of these impacts; they played and continue to play an active role in molding their representation and, in turn, affect the EBCI's concept of representation.[88] The reshaping of small-business identities comes from the perspective of the business owners themselves, but in the process, it alters how they, and their entire community, are viewed by others—especially tourists. Small businesses, which have the most interaction with tourists, educate those tourists to a significant degree while also bolstering community knowledge.[89] In also selling goods that the community needs—say, corn beads for artists—they have to know about the products and are, thus, one of the many keepers and distributors of this knowledge (the quality of the corn beads, what the season has been like for growing them, and so on). Therefore, small-business identities, as expressed through their physical forms, inventory, and business philosophies, recursively form and are formed by the identity of their community in a dynamic socioeconomic process.

Seeing the Authentic

Another popular event that some small businesses offer is personal appearances of artists at their store. Tourists in general have always been fascinated by viewing and interacting with local community members—especially artists. Tourists who specifically seek out businesses where an artist is actively creating a product will also be willing to spend more money on that artist's pieces. Some have labeled this practice as racist as it implies an "othering" inherent to tourism.[90] I believe that there is more complexity to this activity. Meeting an artist is an extension of the validation many people seek when conducting business in general. Consumers are often more comfortable doing business when they can see the owner and feel that there is a measure of accountability. It is no coincidence that this is particularly acute today, when corporations are alienating consumers more frequently, as reflected in the increasing discourses on social relations of consumption, production, and distribution; consumer alienation; and consequences of corporate deregulation. Part of the lure of tourism—and this is especially relevant in heritage and cultural tourism—is that you *do* get to make a connection with the person making the item. It validates tourists' desire for "authenticity" beyond the IACA stamp and serves to reinforce that they are without a doubt supporting a local artist (a sometimes-difficult feat when they have little knowledge of how the products are being produced). The tourist can (and does) ask, "Are you Cherokee?" as she sees the person creating her piece of art. As Pooh related to me:

When I did the craft shop, I pulled together eight of my favorite Cherokee artists that I wanted to really promote, and I launched a website. Well, I brought them all together, had it catered, and hosted for them at my shop. . . . I said, "I want to do one show where you'll all come up for two days, give your time, you sell everything at retail. Because what I find is that people want to meet you guys, for me to build a collector base for you all, they've got to come and meet you. They've got to know about you. They've got to be able to connect with you the person." They did it. It was successful. We added a second show.[91]

This also often applies to the small-business owners themselves. While I sat in stores during the afternoons, I would often hear tourists asking for the owner by name. They would come in from out of town specifically to see the owner, to purchase a product from a real person. In Bethany's case, most people who came into the store would ask if she was in that day. In reference to this close relationship with her customers, she said,

That's one of the things I try. I'm not going to say that what I do works for everybody, but [the customers inside the store at that moment] just reminded me of one of the things. They were in here earlier. . . . He said, "Well, is this made here? Is that made here?" I said, "Yes." I said, "Have you ever been to the Indian village?" He said, "No, but that's what I want to do." I said, "Well, you need to go up there first and then decide what you would like as a souvenir." He said, "Do they have a store up there?" and I said, "They sure do, and when you get through there, you'll go right into that store and they have all the things they make up there." But he came back here because I didn't try to corner him up and say be sure and come back and shop with me, because when people leave, I want them to be happy. That's another thing. If I lose ten dollars on a sale, they're going to leave here happy, but most [business]people are not going to do that. See, that's not real good business-sense in the books, but like I say, I'm probably not a good one to go by the books. I'm just not. I'm just not that way, but it does work.[92]

In Bethany's case, even though she is not an Eastern Band citizen, her intimate knowledge of the market, her close relationship with Eastern Band craftspeople, and her near lifetime of working on the Qualla Boundary gives her customers a feeling of connection and authenticity.

The new EBCI emphasis on authenticity, however, also feeds the internal pressure on artists and business owners to maintain this new "heritage" form of representation—to produce and stock the more expensive local, handmade products. Artists and small-business owners struggle to balance the transformation of the EBCI's public representation with the need to offer consumers the items they want to buy in order to stay in business. As Natalie says of her experience as an artist, "I think that every artist has that concern. And there's no shame in making art to sell. And those who make art to sell know it. And those who don't know that they're making art to sell, I don't know. [In other words,] there are those who don't know that they're making art to sell and those that do know it. And that's all." Natalie and other American Indian artists must choose between two competing interests: to create salable artistic works within the genre of "Indian-Themed Art," which have a greater chance of selling (especially in Cherokee) and are more likely to allow the artists to make a living solely off their work, or to follow their creative impulses, which might not be so eagerly consumed by the public.[93] As we saw with "Chief" Lambert, this (constructed) choice between serving the public and selling the products you believe in (which are certainly not always mutually exclusive) can have significant consequences.

The Sequoyah Fund began a program in 2013 that attempts to address these particular issues, among others relating to authenticity, with its new "Authentically Cherokee" brand. The program initially partnered with ONA-BEN (Our Native American Business Network) and rolled out a website in 2015, focusing on the branding, marketing, and distribution of Eastern Band artists, especially those whose work is "more modern and a little different," working to "preserve Cherokee culture in a contemporary way."[94] This illustrates the place of branding in Native Nations' asserting control of their representational identity, but it also highlights the work of contemporary artists in tackling the representational challenges they face in producing art for the public. In doing so, this program also sees itself as a version of "buy local" for Eastern Band art entrepreneurs, with the brand logo also acting as a type of certification of Eastern Band citizen status. This program thus defines both *authenticity* and *Cherokee* as first (and most importantly) rooted in citizenship and second, the continuance of Cherokee traditions, while framing these traditions as contemporary actions and expressions. Although this program focuses on a specific segment of the artist population (eleven artists in 2018), the brand itself could be extended in the future to include a wide range of producers and products.

· · · · · ·

Tourism on the Qualla Boundary, along with the small businesses that power and support it, has experienced many transformations. From its nascency (before the GSMNP was even established) to the Red Power movement and casino installations, this industry has weathered many exogenous shocks and endogenous changes. Their prime location at the entrance of the GSMNP has given these small businesses a decided advantage over Native Nation tourism locations that are more difficult to reach and less populated with returning visitors, but it cannot entirely shield them from economic recessions or from tourists' potentially fickle preferences. After the EBCI faced multiple threats to its formerly profitable tourism industry, from rising gas prices to the waning of Western films and thus interest in American Indians, it took a calculated, strategic risk in opening a casino. The success of the Cherokee Casino elevated the EBCI's economic power, allowing it to slowly recraft a new tourism-industry representation.

This recrafting and deploying of representation and "authenticity" continue to be a topic of discussion, from the regulation of small-business signage to the determinations of who can participate in chiefing. Although many of the preferences of tourists to Cherokee have changed over the years, one request has stayed the same: to see "the Indians." This desire is driven by many motivations; some come to learn about the EBCI from the EBCI, some to help support the EBCI economy and Eastern Band businesses (at times associated with white guilt), some to reclaim what they believe to be their Indianness (in which "othering" meets "selfing" in crafting one's own family mythology of descendancy), and some to see and capture a piece of the Indians—whether in photos or in craft purchases, with the crafts representing indigenously "pure objects (art) and pure persons (artists)"[95]—before they purportedly disappear. How the EBCI and small-business owners negotiate this tourist demand has changed dramatically over the years; it now encompasses an assertion of their own perspectives, words, and representations as "the EBCI" and as Eastern Band individuals via small businesses and artists. In doing so, the EBCI and its citizens continue to exercise their agency and economic sovereignty by developing a tourism industry that provides a successful base for their economy.

FIGURE 2.6
Granny's catering
for an EBCI event at
Kituwah. Photo by
author.

While the success of the Cherokee Casino enabled much of this self-authoring, small-business owners, who often serve as the individual faces of the Eastern Band to tourists, have been vital in recrafting the representation of the EBCI. The long-term sustainability of tourism as an economic development platform for communities in need is much debated, though, especially within the field of tourism studies.[96] The EBCI has shown, in its case, that despite the vacillating nature of tourists' interests, tourism as a long-term sustainable industry is possible—at least for the one hundred years that the EBCI has officially engaged in it so far. However, no matter the industry choices of the EBCI and Eastern Band small-business owners, in order to support an entrepreneurial culture, they will need to contend with the boundaries that come with American Indian small-business ownership: property, citizenship, and representation.

3 Bounding American Indian Businesses

. . . .

During my fieldwork, I frequently drove a winding, two-lane road that climbs steadily up one of the oldest mountain ranges in the world to reach the Qualla Boundary. Hairpin turns through the forest start appearing an hour past Asheville, the last major city east of the GSMNP. Occasionally, the dense forests break just long enough to catch a glimpse of the Great Smoky Mountains' rolling blue vista, which draws about eleven million tourists a year.[1] As hotels begin to appear, there is a sign announcing, "WELCOME Cherokee Indian Reservation," marking the beginning of the geographic boundary where my research takes place. This space, known as the Qualla Boundary, consists of approximately fifty-six thousand acres, held mostly in federal trust. The population I work with is also bounded, as the EBCI is a federally recognized Native Nation, whose citizenship qualifications are now determined primarily internally but remain subject to federal law.[2] The representational aspects of this particular space, in addition to issues that emerge when looking at the tourism industry, have also been reified into a boundary of sorts through federal laws drawing on citizenship, such as the Indian Arts and Crafts Act, along with internal EBCI regulations. Historically, the EBCI has had to persistently pursue and reaffirm the parameters of each of these boundaries. Examples of this agency include its decades-long battle for North Carolina citizenship, its deployment of strategies and tactics to retain its land during federal attempts at Cherokee relocation, and its strategic approaches to crafting its own image for the tourism industry.

Every Native Nation is a "border nation"—physically, economically, politically, and legally. As such, the volatile topic of these Native Nation boundaries is historically and contemporarily enmeshed with contestation and conflict, not only in the larger political actions of these states but also as it is felt in the daily lives of American Indian peoples. Boundaries of territory and citizenry in particular have always been crucial to the subject of American Indian rights. The most dominant strategy to reduce—or eliminate entirely, in some circumstances—American Indian rights is through the manipulation of these boundaries. This happens on a federal level in the pendulum-like policies of the U.S. government, which have swung between the extremes of either attempted elimination of Native Nations or support for Native Nations' inherent sovereignty. These vacillations expose underlying colonial ambivalence as to the status of Native Nations.[3] Although it would seem, at first glance, that these boundaries are currently fixed, the complex reality is that these politically tied boundaries continue to be both actively ignored and aggressively assaulted, in part through acts of economic colonialism. The EBCI today continues to oppose outside attempts to dissolve or manipulate its boundaries and has been at the forefront of negotiations with external state powers while simultaneously expressing its right to craft and recraft its own boundaries. The delineations of these boundaries, then, have complications and consequences for the exercise of EBCI economic sovereignty as well as for the small-business owners who choose to operate there. These boundary formations are critical to understanding the contextual distinctiveness of federally recognized American Indian entrepreneurs through land rights, formation of citizenship requirements, and issues of representation (especially in relation to citizenship). For the EBCI, this context begins with land.

Origins of EBCI Land and Citizenship

The formation of Cherokee territories as we know them today began with the Cherokees' knowledge of a great migration that eventually brought their people, numbering so many "that [they] covered most of the eastern seaboard,"[4] to settle in what are now the states of Alabama, Georgia, Tennessee, South Carolina, North Carolina, and, to a lesser degree, Kentucky and Virginia.[5] This territory stayed relatively intact until 1721, when treaties (here, with the governor of South Carolina) began to officially whittle away at this land base. By the 1820s, the states that were settled on Cherokee Nation territory, most notably Georgia, began to take measures to force the Cherokees west of the Mississippi River. In 1830, Congress passed the Indian Removal Act, authorizing the president to negotiate the removals of Indians east of the Mississippi. In its aftermath, two key U.S. Supreme Court cases established the relationship between the states, the federal government, and the Cherokee Nation. In *Cherokee Nation v. Georgia* (1831), the Cherokee Nation sought status as a "foreign state" and an injunction against Georgia, which was enacting oppressive state laws in violation of Cherokee Nation sovereignty. Although the Cherokee Nation lost this case in the sense that they were not declared a "foreign state" (and thus could not sue Georgia as one), the court did declare them a "domestic dependent nation," thus defining a legal status for Native Nations. *Worcester v. Georgia* (1832) soon followed when the Georgia Guard arrested missionaries Samuel Worcester and Elizur Butler after they refused to recognize Georgia's state law prohibiting whites from living within the Cherokee Nation without taking an oath of allegiance to the state. While this case was a legal victory for Worcester, the missionaries were not freed from prison until two years later, when they agreed to leave the state.

While seminal for clarifying Native Nation governmental relationships with the United States, these court decisions did little to aid the Cherokees in their fight against removal efforts. Furthermore, although these American Indian removals were legal under the Indian Removal Act, the Cherokees who signed the Treaty of New Echota, which provided for the Cherokee Nation's removal, did not have the authority to do so, thereby making their acts illegal under Cherokee Nation law.[6] There was no official death toll from the Trail Where They Cried—more accurately called Nvnohi Dunatlohilvyi (ᏃᏘᎯ ᏕᎾᏠᎯᎸᎩ) in the Cherokee language—but estimates suggest that this process of relocation (1838–39, a time period Cherokees call the Removal), first to concentration camps within their homelands and then to the Indian Territory (what is now Oklahoma), caused the loss of approximately four thousand lives.[7] The U.S. government purposefully undertook this act to, among other motives (e.g., as always, access to land), weaken the thriving Cherokee Nation by separating it from its economic land base and thus from the means by which it had very successfully supported itself (food, schools, courthouses, medicinals) as well as from prime locations of commerce.[8] During this tumultuous time, some Cherokees continued to live in the mountains of North Carolina and others fled from the relocation efforts to western North Carolina. The descendants of many of these Cherokees would later be recognized as the Eastern Band of Cherokee Indians.[9]

The Cherokee Nation was politically active and legally astute and thus was very much aware of the possibility that their efforts to combat U.S. attempts at removal could fail.[10] The Cherokees living in western North Carolina—specifically the core group of Qualla Indians who would later become the EBCI—resisted removal by pursuing their claims to North Carolina citizenship (and thus dissolving their citizenship in the Cherokee Nation West) based on the previous land treaties of 1817 and 1819.[11] These treaties permitted heads of Cherokee families to remain in western North Carolina and apply for 640 acres of land. The state of North Carolina finally legally authorized the North Carolina Cherokees to stay in 1837.[12] Unfortunately, the matter of citizenship would continue to be contentious for the North

Carolina Cherokees. The federal government periodically affirmed their citizenship (via a series of acts of Congress through 1930), while the state of North Carolina refused to acknowledge them as state citizens (including refusing them the right to vote). Part of this flux would be resolved when the federal government formally recognized the North Carolina Cherokees as distinct from the Cherokee Nation in 1868, but it would not be until 1946, after continuously fighting the state of North Carolina for nearly a century, that North Carolina finally conceded the EBCI full and practicing state citizenship, thus allowing Eastern Band citizens to vote.

During the time in which their citizenship status was clouded, the North Carolina Cherokees needed a stable solution to the issue of their land ownership. William Holland Thomas was a white North Carolinian lawyer and businessman who had been a lifelong ally of the North Carolina Cherokees; his actions feature prominently in their history, especially during their legal battles of this era. Thomas worked jointly with the North Carolina Cherokees to buy large amounts of land on their behalf, totaling nearly fifty thousand acres by 1842, and hold it in his name.[13] The lands were purchased using both Thomas's money and monies owed to the North Carolina Cherokees by the federal government. By having Thomas purchase these lands on their behalf, the North Carolina Cherokees created a legally recognized and relatively cohesive EBCI land base.

In order to further protect the common ownership of the land, the North Carolina Cherokees incorporated for the first time in 1847 as a sugar and silk Cherokee Company. Owing to the lack of incorporation laws in North Carolina at that time, this was accomplished by a proclamation from the governor.[14] It is little coincidence that the EBCI considered incorporation at this time. As Joanne Barker describes, 1819 marked the *Trustees of Dartmouth College v. Woodward* Supreme Court decision in which corporate charters were determined to fall under constitutional protections: "Protected as a constitutional right, corporate property rights trumped tribal territorial claims, even when secured by a treaty, and even when corporations acquired the lands by fraud. *Fletcher* [*v. Peck*] and *Dartmouth* thereby represented the rearticulation of 'Indian tribes' into a legal and economic structure predicated on imperialist capitalism without any corporate accountability."[15] Thus, one way to increase, although not guarantee, Native Nation protections was to choose to incorporate ("choose" being the operative word, compared to, for example, the incorporation of Alaskan Natives).[16] These EBCI actions—from buying its own land to incorporating for legal protection—represent acts of "positive refusal" (and "failure to consent"), as elaborated by Audra Simpson, to having their boundaries legally defined in a way deemed necessary, acceptable, and appropriate by the settler-colonial state; as Simpson argues, these are acts of refusal of settler dominion over territory.[17] Because of these hard-won battles for their homeland, Eastern Band citizens refer to their land base as the "Boundary" rather than a "reservation." This reflects the distinction that EBCI land was not reserved for them as a result of some cession; rather, it is their own homeland, which they gained control of on their terms.

While this incorporation put the North Carolina Cherokees in a more peculiar legal position than other Native Nations at that time, it is important to acknowledge that federal and state protections of landholding could only be realized by having Thomas, as a white male, ultimately hold title to the land as its trustee. This was a precarious and vulnerable arrangement for the North Carolina Cherokees. Unfortunately, after the Civil War, Thomas's mounting tax and personal debt, as well as his health problems, overwhelmed him, and a lender eventually claimed Thomas's landholdings. Eventually, the North Carolina Cherokees brought action against Thomas, and the court ultimately conferred the land's ownership and outstanding debts to the EBCI in 1874.[18] It would not be until 1925 that the federal government would take trusteeship over EBCI land, thus relieving them of the state property taxes they had paid since the Trail Where They Cried.[19] During the Collier administration, the EBCI would again use incorporation as a mechanism for asserting sovereignty, arguing in 1938 against U.S. governmental (via the Bureau of Indian Affairs [BIA]) control over its internal affairs. In this case, the EBCI Tribal Council voted down a new constitution under the 1934 Indian Reorganization Act (also known as the Wheeler–Howard Act), thereby rejecting BIA authority over the Qualla Boundary, EBCI governmental affairs, and the rights of their citizens.[20] The EBCI's decision to incorporate, along with its use of Thomas as its landholder, demonstrates its agency even (and especially) in times of crisis through the exercise of its economic sovereignty. These actions innovatively appropriated U.S. economic-based legal mechanisms to secure, as best as possible, protective measures for the EBCI's land, resources, citizens, and nation.

Through the years, the issue of internal EBCI membership and citizenship has been as complex and has undergone as many transformations as the EBCI's land-ownership status. Mikaela Adams notes:

> In the eighteenth and early nineteenth centuries, Cherokees had
> defined their communities by kinship. As a matrilineal society, the

Cherokees had long traced tribal belonging through female kin. According to this system, anyone born of a Cherokee mother was automatically a full member of the community, no matter the father's racial identity. Over the years, however, kinship patterns changed as the Cherokees interacted with non-Indians and became acquainted with patriarchal customs. Even before the removal of the 1830s, Cherokee men had secured the rights of citizenship in the Cherokee Nation for their children born of non-Cherokee mothers. Cherokees who remained in the east following removal continued to intermarry with non-Indians, and many of them considered their children to be Cherokee, regardless of the sex of their Cherokee parent.[21]

In 1874, the court case that granted the EBCI final legal title to its land also began to tie economic interests to political citizenship, extending the definition of citizenship beyond merely blood. Adams describes this moment:

> Ancestry was important, but blood alone did not make someone an Eastern Band citizen. The tribal council also restricted citizenship to those Cherokees who had participated in rebuilding the Band's land base in North Carolina. . . . The tribal council argued that only those Cherokees with "pecuniary interest" in the land should have rights as tribal citizens. . . . In particular, they or their ancestors had to have been present on the land at the time of the 1874 court decision. . . . The decision to include "pecuniary interest" through residency as one of the criteria for inclusion illustrated that the Eastern Band conceived of itself as more than an ethnic group or racial minority in the South. It was a political organization with economic interests. It was not enough to claim racial heritage as Cherokee; *individuals also had to prove their political citizenship in and economic ties to the Band.*[22]

The critical use of economic elements to cement political actions and sovereignties followed in 1889, as the EBCI incorporated once again under the newly implemented North Carolina incorporation laws. This charter of incorporation, along with its 1895 amendment (Section 22) that set a one-sixteenth minimum blood quantum for rights to EBCI assets, was significant, as it would serve as the EBCI's governing document, helping to solidify the EBCI as a political body. Three heavily contested censuses occurred after the incorporation (the 1907 Council Roll, the 1908 Churchill Roll, and the 1909 Guion Miller Roll). One reason underlying these contestations was the common practice of paying a lawyer a fee plus a commission to fight for an individual's inclusion on American Indian rolls—instigating the use of the phrase "five-dollar Indian" for individuals who gained roll placement in this manner.[23] Additionally, economic incentives from timber shares, land allotments, and court-ordered treaty recompenses added to the scramble for placement on the EBCI rolls. In referring to these actions, Adams notes: "This stance [on citizenship requirements] was not only about protecting Cherokee resources for core members of the Cherokee community, it also was about protecting Cherokee political rights for individuals who cared about the Band's future. *Without its economic base, the Band's political independence would be meaningless.* If individuals with no interest in Eastern Band affairs claimed a significant portion of tribal resources, the Band's political structure would collapse."[24]

It was the fourth census, the 1924 Baker Roll, that would become the base roll for the EBCI. The U.S. government, specifically a man named Fred A. Baker, would determine who would be included in the Baker Roll, and his determination required no EBCI approval. The EBCI Tribal Council did, however, negotiate many elements of the rolls, including the addition of specific individuals. Yet despite this EBCI Tribal Council involvement, Baker ultimately chose to disregard the EBCI's 1889 charter stipulating the citizenship criterion of a one-sixteenth minimum blood quantum in favor of a one thirty-second, and sometimes even lower, blood quantum.[25] Additionally, the economic incentives for being added to the EBCI rolls meant that during the Baker Roll determination, nearly twelve thousand additional individuals applied for inclusion in the roll. After Congress asserted that it alone (not individuals, such as census takers, or even the Native Nations themselves) determined the EBCI citizenship qualifications, the Baker Roll was finalized in 1928 and consisted of 3,157 citizens.[26] (It is important to recognize here that these Native Nation rolls, compiled by the U.S. government, were originally meant not to determine Native Nation citizenship but to serve as a vehicle for the dissolution of Native Nations through such means as exclusions and allotments.) According to Adams, "In 1931, Congress followed the Department's recommendation and passed an act that suspended the allotment of the Qualla Boundary and provided that, from then on, no person with less than one-sixteenth Eastern Cherokee blood would enroll in the Band."[27]

For the EBCI and other Native Nations, the subject of blood quantum and citizenship began enmeshed in controversy and remains so today. The Cherokee Nation in Oklahoma (like nearly one hundred other federally recognized Native Nations) has never used a minimum blood quantum for citizenship purposes, instead basing its citizenship on lineal descent from the Dawes Rolls of 1906, stating, "All citizens of the Cherokee Nation must be original enrollees or descendants of original enrollees listed on the Dawes Commission Rolls."[28] However, the much smaller nation of the EBCI (approximately 14,000 versus 300,000 Cherokee Nation citizens) has primarily continued to use a one-sixteenth minimum blood quantum, calculated from the Baker Roll, as a basis for citizenship, and has audited its rolls and amended its charters over the years (in 1967, 1986, and 2009) to determine whether some enrolled citizens did not meet the EBCI's criteria for citizenship.[29] This emphasis on the importance of blood quantum for the EBCI (as well as for other Native Nations that choose to incorporate it) reflects more than just political and economic motivations at a government level; in 2015, the *One Feather* posted a poll asking, "What do you feel gives you Native American identity?" The results were 41 percent blood quantum, 37 percent history and culture, 14 percent language, 7 percent enrollment card, and 1 percent arts and crafts.[30] Given the gravity of the consequences levied by the U.S. government on Native Nations and American Indians based on "politics of perception" and settler-colonial reified conceptions of "authenticity" (e.g., the Termination era), paired with blood quantum's place in securing the safety of EBCI economic assets and political incorporation, this internalization of blood quantum as an indicator of identity is not surprising. As this brief history demonstrates, the complexities of citizenship and land boundaries and their impacts on Native Nation economic sovereignty are numerous. By focusing on issues that Eastern Band small-business owners face today, we can see how individuals experience these complexities.

Functions of Land and Scarcity

Land has always been at the foundation of indigenous and settler-colonial relations. The physical layout of land that shapes the Qualla Boundary business sector reflects the importance of who controls this land and how, affecting individuals' choices and EBCI practices of economic sovereignty. In its most simplistic form, there are three main categories of landholdings that jurisdictionally affect Native Nations in Indian Country today. The first is trust land, which encompasses land titles held by the U.S. government in trust for the exclusive use of American Indians, in which the state has no authority (with certain exceptions). The Qualla Boundary is exclusively trust land. The second is fee simple land: private land ownership with a deed that the owner holds for the land. This is the most common form of general land ownership today. The third is land owned and controlled by U.S. governments, such as roads and parks. In the case of the checkerboarding of American Indian lands, trust and fee simple lands owned by both Natives and non-Natives are interspersed and can be noncontiguous. This physical interspersion compounds jurisdictional issues between the county, state, and federal governments and Native Nations. In practice, there are many more variations between these types of landholdings (e.g., a Native Nation can own land without having it held in trust). In a business context, the key question is about who can have access to this land and, by extension, to its economic markets. The overriding issue for the EBCI is that of scarcity.

Because the EBCI was not subject to allotment in 1887 and was able to purchase its own land, the land is represented as fairly contiguous. Although Snowbird and some recently purchased land in Cherokee County are separated from the main area around Cherokee, the area does not reach the allotment-level checkerboarding extreme seen on some reservations.[31] This land *does* remain partitioned by other jurisdictional issues, however. Instead of reservation land being primarily divided between the EBCI and noncitizens, as is the issue with checkerboarding, it is divided between the EBCI and U.S. government entities, as in the case of roads. Because of the Qualla Boundary's singular location, providing an entrance to the GSMNP, there are major freeways alongside the Qualla Boundary, as well as small highways that go directly through it, owned and managed by the state of North Carolina. This means that the state must approve any improvements or modifications. Everything relating to these roads—from repairing a bridge to adding a pedestrian greenway to make it safer for Eastern Band citizens to walk to work and for tourists to walk between the attractions in Cherokee— must go through a lengthy approval process at the state or federal level in addition to EBCI approvals and possibly BIA land-management approvals. Furthermore, the area around Cherokee straddles two counties, Swain and Jackson (a product of an attempt to split the EBCI vote in 1871, when Swain County was created from both Jackson and Macon Counties), adding to the government-approval complications.[32]

The repercussions of this process have stifled the growth of many businesses. One example of this difficulty that was conveyed to me during discussions with small-business owners, and that is rarely addressed in this context, is internet access. Most major telecommunications companies have refused to invest in adequate (if any) internet infrastructures in rural areas due to the low profit margin.[33] As a result, the EBCI initiated and now owns its own fiber-optic network, BalsamWest. This network provides internet access to three states and countless small rural communities that had previously been considered too small to provide access to.[34] The unfortunate reality of the situation, however, is that only a handful of the business owners I spoke with during my initial research had internet access at—let alone websites for—their businesses. The complication was that although the cable lines were near their businesses, the roads were owned by the state and would have to be modified to get the line to their side of the road. The state approval process is such a lengthy hurdle that this project, considered of no urgency, was simply shelved. In 2009, the Cherokee Broadband Enterprise was finally approved by the EBCI Tribal Council: "[This] tribally-owned enterprise . . . is working to provide internet connectivity to the most challenging parts of the Qualla Boundary and to offer quality, competitively priced service to those who already have internet service. Cherokee Broadband Enterprise has been in existence for approximately two years and is working hard to complete the construction of the towers and systems necessary to reach as many unserved residences and businesses as possible. Cherokee Broadband also provides wireless internet service to the downtown Cherokee business district, Saunooke Village, Ceremonial Grounds and the Expo Center."[35]

· · · · · ·

There is also the issue of general land accessibility on the Qualla Boundary. Much of the land there—and, indeed, throughout western North Carolina—is unusable for development due to its mountainous terrain. First, it is financially impractical to build on, as construction costs often include leveling hills and mountainsides—*if* this can be physically accomplished at all. Second, the scenery, forest, and land are of major importance to tourists as well as residents who still use these resources extensively.[36] The result is that most of the EBCI's land cannot be feasibly used without massive destruction of the environment. As Chief Hicks commented regarding the land and cultural representational issues, "We don't have the land base to compete with the people over the mountain. Arts and crafts—that's where this Tribe needs to go. We have got to create a specific market. We have to display, in the right way, our abilities."[37]

Leasing

There is one primary (but winding) business corridor, made up of subdistricts, in Cherokee. Most of this serviceable land, and the buildings on it, have been owned and leased by the EBCI government, or have been in possessory holding by individuals, for decades. Possessory holding is trust land ultimately held by the EBCI, but which operates as if it were fee simple (i.e., land owned by an individual). Subject to some restrictions and committee or EBCI Tribal Council reviews, the land can be built on and transferred to another Eastern Band citizen or leased for generations.[38] Land leases of fifty to one hundred years are not uncommon, and some leases can be passed down via inheritance. This means that the rental price to a new businessperson who is not part of a family that owns the land is very high, if available at all. To compare, in neighboring Bryson City in 2009, lease prices were about $4 to $8 per square foot, while in Cherokee, they were $12 to $16 per square foot, putting the price of some small shop leases—roughly eleven square feet—at $1,936 per month. Additionally, the EBCI leasing office required at that time that renters buy a bond for a retail lease, a practice that is decades out of date.[39] Subsequently, many of the businesses on the Qualla Boundary are family owned and passed down through that family in one form or another (i.e., sometimes closing down one shop and opening another type of shop in its place as it is passed down).

The proximity of this land to the entrance to the GSMNP makes this prime property for tourist-based businesses, further adding to the price of rent and business ownership, as businesses compete to be located in the principal areas reachable by tourists. The competition for space is also increased through the EBCI's recent efforts to promote small-business ownership on the Qualla Boundary. Compounding these issues at the time of my fieldwork was the problem of the lengthy BIA delays for leasing changes. As Joel Queen stated,

> You have to wait six months for the lease to clear the BIA. That's how backed up the paperwork is. Six months. People have made the mistake and said, "Yeah, we'll go ahead and lease you the place; we'll get the paperwork done and get it down to the BIA." Well, before the lease gets back from BIA, they've had a disagreement with the owners and they've already lost their lease before the original lease comes back.

They're already kicked out of the building before they're even legally supposed to be open. People would put their time and money into different businesses. They've opened up coffee shops and other things and borrowing money for it and everything else and then end up being kicked out of the building before the lease ever gets back because of something that the landlord didn't do or some disagreement between you and the landlord.

In late 2011, the U.S. Department of the Interior proposed comprehensive changes to the Indian land-leasing regulations. These mainly addressed troublesome bureaucracy issues at the BIA, including the long delays and the lengthy approval process. For example, one proposal dictates that BIA decisions must be made within thirty days, and another that approval must occur unless there is compelling evidence not to. It remains to be seen whether the newly proposed changes to the BIA procedures (via the Interior Improvement Act [S. 1879]) will rectify some of the situations described here as well as the more recent troublesome land transfer cases detailed at the 2017 EBCI Housing Summit.[40]

All these factors come together to create a scarcity of available business locations, which unfortunately means that citizens sometimes need to locate off-boundary, significantly reducing their access to both tourists and local markets.[41] It should also be noted, however, that it is the EBCI and its citizens who logistically control the land, and therefore leasing is in and of itself a part of the overall economy. Leasing provides a steady and reliable income stream that circulates within the community to some citizens and the EBCI, either through the practice of leasing or through owning a business on it themselves. The ability to control and use these leases is a key component of economic sovereignty, ultimately evincing authority over land in implementing economic decisions.

To counter some of these land-quantity constraints, the EBCI exercised its economic sovereignty by purchasing new parcels of land for future development, including, as would be revealed later, development of a new casino. In 2010, the EBCI bought 793.58 acres in Cherokee County at a cost of $6,414,828, which included both trust and non-trust land.[42] This is, in general, a delicate undertaking, as putting Native Nation–owned land into federal trust takes it out of the non–Native Nation tax base; as a result, it is not welcomed by many states and counties.[43] On the other hand, if a Native Nation, like the EBCI, is acquiring land for economic development, the new economic stimulus may offset the loss of tax revenue for that county and state. Businesses located on and around this land would most likely have a substantial amount of support (e.g., in new infrastructure) from the EBCI, county, and state to help ensure economic success. This optimism was reflected in ads circulated online, such as the following:

> What does this [purchase of lands by the EBCI] mean for area land values and to you? As in past developments such as this and in a market that is at the lowest it's been, prices should rise rapidly. With construction of the [new EBCI] casino, comes jobs and with people moving to the area, comes the need for great locations in residential developments. [The EBCI is] pumping institutional money into the area and sophisticated investors have begun purchasing. Most people want to invest alongside others that have already begun the new upward trend with the stagnation of the stock market, this is an opportunity! Developers are very motivated to move land and many great deals have been made. . . . The upcoming *Great American Land Sale* [near Murphy in Cherokee County is starting]. Make your move today and invest in your future.[44]

The promotion of this as a "Great American Land Sale" is as complex as it is ironic. This 2010 land sale is typical in a settler-colonial context, as it was instigated by (here, changes in) Native Nation and American Indian economic bases and assets. Furthermore, this particular land was Cherokee land; the current town of Murphy is known as Tlanusiyi, the "Leech Place," and the county is *Cherokee* County, formed in 1839 (the year after the initiation of Removal) and so named to "honor" Cherokees. The necessity of the EBCI buying land that is its own in order to further practice its economic sovereignty is an issue that is common across Indian Country.[45]

Scarcity as a Benefit?

Although land scarcity has had a negative impact on business expansion on the Qualla Boundary, this scarcity of land also keeps the physical tourist market bounded, which, paradoxically, may be a contributing factor to its longevity. This scarcity is beneficial for businesses already located in Cherokee, as the tourists are concentrated in a few specific areas, and the businesses generally see more consumers as a result.[46] But this raises the question, Why don't the business owners without access to these concentrated tourist areas on the Qualla Boundary move their businesses off-Boundary, just over the reservation line? After all, the consumers are not physically confined to shopping only on the Qualla Boundary. Part of the answer is that some business owners *do* relocate off-Boundary. But locating off the Qualla Boundary affects more than leasing rates. Drawing loosely on Pierre Bourdieu's concept of cultural capital as well as the preceding discussions of representation, I argue that the land, bounded as it is as a marked space of indigeneity, has become a representation and extension of the Eastern Band people in the eyes of tourists as well as many locals.[47]

The easiest comparison of this spatiality to Cherokee, both in issues of perimeter boundedness and in cultural capital, is nearby Gatlinburg, Tennessee. This town is similar to Cherokee in that it also sits at the entrance of the GSMNP and has a business-intensive downtown area. However, although its location brings many tourists (unless you are familiar with the alternate route, you are forced to drive through the wall-to-wall traffic of the downtown area), its content is similar (if not exactly the same in some cases) to many other tourist towns surrounding the GSMNP—all of which bank on their identification as a "mountain town." It has many of the same stores, same fudge, same T-shirts, and so on. In other words, the physical space of Gatlinburg provides no *unique* cultural capital that cannot be accessed in another tourist mountain town. Greg Richards, a tourism studies scholar, sums up these links between cultural capital and land: "Cultural capital is not only a means of personal distinction, but *can also be an attribute of place.* In order to attract investment capital and the spending power of the middle class, regions now differentiate themselves by emphasizing the aesthetic qualities of material commodities and services that represent symbolic capital. Examples of this can be found in the use of museums, monuments and other heritage attractions in regional economic development strategies."[48]

Although Richards's analysis does not make it explicit, in order for a "place" to be distinct, it must have some reckoning of fixed boundaries. This is a problem for Gatlinburg, whose lack of unique cultural capital is compounded by its sprawl. Because there is no physical boundary per se to Gatlinburg (i.e., one that is demarcated to the visitor as being "on" or "off" of Gatlinburg-as-cultural-capital land), businesses can and do extend farther and farther out from the epicenter of the town. Factory outlet malls, Dollywood, enormous mini-golf and go-cart parks, and elaborately large restaurants line the highway for miles. Sharon Zukin's work on gentrification and Disneyland specifically highlights the importance of the fixedness of this space and "the spatial structuring or embeddedness of new forms of consumption, both locating consumption in space and localizing specific features of a service economy."[49] Unfortunately, the farther you get from the epicenter of Gatlinburg, the more diluted the steady stream of actual tourists-consumers becomes. Businesses that hope to sell to the crowd brought in by the GSMNP find that the competitive sprawl makes their longevity less likely because consumers are faced with a seemingly endless supply of repetitive choices.

This perspective on the issues of sprawl informs our understanding of land scarcity. Although scarcity can create problems, in Cherokee, scarcity may also provide one of the foundations for solid, long-term economic markets. Ultimately, it is the fact that reservation land is bounded, fixed, and scarce that allows it to convey a heightened level of cultural capital to those outside it. Even though *all* U.S. lands are American Indian lands, it is only designated reservation lands that currently carry the cultural cachet of "Indianness" for settler-colonial society. The constant battles by Native Nations to protect sacred American Indian spaces located outside federally designated Native Nation areas speaks clearly to the settler-colonial ideological divorcing of Native peoples from their lands in non-bounded contexts. As can be seen in Cherokee, the physical land of the Qualla Boundary provides its own cultural capital, which can only extend past the boundary line weakly, if at all.[50] Businesses past the Qualla Boundary line are just not considered as *Cherokee* (read "authentic") as those within it.[51] The land itself and its designated boundaries contain the cultural capital that tourists seek—and, as we have seen, small businesses on the Qualla Boundary can provide that capital.[52]

Furthermore, as Steve Britton maintains, for "the inclusion of the touristic experience or attributes of [a] place into a saleable commodity (a tour, the ambiance of a hotel in close proximity to a significant site, souvenirs, or symbolic image with recognizable connotations) . . . spatial proximity is often crucial, as the special ambiance of a hotel or authenticity of a souvenir is largely dependent on its direct association with the sight [*sic*]."[53] Britton also briefly touches on indigenous tourism in this respect when saying in regard to Australian aboriginals, "[This] extends to the native peoples as well, because the mystic [*sic*] of the [Uluru] Rock is inextricably bound up with White Australia's notion of aboriginality and the social position of the Aborigines at Uluru and in the wider society. Tourists expect to have an experience with the local Aborigines, something intangible which they can take away with them. By having contact with Aborigines as tour guides, park rangers, artisans, or simply as part of the backdrop to the monolith, the tourist experience is more meaningful and 'authentic.'"[54] Taking this notion further and applying it here, businesses located within the Qualla Boundary may gain an association with place that bestows on them a type of Cherokee-ness in tourists' eyes, whether they are owned by Eastern Band citizens or not.

The cultural capital gained by locating a business on the Qualla Boundary equally applies to non-tourist businesses, as having a business located within this boundary signals both social capital (via networks formed within the Qualla Boundary) and cultural capital as an Eastern Band community member. Many of the business owners I spoke with conveyed that they located on the Qualla Boundary partially out of an unspoken obligation, both economically and in terms of loyalty, to this community. As Natalie describes, "We knew we wanted to open a place for Cherokee. There was no place where we gathered in public. We're the only place still right now. There are no bars. There are no pubs. [Although] there are restaurants where people gather. . . . [We wanted to show] that we're here to stay. That we're not just here to make our money and leave. That kind of thing. And we're not here to exploit the Cherokee culture."[55] As we watched a group of Qualla Boundary residents in discussion, Bethany noted of her store, "See, that's something else I do. I am a networker here, and the local [Eastern Band] people use it for their office. I love that. They have people meet them here. I just love it."[56]

The fixedness of this land boundary is not, however, as permanent as it first appears. Native Nations continue to exercise their agency, using their inherent sovereignty to reform and expand the boundaries of their land. One method is to simply buy land, as in the EBCI Cherokee County case. But there are other ways that Native Nations can challenge their land boundaries. A small but significant case involving wild plant harvesting in 2009 in the mountains of the GSMNP brought to light land-boundary issues for the EBCI.[57] It was revealed during this case that the EBCI GIS (geographic information system) manager, in his analysis of roughly 1.8 million documents from five sources (the Bureau of Land Management, the Department of the Interior, the U.S. Census Bureau, the North Carolina Land Records office, and the Bureau of Indian Affairs), found that there were inconsistencies across all sources as to where the Qualla Boundary's boundaries actually lay. Additionally, there was an issue of unaccounted-for land that had been purchased by the EBCI. Of the 100,000 acres of land that the EBCI had purchased before the 1880s, only 56,000 acres now remains in trust. The EBCI continues to research both of these items, which have the potential to reform its current land boundaries. One manifestation of this issue of claiming, and claims to, Indian land came to a head during my initial fieldwork and would not be resolved until 2016.

In early 2010, the Eastern Band people were confronted with a new economic-development conundrum: should they have consistent electrical power supplied to their homes and businesses but, in doing so, desecrate what some consider the most sacred piece of Cherokee land? This dilemma emerged when it was revealed that Duke Energy was building a massive, thirty-two-acre substation on the mountainside alongside Kituwah—the "Mother Town" for all Cherokee people. As the details of the plans were released, many Eastern Band citizens chose to oppose the substation.

It was numbingly frigid the morning of the Rally for Kituwah, a protest against the destruction of our Mother Town. As we stood around waiting for stragglers, I felt the cold creeping into my bones, despite having lined my pockets with hand warmers. It was the last day that I would be a resident at my field site, and truth be told, I was supposed to be loading our moving truck to leave in a few hours. The rally that day, though, was the culmination of many weeks during which I had watched the mysterious clear-cutting of the mountainside, kept a close eye on the *One Feather* as people tried to determine what was happening, attended government meetings about (what would be) this Duke Energy fiasco, and talked with people who lived in the area about how this would affect them. I could not miss the rally now. It had been organized in a hurry, as it had not been formally announced that on that particular morning the president of Duke Energy, James Rogers, was coming to meet with Chief Hicks for a closed-door meeting to discuss an agreement. Unfortunately, most people could not get out of work or school on such short notice, and only nine of us were able to march to the EBCI council house. By this time, the other EBCI council members had heard about the meeting and demanded that they, too, be included. We protesters stood outside the council house, shivering, with our signs, until Mr. Rogers drove by. Apparently word of our modest rally had spread, and it had been determined that the EBCI police should escort him to the back of the council house, where he would enter and thus avoid any possible incident. Shortly thereafter, an EBCI police officer came to speak with Natalie about our lack of a permit (in actuality, there was no ordinance for rallies on the Qualla Boundary, and he was basing his argument on a parade permit). He was polite and agreeable, merely giving us a warning for "next time."

Natalie had been the most public voice in the charge against Duke Energy, despite the potential negative impacts to her business if Duke refused

FIGURE 3.1
Save Kituwah flyer.
Photo by author.

to build the substation at all (see figures 3.1 and 3.2). Winters on the Qualla Boundary saw regular power outages. Storms would knock out power to large swaths of land, homes, and businesses for days—or longer—before Duke Energy resolved the issues. Natalie's coffee shop was one of those businesses regularly affected, often closing due to substandard power access. Despite the lure of reliable power to keep her business operational during the winter months, she chose to make Tribal Grounds one of the epicenters for the transmission of knowledge about Duke's plans to build on the sacred site, offering it as a meeting place to form collective action against this building plan. It had been rumored that during this particular winter, as the Kituwah fight lingered on, the Duke power-outage response units were taking just a little more time than usual to respond.

At this point in our protest, council member Teresa McCoy from Big Cove Township arrived, furious that Eastern Band citizens were being forced to stand in the cold. She suggested, strongly, to the tribal council house police that we should be allowed into the building to warm up, and she promised to see if we could sit in on the proceedings. She made good on that prom-

FIGURE 3.2 Billboard on Qualla Boundary. Photo by author.

ise, and we did indeed get to see the whole proceedings. The meeting turned into an "airing of grievances," but it was also rife with twists and turns. The Duke spokespeople were overheard commenting among themselves that certain slides of their presentation "should not be shown to the public"; the council members and chief angled for a land swap that would lead to a site move; the public complained about violations Duke had already committed during this construction project, which had resulted in at least one house being buried in a muddy landslide; and the Swain County commissioners were rightly incensed that Duke had ignored them entirely while providing neighboring Jackson County an entire detailed presentation (which Jackson County required by law)—complete with an environmental impact study—before beginning construction on the Jackson County site. The intrigue surrounding Duke's plan did not stop with that meeting. Over the coming weeks, Duke would be accused of many incidents of misconduct, including destroying archaeological sites by leveling the site area by forty feet, down to sterile subsoil, before thorough testing was done;[58] misidentifying streams on environmental reports; and erroneously claiming that a thirty-two-acre power station could be classified as an "upgrade" to a minor power line (this last item was the point the company used to claim that it did not need to inform anyone of its activities).

This controversy illustrates many aspects of economic conflicts: the feeling of entitlement and untouchability that large corporations embody, the tenacity of citizens when confronted with corporate threats, and the choices made by politicians to address national resource protections as they relate to the broader good of the nation. However, I believe that this example best illustrates the complexities resulting from economic development by Native Nations in particular, like the EBCI. That winter of 2010 had already been a challenging one for the Qualla Boundary. Rockslides and snowstorms blocked people trying to travel to and from it, and power had been down for days on end, leaving people trying to warm their homes with only wood stoves (this, as well as other power-outage-related issues, has unfortunately led to fatal house fires).[59] Some businesses closed completely. On top of this, a new tower was being added to the Cherokee Casino, which would require even more energy. Duke Energy's promise (delivered after its plans for the substation were exposed) was that this power station, to be built on what some consider the Cherokees' most sacred location, would solve all these issues.

The heart of this problem, however, was that the EBCI did not own this part of the land. As we have seen, in the mountains, land—especially usable land—is scarce and expensive. In 1996, the EBCI purchased the sacred Kituwah Mound from a farming family who had owned it for generations. But as news spread that the EBCI was buying land, those who owned nearby parcels assumed that with the establishment of its casino, the EBCI was now in a position to pay any asking price. The prices quickly skyrocketed beyond the EBCI's budgeted funds. The EBCI was ultimately unable to buy much of the land it wanted, and the lack of EBCI property ownership around the Kituwah Mound left it in a weak position against the Duke Energy behemoth.

Put into an economic context, Native Nations often do not have ownership of—nor, critically, are they able to *gain* ownership of—their sacred lands. This is the result of the economic violence and hegemony that first separated many Native Nations from their sacred sites and then created poverty (both deliberately and inadvertently), ensuring that they would not have the economic means to reacquire those sites.[60] For Native Nations to protect these sacred areas, they must be economically empowered. But, as in the case of the EBCI, economic empowerment can then, ironically, put these very locations in peril, as landowners significantly raise prices in response to demand from a now economically empowered Native Nation—which once again puts the land out of the Native Nation's grasp.[61] In 2016, this case finally closed as part of a larger settlement with Duke Energy. As payment for a massive 2009 fire, which burned for a week and damaged 2,300 acres of EBCI land as a result of a faulty Duke Energy power pole, the EBCI received $1.7 million. Most interestingly, and more importantly in many ways, Duke Energy also transferred its purchased (and now unused) portion of the thirty-five-acre tract of land adjacent to Kituwah to the EBCI. As council members reiterated, this was a historic moment.[62]

Constructing Citizenship and Economic Development

The agency displayed by Native Nations in re-forming their geographic boundaries is echoed in citizenship determinations. Native Nations are recognized in federal and individual Native Nation law as having an inherent sovereign right to determine their own citizenship—subject to certain federal limitations, of course. For example, federal policy prohibits a person from being a citizen of more than one Native Nation, even if each parent is a citizen of a different nation. This specific barrier has far-reaching consequences for Native Nation citizenship, beginning with the loss of one's citizenship via a blood quantum that does not meet the minimum requirements of some Native Nations. For example, the child of two 100 percent blood-quantum ("full-blood") citizens of differing Native Nations would be considered 50 percent American Indian blood quantum by the federal government. It is easy to see the implications of this policy of erasure (following the logic of elimination), especially when considered alongside the counter logics of other historical racializing policies, such as the "one-drop" rule for African Americans, designed to increase populations. It is important to note, however, that many Native Nations have their own policies allowing for dual enrollment of citizens in defiance of this federal policy (this does not currently include the EBCI, which excludes dual enrollment in Section 49-3 of the Cherokee Code, but this potential is being casually discussed among its citizens); this practice is more common among Alaskan Native Corporations, especially with respect to minors, than in those Native Nations located within the contiguous United States.

As with land, this very basic introduction merely scratches the surface of the highly complex practices of Native Nation citizenship. On the private-business level, the boundary of citizenship is important because it addresses the question of how the EBCI allows and, even more so, encourages both citizens and noncitizens to participate in its small-business sector. As with other nations, complications of citizenship arise and can have adverse effects on small businesses. For the EBCI, the issues of citizenship are made more complex by its blood-quantum system. In the most simplistic terms, this means that if an Eastern Band business owner whose blood quantum is legally one-sixteenth marries a non–Eastern Band citizen (American Indian citizen or not), their child would be under the minimum blood quantum for EBCI citizenship and would be designated instead as a first descendant. *First descendant* is the legal and common-use term for people whose parent(s) are EBCI citizens but who do not qualify themselves for full citizenship benefits (e.g., voting rights) due to their blood quantum falling below the minimum.[63] If this first descendant does not marry an Eastern Band citizen of sufficient blood quantum, they will not be able to pass on a Qualla Boundary business to their spouse or child. When the first descendant dies, the business is evaluated, and if a new lease is not granted to the children, they are given the business's fair-market value from the EBCI government in compensation.[64] For a liminal first descendant (neither full citizen nor noncitizen) or the child of a first descendant, this policy creates a conflict between responsibility to community, which wants businesses to locate on the Qualla Boundary, and responsibility to family, which requires locating off the Qualla Boundary to ensure the business's continuation. This precise conflict has played itself out many times as business owners struggle with the decision of where to locate. (See appendix D for specifics on enrollment numbers and related information.)

The best way to understand these complexities is to see how they unfold on the ground and how these business owners choose to work within them. As Abe Smith, a small-business owner and first descendant, explained to me:

> That's the whole thing. . . . I can't even inherit what [my parents have] worked [their] whole life for. The only thing that I kind of regret, and I say just kind of but not really, but I kind of wish there were times that [they] would have helped me start a business somewhere else, because I would love to do what I'm doing but I wanted to have a trading post that might still be standing there in a hundred years that maybe my grandkids or my great grandkids would be running, because that's the kind of business that I'm in.[65]

Abe grew up in one of the most prominent business-owning Eastern Band citizen families on the Qualla Boundary; however, his legal blood quantum rendered him a first descendant. His father was one of the first to open large hotels on the Qualla Boundary and had amassed an enormous amount of business property spanning nearly the entire length of the downtown-area highway through what is now known as the Cultural District of Cherokee. Abe's father's businesses began over forty years ago and now include hotels, restaurants, and gift stores geared toward both tourists and locals. His dedication to the health of the EBCI economy and his service to the community are known throughout the region. This dedication to the EBCI economy took many forms, but the most noticeable was his insistence on locating all of his businesses physically within the Qualla Boundary. This is especially provocative when you take into consideration that at the time, Abe's father had no legal heirs to continue his businesses on the Qualla Boundary once he passed.

The EBCI's sovereign right to determine its own enrollment qualifications internally was restored in 1957. From 1959 to 1963, the minimum blood quantum was one thirty-second, but the one-sixteenth minimum was reestablished by vote after 1963. For the 1986 charter, it was decided that citizens with a one thirty-second blood quantum would be grandfathered into the new citizenship laws; this allowed a citizen with one thirty-second blood to stay on the rolls but not their children (in the case of the other parent not having enough blood quantum to result in one-sixteenth for the children). For Abe, this ruling means that he and his siblings do not have enough blood quantum to be Eastern Band citizens. His father did, however, have a hand in advocating for another section of the charter that stated that "first-generation descendants" (e.g., Abe and his siblings) *could inherit* from an enrolled member, thus assuring that his business stayed in the family for one more generation.[66] This extension of benefits to first descendants also includes access to some EBCI resources, such as schooling and health care.[67] As a result of this amendment's inclusion, Abe could now inherit his father's businesses.

But the fear of loss has had an impact. Recently, Abe has begun to consider moving his remaining business ventures off the Qualla Boundary in anticipation of eventually being able to pass them on to his children. This is not an unusual strategy, as in the 1980s, another prominent business family in Cherokee began buying land adjacent to the Qualla Boundary specifically to build a substantial number of businesses there. Although there are several reasons for moving a business off-Boundary (access to more land, cheaper land, and prime locations), choosing these locations ensures that the businesses will always be next to—if not within—the community and retains more secure property rights for intergenerational transfers of the businesses to noncitizen children.

This fear of property loss due to citizenship status is also justified beyond intergenerational transfers. The newest roll audit approved by Eastern Band voters was completed in February 2010 by an external agency and identified 1,405 "actionable" citizenship files. The reasons for being placed on this list ranged from lack of birth certificate to no verifiable link to the Baker Roll. This means that many current citizens could possibly have their citizenship revoked at some point in the future, although the EBCI Tribal Council and Enrollment Committee (formed for this review) have taken no action or made any decision at the time of this writing. (See appendix E for "Loss of Membership," Disenrollment Code, Section 49-9(b).)[68] In addition, a complicated incident arose in 2011 in which the EBCI government took over land without compensation after a will had been found to be insufficient to pass the land to the first descendant.[69] Although this issue involved a specific set of unusual circumstances, the reverberations were felt, as the implications for business owners could be profound in such cases. This feeds a well-founded concern about business longevity for owners choosing to locate on-Boundary. The EBCI has since passed more citizenship regulations that further bound enrollment. For example, the EBCI has chosen to mandate DNA testing for paternity (at a cost of $140 [$195 per family unit], to be paid by the individual) for all new enrollment applicants (including adoptees); this decision was ratified in June 2010.[70] Age limits on application for enrollment have also seen many changes over the past three decades. Since 1995, the enrollment deadlines have steadily expanded from the requirement for enrollment before the third birthday (1995) to that of no age deadline (1999–2011).[71] At the EBCI Tribal Council meeting in September 2011, an ordinance was passed (ratified on December 1, 2011) once again limiting enrollment into the EBCI to those persons under the age of nineteen but removing applicability to adoptees.[72] This ordinance positively affects those who have experienced complications from adoption (e.g., limited access to adoption records) while still placing a limit on those adults who presumably have not been active community members for most of their lives (see appendix F for Section 49-2).

Most of these changes in the boundaries of citizenship have been contested and, at times, hotly debated within the Eastern Band citizenry. Individual citizens can exercise some agency within the constraints, as Ron from Talking Leaves does when he states his belief in relationships over identity cards: "I never ask [local] people for their enrollment card. You just know people. I have never asked somebody for it, and I won't. It's none of my business." Unfortunately, these types of inheritance issues can cause successful businesses to leave the Qualla Boundary, taking away valuable tax dollars—and perhaps something more valuable: the knowledge of how to craft a successful business.

Brain Drain, Networking Loss, and Economic Drain

Both land and citizenship boundary challenges raise the specters of brain drain (the loss of knowledge when residents physically leave), networking loss, and economic drain. When successful business owners (such as Abe Smith in the previous example) decide to locate off the Qualla Boundary, they potentially take generations of Qualla Boundary–specific business knowledge with them. The networking resources offered by businesses in close proximity in a supportive, collegial environment also vanish. The importance of these intangible resources can be seen in Natalie's description of how she managed to keep her business stable in a rural environment, emphasizing her reliance on community:

> Another good thing to do as a business is to make friends with your local businesses. Whether you're selling stuff from them or not is irrelevant. If you can go and eat breakfast at the local breakfast place on a regular basis, somewhat regular because we own a business, but if you can be a customer to other businesses, then when the time comes for you to need some inventory—like I need spoons right now. I'm going to go to Peter down the road and ask, "Please, can I buy some spoons from you" or "Please, can I buy some register paper," because you might not have the type of register paper in your community that you need right away. And your food service dude is not on the phone or is on vacation because he sold you things that are way too high priced and now he's in Maui. And he can't meet your needs.[73]

Proximity encourages a support network that is stronger than the sum of its parts. The entire system is weakened when businesses leave. Not only is the physical connection lost—for example, buying items in times of crisis—but the exchange of information regarding how to run a business (especially the intricacies and specificities of being located on a reservation) is also lost. In addition, the camaraderie that comes from this shared experience is gone. These are more than feel-good benefits; these interactions are the basis for exchanging valuable information on the current business climate and for taking collective action. This can be seen in activities such as the formation of the Cherokee Chamber of Commerce, which was initially created by businesspeople on the Qualla Boundary.

The implications for the economic drain produced by businesses moving off-Boundary are just as concerning. When citizens choose, or are forced, to operate off of the Qualla Boundary, the EBCI may lose its levy, leasing taxes, and the ability to keep money circulating within the community, among other consequences. In some cases it is not just the business that relocates off-Boundary. It is not unusual for the whole family to move for the convenience of being near (or living in the same physical space) as the business; the community thus loses an entire family's economic contributions. However, in acknowledging these potential negative impacts of restrictive citizenship boundaries, I would be remiss if I gave the impression that all Eastern Band citizens were against these policies and their ramifications for small businesses. In discussing these issues with potential entrepreneurs, some viewed these possible impending turnovers of businesses and land ownership on the Qualla Boundary as ousting business owners who they perceive to have unfairly dominated the downtown Cherokee market for decades.

Scarcity Benefits Revisited

These issues of citizenry and the scarcity of land are inextricably intertwined. For all the deeply problematic ramifications of the EBCI's inheritance and blood-quantum laws, they also aid in safeguarding the resources that the EBCI and its citizens need to function on both a governmental and individual level, as we saw in Mikaela Adams's research. The EBCI's legal authority to choose to keep its own population bounded via blood-quantum requirements contributes to its ability to provide enough resources for its citizenry in the future through land purchases, entrepreneurial funding, and so on. Even with this bounding of citizenship, however, the EBCI still faces some issues of limited resources for its citizens, as evidenced by the land-access issues previously described, even while other resources (e.g., funding for small-business support) increases.

It would be disingenuous, however, to discuss the strategies of these Native Nations who choose to institute additional boundaries on their populations (beyond those imposed at the federal level), such as blood-quantum minimums, without also acknowledging that reducing Native populations and denying land to Native peoples is the primary tactic of the settler-colonial state. *Scarcity is by design.* The Cherokee Nation in Oklahoma chose to focus on lineal rather than blood-quantum-based citizenship; the consequence of this is that they have approximately 66,000 acres under the Cherokee Nation's jurisdiction and about 300,000 citizens (compared to the EBCI's 56,000 acres and 14,000 citizens); only 70,000 live within the 7,000-square-mile geographical area.[74] Every Native Nation is affected by settler-colonial policies of elimination and reduction, and each nation must make difficult decisions as to how it will best serve its citizens given the current constraints. Because there are no definitive answers to this question, it is not uncommon for conflicts to arise when crafting federal laws based on these boundaries—as in the case of the Indian Arts and Crafts Act.

Asserting Creative Boundaries

The ability of Native Nations to define their own citizenry is crucial—not just for local issues, such as the levying of taxes, but also for larger issues, such as the protection of intellectual resources and cultural assets. One example of this is the Indian Arts and Crafts Act (see figure 3.3). Before the IACA, it was common for artists and mass-production companies, who were not citizens of any Native Nation, to create artwork and crafts while claiming (or heavily implying) that these products were Indian made and traditional.[75] The primary consequence of this deceptive activity was that the market was flooded with misrepresented goods that competed directly with goods made by citizens of Native Nations. This not only left consumers with counterfeit products but drove products made by American Indians out of the market in price and availability. Furthermore, these fraudulent goods, by their claims of "authentic" or "traditional," contributed (and, it can be argued, as Alice did earlier, still do contribute) to an identity construction that is out of the hands of the American Indians they purport to represent.

Congress passed a reinforced IACA in 1990 to address these continuing fraudulent claims of goods that were "Indian made." According to the U.S. Department of the Interior, this act "is a truth-in-advertising law that prohibits misrepresentation in marketing of Indian arts and crafts products within the United States. It is illegal to offer or display for sale, or sell any art or craft product in a manner that falsely suggests it is Indian produced, an Indian product, or the product of a particular Indian or Indian Tribe or Indian arts and crafts organization, resident within the United States."[76] This act now applies to any federally or state-recognized Native Nation. Consequently, it is illegal for an individual to claim that a piece of art or jewelry is "Cherokee made" unless it is, indeed, made by a Cherokee-citizen

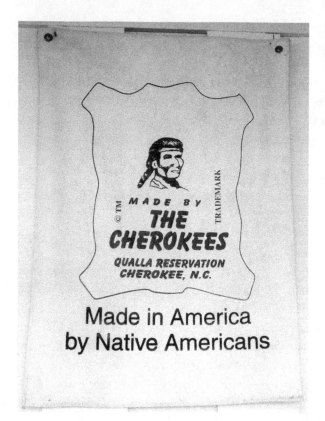

FIGURE 3.3
Sign on a Qualla
Boundary storefront.
Photo by author.

artist, thereby offering some protection to these small-business artists as well as store owners wishing to promote Cherokee-made products.[77]

The IACA received a boost in July 2010 in the form of an amendment that now allows all federal law-enforcement officers to investigate and enforce the IACA laws, which were also strengthened with higher fines and penalties. As summarized by the Department of the Interior, "For fraudulent works with a total sales transaction amount of $1,000 or more, a first-time violation by an individual will result in a fine of up to $250,000, imprisonment of up to five years, or both. A first-time violation by a business will result in a fine of up to $1 million. For smaller cases with first-time violators, if the total sale amount is less than $1,000, an individual will face a fine of up to $25,000, imprisonment of up to a year, or both, and a business will face a fine of up to $100,000. In the case of a subsequent violation, regardless of the amount for which any item is offered or displayed for sale or sold, an individual could be fined, imprisoned for up to fifteen years, or both, and a business could be fined up to $5 million."[78]

Further, in 2008, the Cherokee Tri-Council, comprising the three Chero-kee Nations (the EBCI, the Cherokee Nation, and the United Keetoowah Band), issued a joint resolution condemning anyone advancing their career by claiming to be Cherokee who is not a citizen of one of the three Chero-kee Nations. The EBCI Tribal Council bolstered this joint effort in 2011 by passing a resolution (No. 6) to establish the Cherokee Identity Protection Committee to combat the nearly 212 groups claiming to be Cherokee tribes (as of 2016, as compiled by the Cherokee Nation's Fraud List).[79] Many East-ern Band citizens told me that they supported this resolution, but others (some speaking to me personally and some speaking publicly in the *One Feather*) were careful to note that if the BIA does recognize one of these al-leged tribes, they will respect that decision, specifying that they primarily take issue with the incredibly problematic processes of state and self-recognition. While I attended the historic 2015 Cherokee Tri-Council meet-ing (the first tri-council meeting at Red Clay since the Removal period), the council again passed several joint resolutions, including No. 7: "Requiring all cultural or historical presenters or artisans claiming to be Cherokee to be verified by one of the three federally recognized Cherokee tribes."[80] This is a continuation of wider efforts across Indian Country, noted by Lea McChesney, in which there is "an attempt to reverse this institutional au-thority [via the 'politics of possession'], [as] Native cultural organizations increasingly assert control over Native identity [with artists as the symbols of 'pure culture'] by combining Western economic models with expressions of cultural sovereignty."[81] In the Cherokee's case, this is accomplished by invoking political and economic sovereignty in order to regulate market goods. Since my initial fieldwork on the Qualla Boundary began, individ-ual artists have initiated efforts to identify their Eastern Band citizen–made products. These now include tagged and labeled items (see figure 3.4) that read, for example, "This is a genuine Cherokee Indian Handmade Article," along with "Made by" and the name of the piece's creator, or "Handcrafted, Cherokee, NC" with the words "Enrolled, EBCI" (or equivalent) handwrit-ten on a tag. Thus, although there is a federal umbrella of protection in the IACA, individual Native Nations and individual American Indian citizens can and do bolster these protections in their own way.

For the EBCI, in particular, its new heritage tourism development model once again increased the demand for Eastern Band–made goods. One re-sult of this increased demand is the proliferation of copycat objects. The IACA offers some protections against this, but it offers no defense against two specific categories of copycat occurrences: non-Natives copying and

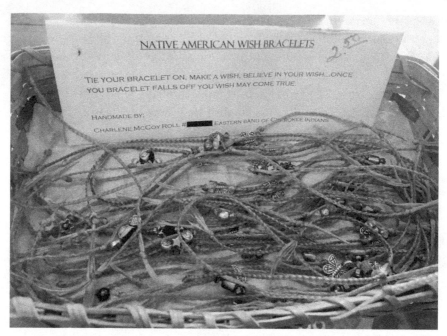

FIGURE 3.4 Eastern Band artist Charlene McCoy, with roll number. Photo by author.

selling Native arts and crafts without fraudulently labeling them as "American Indian made" (e.g., fake religious items and bogus clan masks), which relies on the general public's lack of information about the IACA; and the copying of goods, ideas, and techniques within American Indian artisan groups. During the period of nostalgia tourism, these issues with the EBCI's cultural assets did not arise in great number because most consumers wanted easily recognized pan-Indian items. Although collectors, especially those of American Indian art, have always been a part of the tourist market, the considerable expense associated with collecting during the nostalgia tourism period (which was also pre-internet) made them a smaller percentage of the total customer base. But today's heritage tourism market has brought these issues into sharp focus for the Qualla Boundary.

When discussing arts and crafts produced by Eastern Band citizens and sold through businesses on the Qualla Boundary, it is important to mention the less formal protections of intellectual property and business secrets. Some of the business owners I spoke with were extremely protective of their inventory, an issue made clear to me as I walked around the stores in Cherokee. One owner, who had already given me permission to take notes that day, stopped me while I was jotting down ideas about two customers from

Germany who were looking over herbal medicines. He asked to check my notes in case I was taking down the names of artists whose works he had in stock, their prices, and which of their works he carried. After showing him what I had written, which had no recordings of these particular items, he was satisfied that I was indeed an anthropologist and not sent from another store to steal his artists or products (a rare moment when an anthropologist taking notes on a reservation was considered one of the *least* suspicious activities to be engaged in). I stayed and spoke with the store owner for the rest of the afternoon about these issues. This was not a solitary example, as other business owners expressed similar concerns that their products were being "stolen" or undercut by "spies" from other businesses. This was especially true with regard to the works of non-Cherokee American Indian artists, whom business owners expended much time and energy finding.

Many of the artists I spoke with were also unhappy with the lack of design protections; after expending much time and effort creating a new product or style, they had few ways to protect their works from being copied by other artists. This can happen on the national stage, as with Donna Karan's theft of Seminole patchwork designs,[82] but also on an individual level between American Indian artists. As Alice said during our focus group meeting, "Somebody will steal your idea and the next thing you know, it's all over the place. I've had that happen. I made little bitty jewelry boxes. The next thing I know, I saw one. They bought one from me but they didn't know how to do it. They didn't know how it worked. They had to take the whole thing apart to figure out how it worked." While this could lead to concerns about passing on knowledge in general, I found that most artists were, in fact, quite eager and willing to share their knowledge of the general construction of their particular art, be it carving or painting. The line was drawn, however, at a particular style, product, or technique that they or their family had created. These issues, and their solutions, are still unfolding as the EBCI continues to reshape its image in the tourism industry.

· · · · · ·

This chapter merely scratches the surface of the numerous complexities of Native Nation land and citizenship boundaries. The strengthening, and even expansion, of Native Nation boundaries today is a result in part of their consistent work to hone their strategies of economic sovereignty in the face of continued efforts by various levels of the U.S. government to diminish these boundaries in scope or control. These efforts not only span massive historical events like the Removal but also include issues of economic hegemony in the coercion of wage labor, which has been pointed to as another form of "removal" contributing to homeland dispossession; the deliberate use of debt as a tool in the reduction of sovereignties; the mismanagement of American Indian monies; and policies regarding taxation and regulation.[83] All of these have profound effects on Native Nation entities and their individual citizens.

Small-business owners who choose to locate on a reservation must not only learn how to negotiate the complexities of owning a small business but also learn about and negotiate the specific obstacles and advantages presented by these Native Nations' land, citizenship, and representational boundaries. These owners must take all of these aspects into consideration when deciding whether to locate on the Qualla Boundary. The trust status of land, ostensibly in place to protect Native Nation assets, also generates many difficulties for the EBCI nation and its citizens with regard to obtaining lands. This compounds the existing scarcity in accessing leased properties and the complications of transferring these properties between citizens, which then adds to the further entrenchment of intergenerational landholdings. The EBCI's citizenship boundaries—which have protected its national assets, from land to dividends—also compel some businesses and business owners to leave the Qualla Boundary, taking with them their levies and their institutional knowledge. For some Eastern Band citizens and EBCI officials, this loss is minor compared to the advantages that they feel a bounded, blood-quantum minimum citizenship affords them in asset protection and representational control.

The EBCI and Eastern Band citizens continue to exercise their rights to transform these boundaries as economic and political situations require. They are purchasing neighboring lands in order to buy back sacred and historically significant grounds (such as Kituwah, Cowee, and Tallulah) as well as acquiring land for economic development.[84] They have also revised their citizenship criteria several times and, more recently, have audited their rolls. In representation, they have crafted joint resolutions with the Cherokee Nation and the United Keetoowah Band to establish protections of these representations in various artistic forms not covered by the IACA. These boundary transformations, in addition to the changes taking place in the EBCI economic base (e.g., the gaming industry), tourists' interests, and the EBCI's own revised focus on cultural revitalization, all have profound impacts on small businesses on the Qualla Boundary and are intimately tied to the ability of Native Nations to express their inherent sovereignty.

Pillars of Sovereignty

The Case for Small Business in Economic Development

. . . .

"Do you have a passport?"

This was the unexpected, and possibly confusing, question that visitors entering the Qualla Boundary were faced with in the summer of 2010. The question was part of an EBCI Travel and Promotion tourism campaign in which the Warriors of AniKituhwa—official cultural ambassadors of the EBCI—stopped cars coming onto the Qualla Boundary to talk with incoming visitors. The Warriors of AniKituhwa are a group of Eastern Band men portraying Cherokee warriors from 1762; their clothing varies depending on the event and weather, but it includes leggings, period-accurate tunics, feather headpieces, loincloths, accessories (bandolier bag, weapons), and, when projecting a deliberately intimidating look, red and black paint.[1] They are required to undergo training in Cherokee songs and dances, Cherokee language, and various crafts (beadwork, quillwork, and so on).[2] When one of these Warriors approached a car at the roadblock that day, he introduced himself in Cherokee ("ᏆᏙᏓᏍᎳᏫ ᏞᎢᎥ . . ."; "Usquetsiwo dagwado . . .") and asked in English, "When you were planning on coming here did you actually research about having to have passports to come onto our boundary?"[3] Usquetsiwo (Sonny Ledford) explains his take on the underlying message:

> What we've done today is promotional for the Cherokee people here
> on our Boundary. We volunteered to do this to help the tourism
> that comes into our Boundary. They actually get to see what real
> Cherokee warriors look like. Also, when we do these things for
> our people, our schools, things like this, it's made a big impact on
> the Tsalagi people by teaching and educating about our culture,
> our past, the history, and *the truth*. A lot of times the truth isn't
> spoken. . . . From us here as the Warriors of Anikituwah [*sic*], we
> hope that tourism keeps coming and that we keep educating more
> of the public.[4]

Part of the truth that Sonny speaks of here is the overt message that the Qualla Boundary *is* its own nation. This message was also reinforced by

FIGURE 4.1 Billboard found on and off the Qualla Boundary. Photo by author.

billboards surrounding the Qualla Boundary stating again, quite frankly and simply, "Another Country," accompanied by a picture of a Warrior of AniKituhwa (see figure 4.1). As this campaign and these ads demonstrate, Native Nations' sovereignty needs to be asserted on many fronts: not just in courthouses or United Nations discussions or meetings with political leaders but also in the minds of non-Native peoples. On this day, when the visitors inevitably did not have their passports with them, the Warriors gave them one. This "passport" was, in actuality, a coupon book for various businesses, activities, and events in Cherokee.

This event gained some publicity, but it was not widely discussed among Eastern Band citizens. However, the distribution of coupons under the guise of a passport—a common marketing device used to encourage customers to visit multiple locations—has a very unique reading when employed in a Native Nation context. On the one hand, it is an explicit claim to sovereignty; on the other hand, the giving of passports to tourists is curious, as Eastern Band citizens do not have their own EBCI passports (as is the case with the Haudenosaunee), thus making the substitution of national passports with a coupon book both somewhat poignant and a bit unsettling in its linkage of sovereignty with disposability and profitability.[5]

Although the EBCI's conceptual linkage of the claim of sovereignty with economic incentives was seemingly unintentional, the reality is that the practices of political sovereignty, such as nation-building, and the achievement of a stable economy through practices of economic sovereignty are intimately intertwined—and the role of small-business diversity in creating this economic stability can be indispensable. Consequently, these relationships and the situational interdependence of government-owned corporations and privately owned small businesses, especially in the case of the EBCI, are vital to supporting the practices of both political and economic sovereignty.

Sovereignty: Foundations and Intersections

All three tribes are here today. It means a little bit of grief, but it means a whole lot of happiness. No matter what happened in the past, we have our faith, we still have our spirit and we have our sovereignty. . . . The gathering of our Cherokee governments at this sacred site is not only historic, but a strong reflection of our inherent sovereignty. It is because of our Cherokee ancestors' spirit of perseverance that we are able to gather and conduct the business of our people. We must always keep that in mind and protect that right for our future generations.

—Cherokee Nation Tribal Council Speaker Joe Byrd at the 2015 gathering of the Cherokee Tri-Council at Red Clay State Park in Tennessee

The contestations and intersections of the innateness of indigenous sovereignty, the levels of nonindigenous state recognition of said sovereignty, and the ability or lack thereof to exercise this sovereignty coalesce to form spectrums of indigenous nations' experiences, operating in what Thomas Biolsi terms the *"four indigenous spaces."*[6] Even on these spectrums and in these spaces, however, the *form* that federally recognized Native Nation sovereignty takes in the United States, *how* it is practiced, and its *limitations* are particularly unique, and this uniqueness further shapes the contextual distinctiveness of American Indian entrepreneurs. The persistent menace to settler-colonial society that is the inherency of Native Nation sovereignty, combined with general unfamiliarity regarding the theory and legalities of this sovereignty, has often led its expressions to be framed erroneously over time in popular U.S. rhetoric as "special privileges," with implied expiration dates.[7] In reality, the legal expressions of this inherent sovereignty through government-to-government relationships and the agreements (treaties, compacts, contracts) that are derived as a result of this status are not conceptually exceptional; rather, they are contractual obligations, as between any nations.

For Native Nations, sovereignty is the inherent power and ability to create and implement national decisions independently—that is, independently of U.S. governments. As a starting point, according to Jean Dennison, "Sovereignty signals a centralized system of governmental authority that allows for the assertion of independence within and control over a territory" and, in some cases, even beyond.[8] The three aspects of Native Nation sovereignty, elucidated by Valerie Lambert, are as follows: (1) it is legally constructed as a bundle of inherent powers (rather than treated as a monolithic concept); (2) Native Nations must exercise their powers in the context of other overlapping and competing sovereignties (federal, state, and so on); and (3) even when these rights are legally well defined, Native Nations are not always permitted to exercise their sovereign rights.[9] Kevin Bruyneel aptly specifies, in reference to his "third space of sovereignty," that Native Nations will never be fully disengaged from the United States because of their locations. They are nations within a nation; their sovereignty is always compromised to some extent.[10] This means that while the maneuverings of nations worldwide, as they continuously negotiate shifting political and legal boundaries, are de rigueur, for Native Nations, there is the threat that if they push too hard, or not hard enough, or do nothing at all, the federal government can and will attempt to terminate the nation's ability to practice its sovereignty.[11] Even so, Native Nations continue to work to divest themselves as much as possible from the "domestic dependent" status that U.S. governments at all levels have used to attempt to suppress them.

As in the case of EBCI's historical formation, a Native Nation's economic base and its economic sovereignty are foundational components to the practice of political sovereignty. The intertwining of this sovereignty and the actions of economic sovereignty can be seen historically through the impacts of U.S. settler-colonial economic violence and economic hegemony. H. Craig Miner illustrates this when recounting one story of a critical juncture in American Indian history, one that reveals much about the economic and political impacts of uneven power structures between the U.S. government and Native Nations. This moment also conveys how American Indians both resisted and appropriated the practices of the larger settler-colonial society at every turn. "Yet, through Indian Territory–wide meetings and conferences as early as the 1870s, Indians *did* move to solve the intratribal differences that hindered them in their dealings with corporations. They did form their own corporations. They did petition to be allowed to carry out their own negotiations. They did suggest alternative treaty terms. They did learn that a competitive enterprise system has a capability to accommodate diversity and recognize interests, including cultural ones, through contracts. But they found that in the end, politics, not the market, dominated."[12] Miner recognizes here that it was not a "cultural mismatch" that doomed these efforts but the U.S. government's deliberate suppression of their efforts that prevented these Native Nations from exercising their economic sovereignty and, thus, fully exercising their political sovereignty. Politics *is* the market.

Today, Native Nation economic sovereignty is supported by unique hybrid political-economic structures. While political structures in general, of course, have economic impacts and relations (along with collusions, as Barker has examined),[13] Native Nation governing systems have specific hybridizations that can expand their practices of economic sovereignty. The clearest example of this hybridization is that Native Nations as governing entities can simultaneously be for-profit corporations. The range of autonomy regarding how this particular hybridity manifests can be seen from the dictates of federal laws that declared and classified Alaskan Native Nations as Alaska Native Regional Corporations to the choice of Native Nation governments to operate autonomous corporations that include all citizens as shareholders. In North Carolina, the EBCI not only politically coalesced under the shelter of incorporation to protect its national and citizens' assets but also chose to own and manage a variety of government businesses while doing so. This hybridization also manifests legally, as all Native Nations' governing systems are bound by federal laws that specifically target the growth and management of Native Nation economies (from natural resources to businesses), necessitating Native Nation government management of these economic restrictions, as we will see through the EBCI's process of building a gaming industry.

Another expression of this hybridization is the federal protection that Native Nations have in the form of sovereign immunity. Native Nations are protected from the loss of assets in a manner similar to the sovereign immunity benefiting the federal government, states, and local governments.[14] Outside corporations, however, are generally hesitant to enter into negotiations with entities that they cannot sue. In these circumstances, Native Nations have found it necessary to partially waive their sovereign immunity in order to bring in outside businesses, thus increasing their vulnerability. This can be a complex and problematic process, as one Sault Ste. Marie Tribe of Chippewa Indians (SSMTC, also known as "the Soo") court case demonstrates. In this instance, a waiver of sovereign immunity was signed regarding the purchase of a parking garage associated with an SSMTC casino in Michigan, but it was not signed by an SSMTC government official who had been deemed by the SSMTC to have the authority to do so. This led to a court battle, which was decided against the SSMTC in September 2010, reinstating the waiver of sovereign immunity.[15]

Financially, this hybrid structure allows Native Nation governments to aid businesses in ways not available to other political entities in the United States, including direct investment. For example, Native Nation governments can offer loans at reasonable (or zero) interest rates, build and manage business incubators to encourage private business growth, and even allow citizens to use possessory land as collateral, partially circumventing federal government restrictions on American Indian land transfers. Additionally, in the same way that federal, state, and local levels of the U.S. government do as sovereign entities, Native Nations can offer tax breaks and incentives, adjust zoning laws, and provide free education to business owners.

The ability to offer aids such as these is essential, as many Native Nations face economic development challenges, including a possible lack of capital, lack of resources, and so on. Even so, Native Nations have made enormous strides, especially in the late twentieth century, toward expanding their practices of economic sovereignty. Today, there are many Native Nation–backed research projects and economic-development programs designed to provide intellectual resources and direction on how to grow or stabilize a newly rising economy. Because of their hybridity, Native Nations have the opportunity to draw from many alternative systems of business management and sources of income to not only sustain themselves but also to potentially establish themselves as political and economic leaders. For example, Native Nations are creating companies that provide outsourcing services that draw revenue onto the reservation similar to the way tourism creates monetary inflows (e.g., Suh'dutsing Technologies, a division of the Cedar Band Corporation in Utah, which provides various technology solutions to the private and public sectors).[16] These initiatives are enabling Native Nations to emerge as economic powerhouses in their own states. For example, the EBCI is the largest single employer in western North Carolina, as are the Mississippi Choctaws statewide.[17]

This interdependence and balance of economic sovereignty and political sovereignty is crucial to the functioning of Native Nations. The economic collapse of the Menominee Nation after being politically terminated (having been deemed too economically successful to "need" sovereignty) is one example of this.[18] While the necessity of political sovereignty is imperative to economic sustainability, as in the Menominee's case, it is also true that maintaining a stable economy and economic resources to support the practices of political sovereignty is vital. We have seen this in Cattelino's indepth "double bind of needs-based sovereignty" discussion, which has reverberated throughout American Indian studies literature. And as Dennison says about the Osage, "Asserting . . . sovereignty will take time and will require resources from gaming and other economic development."[19]

A more direct example of this interplay is the practice of giving campaign contributions and associated expressions of political support. In these cases, Native Nations use their revenue to support the campaigns of politicians who are "American Indian aware" and who support Native Nation rights.[20] The ability of these Native Nations to throw their hat into the political arena financially may contribute to benefits not just for those select few Native Nations but possibly—because blanket federal laws apply widely—for all Native Nations. Seneca Nation president Robert Odawi Porter explains, "The reality is that in America, more money equals more speech and louder speech, and that same concept applies to Indian Country. There are a few dozen Indian nations that have disproportionate resources, and I think it carries with it extra responsibility."[21] Along those lines, he states that some Native Nations, including his own, are currently working to build a Sovereign Nations Alliance political action committee, which can work as an umbrella organization to support issues that impact the greater good in Indian Country. For the EBCI, the transition from running a moderately successful tourism industry based on small businesses and several EBCI attractions to owning a highly profitable casino has increased its economic power, enabling it to stretch the exercise of its sovereignties and become a major political presence in North Carolina.[22]

Since the 1990s, there has been a steady increase in scholarship on the importance of economic development for Native Nations and, more specifically, the role of economic development in supporting sovereignty efforts.[23] This literature first demonstrates that Native Nations need a stable economic base in order to gain greater independence.[24] The connection between economic stability and the ability to assert sovereignty is then reflected in many of the newest works on modern expressions of sovereignty, such as those of Cattelino and Dennison. When a Native Nation has a level of economic power that exceeds merely sustaining itself, as well as the economic stability to reliably draw from this economic power, it has the ability to control more decisions autonomously—for example, having enough stable resources to train and hire employees to manage and distribute its own federal funds as it sees fit, thus taking fund management out of the hands of entities like the BIA (per the Indian Self-Determination and Education Assistance Act of 1975).

This economic anthropology literature is important because it also directs attention to the sovereignty aspect of "cultural revitalization" that some Native Nations, like the EBCI, are undertaking in an economic development context. Settler-colonial suppression of various societal and cultural practices of American Indians, ranging from religion to language, along with the historical destruction of Native Nations' economic bases, including the removal of peoples from their homelands, resulted in the forced discontinuation of some of these practices. This suppression appears in a range of forms, from overt settler-colonial policies (hegemony and violence, economic and otherwise) to self-suppression as an act of resistance (underground religious practices) to logistical suppression (the inability to use many native languages in current technologies, such as texting and email).

Because these actions are the result of force, I view much of the discourse on "cultural revitalization" as less concerned with revitalization per se than with the *reclamation* of techniques and practices that have been suppressed. While "revitalization" implies a passiveness in languishing or neglect, "reclamation" conveys an active role and agency in taking back what has been forcibly removed.[25] Furthermore, although much of the literature on Native Nation practices situates these suppression efforts in the past (i.e., language use in the boarding-school era), it is a battle that Native Nations continue to fight. This can be seen in individual instances, such as that of the Menominee seventh grader who was suspended in 2012 by a non-Native teacher for teaching a fellow student how to say "I love you" in Menominee, as well as structurally in the U.S. education system.[26] Here, the overwhelming majority of K–12 schools and universities do not allow students to use their Native Nation languages as official "second languages" in practice, despite provisions made by the 1990 Native American Languages Act. These are challenges that the EBCI continues to address in its own language reclamation efforts. The EBCI negotiates for and stumps in support of having high school and college students' Cherokee-language courses count for their "foreign" language requirement and has battled high school course cancellations due to outside determinations of what constitutes a "highly qualified" Cherokee-language instructor.[27] In order to further internal reclamation efforts, however, Native Nation leaders must be able to help provide the means and methods for their citizens to train, or be trained, in these practices. These efforts, as with the training and hiring of language teachers, cannot be accomplished without an adequate capital base, as they require money, time, and access to resources. Indeed, the EBCI pays the salaries of Cherokee-language instructors who teach in the surrounding three counties' schools so that the students attending those non-EBCI schools can have access to Cherokee-language education.[28] Since 2004, the EBCI has also been financially able to operate a total-immersion Cherokee-language school system—the Atse Kituwah Academy of the Kituwah Preservation and Education Program (KPEP)—for Eastern Band children, which provides concurrent language classes for those children's parents.[29] The necessity of financial support, along with the autonomy to make financial decisions, increases even further when a practice has long been suppressed.

Many of the currently prevailing theories about Native Nation economic development are centered on the concept of nation-building. In much of this research, nation-building constructs economic development as a macro-level holistic endeavor—bringing political systems, societal priorities, and economic factors together to shape the whole nation rather than addressing only individual areas of concern.[30] Nation-building itself is a top-down approach emphasizing the Native Nation government as the primary instigator of change for the nation. Unfortunately, nation-building literature can obscure the agency of the individual and the importance of collective actions. While this focus on larger systems and institutions has been prevalent in the wider indigenous economic-development literature, by the late 1990s the dearth of "agents" in the anthropology of development had been criticized, and since then, researchers have begun to explore the role of private business in community development.[31] Much of the subsequent literature has highlighted the interactions between the individual and society, emphasizing the role of social capital in economic development.[32] Work also now focuses on the issues of capital and the individual, highlighting such aids as the much debated microcredit, microfinance, and microloan movements and basic income grants as stimulus for economic development.[33] Research in American Indian studies, such as that of Colleen O'Neill, David Kamper, and Daniel Usner, has made progress in this realm, focusing on workers as agents of substantial change who shape the regional dynamics of U.S. economic development and on sovereignty via "the [workers] who experience and enact it through their everyday lives."[34] These works offer a multivocal, multiposition theory that supports the advancement of a much richer story of development issues as they relate to the entrepreneurial individual, going beyond the binary of the encumbered individual, embedded in social networks, and the autonomous individual. This book's focus on small-business owners on the Qualla Boundary furthers understandings of the entrepreneurial individual, the contextual distinctiveness of the entrepreneurial American Indian, and these individuals as agents of change who play a necessary role in the interplay of economy-building and nation-building. Yet before contemporary individual economic actions and impacts on the Qualla Boundary can be understood, we must address the EBCI's more recently established primary source of economic power: the casinos.

Gaming, Economic Power, and Economic Sovereignty

In August 2011, the EBCI convened a Governing Documents Review Committee to discuss the development of a formal EBCI constitution. One expert brought in for consultation was Manley A. Begay Jr. (Diné), a faculty chair at the Native Nations Institute at the University of Arizona, who asked the audience pointedly, "Who's the self in self-government? Who is the Eastern Band of Cherokee Indians? What does that mean? What are you all about?"[35] One month later, Mary Wachacha, while running for principal chief, further commented on the issue of EBCI sovereignty as practiced from its position as a successful casino-operating Native Nation:

> I have just read the front page of the Asheville *Citizen-Times*, "NC eyes stake in Harrah's money." I cannot believe that the State might agree to live dealers and other games at the Casino, but would agree only if we give the State a share of the Tribe's profits from the Casino.
>
> This Tribe needs to play some hard ball politics. After all, we are one of the largest employers in the state—apparently, it isn't enough that we provide a salary and benefits for casino employees; we are now expected to support the state of NC? What state benefits can Tribal members expect from this forced penalty? Perhaps we should only provide a salary and no health benefits to non-Cherokee employees so that we can cut some of our costs. After all, it is the non-Indian employee who gets the greater gain in health coverage— it certainly is not the Indian.
>
> Apparently the state of NC cannot stand the thought of the Cherokees moving towards self-determination. . . . I hope that by now, the Chief [during his negotiations with the state regarding live table gaming] will emphasize that the state of NC has done very little in the past 200 years for Cherokee Indians to warrant a share of our profits. . . . The initial question the Chief needs to answer is: *Are we sovereign or not?*[36]

The EBCI's economic history provides many examples of its consistent efforts to pursue the dynamic goals of economic sustainability and self-sufficiency. Early in its national business enterprise developments, beginning with incorporation as a sugar and silk Cherokee Company in the late 1800s and later as a lumber business, the EBCI discovered what the Harvard Project would publish in the 1990s—that business and politics do not mix.[37] From these initial management lessons came the Cherokee Boys Farm Club, founded by the EBCI in 1932 to provide Eastern Band citizen services.[38] The Boys Club then started a trash removal service in 1964 to provide the community with an EBCI-owned source of income and jobs. This service expanded to other communities on the western side of the state and was soon the EBCI's most profitable venture, allowing for its future expansion into such areas as office supplies. It continues to run now as a nonprofit, self-supporting "tribal enterprise." The launch, growth, and management of these successful national enterprises gave the EBCI the experience and some capital to begin an entirely new endeavor.

In 1982, the EBCI started a modest gaming venture with the two elements that American Indian economic-development research literature has since deemed necessary for success: a stable government system and a cordial relationship with the state(s) it shares borders with.[39] The EBCI's initial venture was a bingo hall that is still operating today, standing away from the highway on a lesser-used road leading out of town and into the mountains. This was followed by a small casino, which was a rousing success. The success of that casino ultimately instigated the launch of the large Harrah's Cherokee Casino and Hotel in 1997.[40] The year 2011 was the next significant moment for the Cherokee Casino. That year began with the opening of the third tower, bringing the hotel room count to 1,108. This construction was the largest hospitality expansion in the Southeast and the sixth-largest construction project in the entire United States.[41] New signature restaurants were launched, including the then sought-after Paula Deen line (since closed due to public revelation of her various expressions of racism). This marked the first phase of the Cherokee Casino's five-year, $650 million expansion.[42] The EBCI then renewed its contract with Harrah's as a management company for another seven years, locking in the partnership until at least 2018. Per this agreement, Harrah's purchased a $1.2 million MRI machine for the Cherokee Indian Hospital and will provide funds for its maintenance—a total of just over $2 million. Finally, and most significantly, the state of North Carolina and the EBCI came to an agreement on a new thirty-year gaming compact that allows the Cherokee Casino to provide live table games and grants the EBCI sole rights to provide those games in the state west of I-26.[43] The EBCI, in turn, agreed to give North Carolina an incrementally increasing percentage of gross receipts from the table games: 4 percent for the first five years, 5 percent for the next five years, 6 percent for the next five years, 7 percent for the next five years, and 8 percent for the next ten years. The state has agreed to use all of the monies received from the EBCI to help fund the state's public schools.

In July 2011, UNC's Kenan-Flagler Business School issued a report titled *Assessing the Economic and Non-Economic Impacts of Harrah's Cherokee Casino, North Carolina.* This report stated that Cherokee Casino visitor-generated revenue brought in $386 million in 2010 to the surrounding area. During the previous decade, the number of total visitors to the casino had increased from 3.1 million in 1998 to 3.6 million in 2010. It also reported that by 2009 the casino was directly responsible for 5 percent of employment (1,674 employees) in Jackson and Swain Counties and accounted for 8 percent of wages and salary disbursements there.[44] Additionally, in 2009 the casino delivered an estimated $52.4 million in wage and salary income into the local economy, with "household spending generating an additional $8.3 million in economic output, for a total employee compensation impact of $60.7 million in Jackson and Swain Counties."[45]

This revenue has supported an immense increase in Eastern Band citizen services and the expansion of EBCI sovereignty practices. Since the beginning of my initial fieldwork, this has allowed for the building of a new 150,000-square-foot, $82 million hospital (including a primary care and emergency facility that serves everyone, regardless of Native Nation citizenship status, and an urgent care center for all employees of the EBCI), the Analenisgi (ᎠᏁᎵᏍᎩ) Recovery Center, the Kanvwotiyi (ᎧᏅᎣᏘᏱᏍ) Snowbird Residential Treatment Center, the Anthony Edward Lossiah Justice Center, the new K–12 Cherokee Central School campus, and the Atse Kituwah Academy language-immersion building (both schools opened while I was in the field). The EBCI Tribal Council in 2016 also approved the construction of a new homeless shelter (plans and budgets are in the works). The EBCI is now able to self-manage programs, such as its Family Safety Program (foster care, adoption assistance, and guardianship assistance programs) and the Public Health and Human Services (PHHS) division's new administration of a USDA grant, along with the transition of services to the Cherokee Tribal Food Distribution Program.

When discussing the positive outcomes of Native Nation gaming, it is vital to recognize that Native Nations achieved these accomplishments under the constraints of one of the most straightforward cases of continued economic hegemony today. Indian gaming began to make headway as an economic-development enterprise for Native Nations in the late 1970s, following legal and political changes instigated by the Indian Self-Determination Act. By 1979, Native Nations choosing to start gaming enterprises were already facing challenges from state governments. The Seminole were one of the first to face a court challenge, in *Seminole Tribe of Florida v. Butterworth*, which decided in favor of the Seminoles' right to own and manage a bingo enterprise in Florida. This was followed by the 1987 national linchpin case of *California v. Cabazon Band of Mission Indians*. This case was also decided in favor of Native Nations' gaming industries, thereby making this enterprise legal in all applicable states (i.e., unless the gaming enterprise was conducted in a Public Law 280 state that also has specific *criminal* laws prohibiting gaming). Even before this case was decided, the Department of the Interior estimated that in 1985, about eighty Native Nations were offering gaming on their reservations, with twenty to twenty-five grossing between $100,000 to $1 million a month.[46] In the wake of this victory for Native Nation economic sovereignty, however, states renewed their efforts to control Native Nation gaming, this time focusing not on court challenges but on legislative ones. Congress obliged these states' wishes by enacting on October 17, 1988, the Indian Gaming Regulatory Act (IGRA), a federal law that holds Native Nations hostage to state laws and "good-faith" compacts with these adjacent states.[47] This act struck a heavy blow to Native Nation political and economic sovereignty by placing Native Nations' status in a legally subservient position to that of states in issues of gaming.[48]

The IGRA began by categorizing gaming into three classes. Class I gaming is not regulated by IGRA; this class includes "social games solely for prizes of minimal value or traditional forms of Indian gaming engaged in by individuals as a part of, or in connection with, tribal ceremonies or celebrations." Class II gaming includes bingo (as a "game of chance") and card games that "are explicitly authorized by the laws of the State, or are not explicitly prohibited by the laws of the State." Class III gaming is defined as all games not falling under Class I or II—a broad category for most states.[49] Native Nations can have Class II or III gaming only if they are "located within a state that permits such gaming for any purpose."[50] To start a gaming enterprise with a class designation exceeding that which is allowed by the adjacent state, or to start any Class III gaming enterprise regardless of state law, Native Nations are now forced to negotiate compacts with states.

For their part, states are required only to act "in good faith," and if they do not, Native Nations currently have no legal recourse.[51] These compacts, in most contemporary cases, also include various payments to the states, usually a percentage of the gaming proceeds, essentially replacing the state taxes that are forbidden by IGRA. This potentially allows states to charge a higher percentage than what the state taxes would have been.[52] The requirement forcing Native Nations to negotiate with their surrounding state is a clear violation of Native Nations' inherent sovereignty, but it stands nonetheless.

IGRA extends this economic hegemony by further dictating *how* Native Nations' proceeds can be used. For example, gaming profits can be spent in only five preapproved categories:

- funding tribal governmental operations or programs
- providing for the general welfare of the tribe and its citizens
- promoting tribal economic development
- donating to charitable organizations
- funding the operations of local government agencies

Moreover, IGRA prohibits dividend payments that would total over 50 percent of total gaming profits, capping the amount that a Native Nation can choose to return to its citizens in this form.[53]

Subjecting Native Nations to the whims of state politics is a severe blow for Native Nation sovereignty, but forcing Native Nations to funnel much-needed monies out of reservations into the surrounding state, and then dictating the ways in which Native Nation money is spent, are forms of paternalism—recalling attitudes regarding the competency of American Indians to manage their own lands, funds, and resources—that are not enacted on non-Native corporations.[54] The federal government's exceptional regulation of Native Nations as they attempt to achieve a measure of economic power through gaming can also be seen outside IGRA. In 2015, the U.S. Court of Appeals for the Sixth Circuit determined that the National Labor Relations Board (NLRB) had jurisdiction over Native Nation enterprises.[55] However, this extension of NLRB jurisdiction was specifically directed at only certain Native Nation enterprises—those that are for-profit, particularly gaming. According to Kamper, this jurisdictional extension would not extend to nonprofit ventures by Native Nations (such as their health-care-providing entities), which happen to be the enterprises that do not threaten the status quo of economic power-structure relations between Native Nations and various U.S. governments.[56]

Paying Shareholders

Per caps is a term commonly used throughout Indian Country. Short for *per capita*, these are corporate dividend payments made to shareholders—citizens of Native Nations—whose government entity owns a corporation. Dividend payments can be paid from a variety of enterprise industries (although gaming has garnered the most attention), but they are optional, at the discretion of the Native Nation and its citizens. A Native Nation's choice to pay dividends demonstrates an exercise of economic sovereignty in which the nation foregrounds the financial needs of its citizens as a priority; however, the ability to do so, specifically in the case of gaming, is also federally restricted by the IGRA regulation that caps payments at 50 percent of total gaming profits. The EBCI has chosen to pay dividends, and these payments are made biannually to Eastern Band citizens for their government's investment in its casinos. Partially because of misleading nomenclature, combined with stereotypes of American Indian economic identity, these payments have the false stigma of being handouts, often labeled as examples of "special rights."[57] They are, therefore, criticized in ways that non–Native Nation corporate dividends are not, as in the disproven claim that payments disincentivize the poor to work (for the already wealthy, the claim is opposite: that money in the form of, for example, tax breaks, bonuses, and dividend payments incentivizes them to work).[58]

When the EBCI takes the form of a corporation (as in the case of its casinos), its government manages national funds on behalf of its citizens. The shareholders of the corporation are Eastern Band citizens who are considered equally invested owners of the casinos. This means that each citizen (hence the "per capita") receives an equal share of the dividends, which are paid out in the form of twice-yearly checks or direct deposits. These dividend payments for the Eastern Band citizens have varied widely over the past two decades, from the time the Cherokee Casino opened to the peak of its profitability, followed by a drop during the Great Recession of the Bush era. Dividends are calculated by splitting the distributable net revenue 50/50—that is, 50 percent of proceeds are split among the citizens, and 50 percent is reinvested into the nation. Through the early 2000s, payments totaled approximately $3,000 (pretax) twice a year.[59]

Contrary to popular notions, these payments are not a new phenomenon among Native Nations, or even for the EBCI. According to Adams, "The [EBCI] council distributed funds from other timber sales to tribal citizens as per capita payments. In 1900, for example, each tribal citizen received $4.00 from the 'Timber Fund.' The 1906 sale of the Love Tract for $245,000 promised tribal citizens large payouts over several years."[60] The concept of a dividend payment has even been proposed as a contemporary expression of a Native Nation's governmental obligation—as a consolidated representation of its people—to provide and share communal wealth, "just like the meat hunted" would historically be distributed.[61] In this way, the payments of dividends from a communal ownership of a business could be seen as reflecting part of the Cherokee concept and societal expectation of gadugi (ᎦᏚᎩ), roughly translated as the selfless act of working together for the betterment of the community (this concept can also be applied beyond the dividend payments proper to overall casino revenues, as even Eastern Band citizens who refuse a dividend check still reap the benefits of casino revenue through better hospitals, education, and roads).

The most common form of for-profit businesses in the United States are corporations, privately owned entities that are legally distinct from their owners but which simultaneously hold most of the rights afforded to an individual (i.e., they operate as if owned by an individual who can hire employees, enter into contracts, pay taxes, and so on).[62] The United States has few truly large-scale cooperatively owned companies like Spain's Mondragon, a cooperative corporate entity that holds 268 subsidiaries employing 73,635 workers.[63] Becoming more popular in the United States are small cooperative corporations (such as food co-ops), which are owned by their employees and patrons collectively. All of these corporations may or may not choose to pay dividends. U.S. citizens may also be familiar with government-owned corporations. This is "a government agency that is established by Congress to provide a market-oriented public service and to produce revenues that meet or approximate its expenditures"—for example, the U.S. Post Office and the Tennessee Valley Authority.[64]

Comparatively, a "tribal enterprise" is "any business (concern) that is at least 51 percent owned by an Indian tribe" (including Alaska Native Corporations), meaning that the Native Nation must "unconditionally own at least 51 percent of the voting stock and at least 51 percent of the aggregate of all classes of stock . . . or at least 51 percent interest."[65] Unlike U.S. federal businesses, Native Nation businesses are not just put in place to directly provide basic utilities and services for citizens, funded through tax revenue;

Native Nation enterprises often draw a profit from a non-citizen-service enterprise, which serves as a revenue stream for their government to then provide services to their citizens. For Native Nations, this offers a way to provide needed services without drawing solely on the (already possibly impoverished) community. Although these enterprises can be labeled broadly as democratic-socialist modes of production, I agree in this case with Gibson-Graham (and, to some extent, with a similar argument made by Yanagisako with regard to small businesses) that this language privileges a "capitalo-centric" view of indigenous economic activities that cannot take into account the discrete practices, goals, and choices of each Native Nation.[66]

Because privately owned corporations dominate the U.S. media landscape, most people in the United States are not exposed to alternative corporate ownership models and are justifiably unfamiliar with the differences in how an entity like a Native Nation casino operates compared to an average U.S. private corporation or even a U.S. government-owned corporation. This general unfamiliarity with alternative business models helps propagate misunderstandings of what exactly a "tribal enterprise" is, further contributing to the "special rights" rhetoric.

Although these Native Nation–owned corporations function in many ways like privately owned corporations, they also, by necessity, have unique operational practices. The most notable is that for Native Nations that choose to pay dividends, their investors are *automatically all* of the citizens of that nation. This means that children are investors at birth and accrue this money over time, receiving their accumulated dividends when they reach adulthood. As with other companies, there are a variety of ways that Native Nation dividend payments operate, depending on the system the Native Nation deems most positively impactful for their citizens. In the case of the children's accounts (held collectively by the EBCI as the "Minors' Trust Fund"), one payment option is opening the accounts for access at age eighteen, often called a "lump-sum" payment. Until 2011, this was the only possibility available to Native Nations for the distribution of these funds, as the IRS did not permit any other options.

As the EBCI experienced, there were two problems with this lump-sum payment. First was the heavy tax burden of a single, large payment.[67] Second, releasing a five-figure lump sum to an eighteen-year-old is an optimistic venture, as most teenagers lack the experience necessary for serious financial responsibility.[68] Occasionally, these teenagers have, for example, bought cars with the money, depleting nearly their entire account in one fell swoop. There is also possible family pressure to distribute this lump sum. One business owner related a story of his high school employee, who confided that she wanted to refuse the lump sum entirely because her family was already fighting over how it would be distributed among them. One method that concurrently combats these lump-sum issues of large taxes and financial management is a graduated release of the minors' fund distributions. A local high school organization, the Junaluska Leadership Council, researched and petitioned the EBCI Tribal Council for an alternative staggered installment plan once the option became available under 2011 federal law. In June 2016, the EBCI Tribal Council formally approved the new payment plan (three payments at ages eighteen, twenty-one, and twenty-five) for the minors' fund distributions, to be implemented in 2017.[69]

The EBCI has further tackled potential overspending problems with these early payments by implementing several programs, including the Qualla Financial Freedom finance-management program. This program begins teaching money-management skills to children in elementary school and progresses to interactive programs for high school students, presenting them with various financial scenarios that they must manage within their budget.[70] The latest program has been deemed so important that now, per Tribal Council Ordinance No. 401 (effective April 1, 2011), "Any minor member, applying for their minors' trust fund, will be required to complete the online Manage Your EBCI Money Course (www.manageyourebcimoney.org) and include his/her Certificate of Completion to be entitled to receive any monies."[71] The program further claims, "You can be a millionaire before the age of forty if you start investing your money when you're young."[72] A program with a more conservative goal is the Kituwah Savings Program, begun in 2013 and hosted jointly by the Sequoyah Fund (see appendix H) and First Citizens Bank. The Kituwah Savings Program is designed to teach savings and financial-management skills to the kindergarten through fourth-grade students at the Atse Kituwah Academy. The Sequoyah Fund contributes the first $25 to each student's First Citizens account, and the family contributes $5 biweekly throughout the school year, earning prizes, educational field trips, and a $25 bonus at the end of the year if they reach their savings goals. The ability of these new programs to produce financially savvy adults who can manage their money to finance a lifetime of income (if they so choose) should be apparent in the coming years.[73]

The benefits of an unconditional lump-sum transfer in achieving income redistributions and alleviating the impacts of poverty have long been discussed, from Samuelson in "Social Indifference Curves" (with its focus on Pareto efficiency, in which you cannot make any one person better off without making another worse off, and criticized due to its failure to address issues such as income inequality) to Blattman, Fiala, and Martinez in "The Economic and Social Returns to Cash Transfers" and Sulaiman et al. in "Eliminating Extreme Poverty," which demonstrate the long-term positive impacts of such transfers. Another way to address the same issues is through guaranteed annual income (GAI), which can be conditional or unconditional; when unconditional, it is also referred to as universal basic income, in which all citizens receive identical payments. These GAI-type supplements have been proposed in many forms, including substantial universal payouts (Thomas Paine), a negative income tax (George Stigler, Milton Friedman), and even part of U.S. policy (Nixon's Family Assistance Plan in 1970). In 2011, Evelyn Forget published compiled data from the Mincome guaranteed annual income field experiment (1974–79) in Dauphin, Manitoba, Canada. This work revealed that an unconditional GAI increased educational attainment, increased health outcomes, and did not produce a work disincentive. Therefore, we see that a lump-sum payment is one proven way to help mitigate the impacts of poverty but that dividend payments, acting as a GAI permanent income increase (individuals behaving as though it were a permanent change, even with cyclical fluctuations), represent a different mechanism for achieving similar results.

These positive results of GAIs have spurred a tremendous growth in international interest since 2016. Conditional GAIs have been implemented in Finland (est. 2017); Livorno, Italy (est. 2016); and Ontario, Canada (est. 2017) for a portion of their populations. In 2018, Stockton, California, which was the first U.S. city to declare bankruptcy (2012), implemented the Stockton Economic Empowerment Demonstration (SEED) program, which provides $500 monthly to the city's lowest-income citizens.[74] The program is funded by the Economic Security Project (which specifically supports GAIs), the Goldhirsh Foundation for social innovation, and crowd funding. The practice of providing a GAI has also reached directly into charities, such as GiveDirectly, which will donate $22 monthly to every adult in a select hamlet in Kenya for twelve years (impact study to be released one decade after implementation).[75] Relatedly, Alaska's Permanent Fund Dividend (est. 1982) mimics Native Nation practices by paying dividends related to oil revenues to qualifying residents (those with felonies excluded).

Because the EBCI provides a lump sum to its eighteen-year-olds, as well as dividends that act as a GAI, we see both mechanisms being instituted to a demonstrably positive effect. (One interesting negative impact that did emerge was an increase in youth obesity.)[76] The results of dividend payments specifically for Eastern Band youth and their parents have received much research attention since publications began to emerge after the 1993 launch of Costello et al.'s comprehensive and ongoing "Great Smoky Mountains Study," followed by Akee et al.'s additional study of this data. These studies demonstrated a marked reduction of mental health issues for children, with a drop of roughly 30 percent in psychiatric problems and 40 percent in behavioral problems, including an increase in on-time graduation rates and higher levels of educational attainment, accompanied by declines in minor crimes committed by youths (now under the rate of non-Native youths in the study, mirroring the results seen in Forget's Dauphin study).[77] Akee further argues that these reductions also act as cost-savings measures for the EBCI, as the level of government services needed to address social problems is reduced, possibly surpassing the dividend payment amounts by the time the Eastern Band individual turns twenty-four years of age.[78] One explanation Akee offers for this rise in positive youth outcomes is increased "parental quality" through reductions in parental issues that correlate with poverty, such as a reduced rate of arrests among fathers. It should also be noted that contrary to notions of supplemental incomes creating a disincentive to work, neither mothers nor fathers were seen leaving the workforce as a result of the additional income.[79]

But not all Eastern Band citizens accept dividend payments; some choose to "opt out" (as it is described locally). The EBCI nation as a collection of citizens voted to collectively invest and distribute dividends based on a majority approval, but not all EBCI citizens approved of the casinos or the dividend payments, and some chose to refuse payments for a variety of reasons. In 2010, while I was in the field, the Cherokee Casino launched the sale of alcohol on its premises after an Eastern Band citizens' vote. This was no simple task, as the Qualla Boundary is otherwise completely dry and remains so after subsequent voting.[80] This addition of alcohol sales angered many, including small-business restaurant owners who remained unable to sell alcohol and were thus put at a disadvantage compared to the casino restaurants, which could now serve wine, beer, and eventually liquor.[81] Many other citizens objected to this alcohol allowance on moral grounds, citing perceived problems with alcohol abuse and contemporary inaccurate perceptions of American Indians as having a proclivity for alcohol abuse.[82] While shareholders in standard corporations have made a choice to invest in the companies in which they own shares, Eastern Band citizens are born into their shares and are therefore automatically included in the dividend system. If they have an objection to a casino-associated action, moral or otherwise, one recourse is to opt out of the process by rejecting the dividend payments. Although the number of opt-outs is small, it is important to recognize these individuals' choices as an exercise of agency, even within these corporate bounds.

Mitigating Gaming Precarity with Small-Business Diversity

Indirect negative repercussions of casino ownership, such as those emerging from the Duke Energy conflict, are only one of the challenges faced by casino-based economies. When casinos are highly successful (which is not the case in most instances), their wealth can seem to so far surpass other income-generating revenue streams that it is easy to leave other opportunities by the wayside.[83] Additionally, although there are many benefits of successful casino ownership and management, there are also several substantial risks. First and foremost is the ever-looming threat of economic collapse should the casino fail at some point. Previous to my graduate work in the temperate climes of North Carolina, I lived in Michigan. My house was on the edge of Detroit, about five hours from Sault St. Marie, located in Michigan's Upper Peninsula ("the UP"). It is here that the Sault Ste. Marie Tribe of Chippewa runs five gaming enterprises. These successful casinos were a prime destination for busloads of gaming enthusiasts, as the state of Michigan itself did not permit gaming, meaning that the SSMTC's enterprises were some of the only nearby options for this kind of entertainment— and a robustly popular one at that. In 1996, a statewide ballot initiative intending to stimulate the economy cleared the way for gaming in the state of Michigan, with Detroit hosting the three available locations. The SSMTC managed to secure one of these slots (the Greektown Casino). If it had not, it faced the possibility of incurring a great financial loss. The population of the Detroit metro area, along with that of surrounding states, would have easy access to three casinos concentrated downtown (including another just across the bridge in Windsor, Ontario), instead of having to drive hours into rural Michigan for gaming entertainment.[84] Although projecting one specific set of circumstances onto a different set is problematic (here, between Michigan and North Carolina), the SSMTC's potential financial loss is echoed in concerns of Eastern Band citizens on the Qualla Boundary, especially during political debates.

In 2011, Juanita Plummer Wilson, a candidate for principal chief, stated, "It's a dangerous trend that we're seeing. Tennessee is looking at getting its own casino going. What happens when that happens?"[85] The following year, Gary Ledford, 2011 EBCI public safety director and candidate for principal chief, reinforced that sentiment: "At very great financial risk, we've put all of our eggs into one flimsy non-double-weave basket. . . . We have effectively turned our back on the small businessman by focusing all efforts on the casino, in a declining casino market."[86] And, finally, Mary Wachacha (retired, former lead consultant for the U.S. Department of Health and Human Services' Indian Health Service) warned in a commentary written for the *One Feather*, "Let's not get caught-up in the state dangling a carrot before us by the state saying we can have a casino anywhere—they are also saying that anyone—not just the Tribe—can have a casino anywhere. These casino companies such as Caesars, MGM Grand and others have a lot more money than this Tribe to build new casinos. If gaming is allowed statewide, these companies are going to be first in line to build new casinos in the state. The Tribe will have to go further into debt to build another casino."[87]

These comments reflect very real concerns about the precarity of Native Nation gaming. First, there are routine business failures (lack of customers, poor management). These can potentially leave a Native Nation heavily indebted, with no income stream to reduce that debt, while bearing the burden of reduced legal sovereignty as well via IGRA, state compacts, and possible sovereign-immunity waivers. But even successful (understood as stable and consistently profitable) Native Nations gaming enterprises face a variety of challenges: if the Native Nation produces a highly profitable gaming enterprise, the state may legalize gaming—especially in a time of financial crisis, as was the case in Michigan. This increases competition, thus reducing visitors and overall profits. This is especially detrimental for Native Nations whose casinos are far off the beaten path, as many reservations are by federal design. If the state does not legalize gaming, other nearby Native Nations may start up their own gaming enterprises.[88] Finally, there is the possibility that if a Native Nation chooses to open a gaming enterprise in a state in which gaming is illegal, the state could respond by challenging the Native Nation's sovereignty in court in an attempt to oppose the casino.[89] It is easy to see that in nearly every scenario—whether gaming succeeds or fails—reliance on only the gaming industry compromises a Native Nation economy's adaptability and, thus, stability, while also compromising the Native Nation's sovereignty.[90]

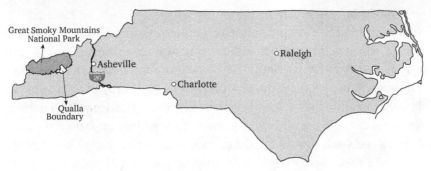

MAP 3 Location of I-26. Design by Christopher Kaminski.

Despite the consistent and diligent work of the EBCI to mitigate these potential issues, it is facing some threats. In the latest 2010 compact made with the state, the EBCI secured rights to casino ownership west of I-26, which runs near Asheville, about an hour and a half away from the Qualla Boundary. This might seem like a well-planned buffer, but if the state hits hard financial times (which it is facing at the time of this writing), this compact clears the way for statewide gaming everywhere else outside that small western sliver (see map 3). Furthermore, the EBCI faces potential competition from the Catawba Nation, which hoped to acquire trust land to build a casino near Charlotte; the state of Tennessee, which is entertaining the idea of entering the gaming industry; and Georgia, which is actively pursuing gaming legislation.[91] For the EBCI, then, the key question when managing this venture is how to shape a stable economy that can support its community in light of these challenges.

As a government, the EBCI continues to develop ways to protect its national income streams through gaming upgrades (progressive upgrades to the Cherokee Casino itself—tower expansions, concert venue, Asian gaming room, a conference center, and so on), the addition of a new gaming venue away from the town of Cherokee, and critical revenue diversification into non-gaming EBCI-owned enterprises. These efforts include tourism-related enterprises, such as an indoor–outdoor adventure park, tours, and fishing camps, as well as non-tourism enterprises, like Cherokee Bottled Water and knowledge industry ventures.[92]

One of the most impressive steps taken by the EBCI in its pursuit of self-sufficiency and economic diversity enabled by casino revenue was the establishment of its BalsamWest FiberNet company. The Qualla Boundary is physically far away from what existing communications companies considered viable infrastructure locations, thereby excluding the EBCI and its citizens from new communication technology opportunities. This meant that the whole community, as well as most of western North Carolina and surrounding counties, was lacking in communication services for education, health services, governmental services, and so on. A project called Appalachian Access, initiated at Southwestern Community College (SCC) in 1999, examined these issues and demonstrated their stifling impact on the area. This spurred Cecil Groves of SCC to encourage collaboration between the EBCI and Drake Enterprises to form what would become BalsamWest. The EBCI agreed to this collaboration and jointly started its fiber-optic communications company in 2003 with $12 million of its casino operation revenue. The new company then laid three hundred miles of underground fiber in ten counties in North Carolina, Georgia, and Tennessee.[93] The switch was flipped, so to speak, in 2006, and the resulting network was so successful that telecommunications company MCI has signed an agreement to connect to the network. This network, although still growing, has provided much-needed internet access for schools, hospitals, and the community, as well as some of its small businesses.[94] Ownership of this company also enables the EBCI to consider either expanding its government-owned enterprises into, or attracting outside businesses from, the knowledge industries sector; to this end, a new $100 million Mission Critical Data Center was approved in 2016.[95]

The EBCI, which had the advantage of seeing other Native Nations pursue the path of gaming before launching its own endeavor, has tried to anticipate and mitigate similar potential financial issues. It has put in place a debt fund generated from casino profits solely for the purpose of paying off EBCI debt.[96] In 2016, with the Great Recession in decline, the newly elected Chief Lambert (who took office in October 2015) and the EBCI Tribal Council exercised this option to become free of EBCI debt (which does not include Tribal Casino Gaming Enterprise business debt) by paying $96 million toward the community's new hospital and new water treatment plant.[97] But as EBCI citizens keenly felt during the recession, attaining the economic stability necessary to continue providing for citizens in the midst of outside shocks is one of the biggest challenges the EBCI will face. The students who were set to draw their funds at age eighteen in 2009, much like most retirees across the United States during the recession, found that they were down thousands of dollars from what their classmates earned in the preceding and following years.[98] The investment choices made for the Minors' Trust Fund were a blessing when they were earning interest and a curse when they lost money during the recession. Casino attendance also fell during this time, exacerbating the problem by reducing the profits going into the fund.

But situations like the Great Recession are exactly those in which small businesses shine. In stark contrast to running a large enterprise, a small business is usually more agile. A small business can change inventory, scale back on hours, or even relocate if needed, while the casino is locked into position, events, and offerings (in terms of dining, shops, and so on), sometimes years in advance. And by its collective nature, there is rarely a singular competitor to the entire small-business sector, unlike the gaming industry, whose profits are likely curtailed by the emergence of even one nearby competitor. For these reasons, the EBCI has begun to focus on small businesses and entrepreneurship in addition to its government enterprise diversification efforts. One piece of this effort is directly funded by casino revenues: the Cherokee Preservation Foundation (CPF, see appendix H), established in 2000. Today, many of the cultural reclamation (such as KPEP), economic development, and environmental preservation projects occurring on the Qualla Boundary are funded to differing extents through the CPF, whose motto is "Weaving Partnerships to Improve the Quality of Life of the Eastern Band of Cherokee Indians and Strengthen Western NC."[99] The CPF is composed primarily of an Eastern Band citizen staff and a board of directors, along with nonprofit partners. Together, they award grants with monies drawn from casino revenue to projects that support the CPF's mission.[100] To date, the CPF has granted over $166 million for "preservation, research, restoration, and/or development of the history, tradition, culture, language, arts, crafts, heritage and overall well-being of the Cherokee people."[101]

To regain lost crafting methods while supporting local artists, the CPF sponsors programs such as the Cherokee Pottery Revitalization Project, which paired archaeologists, including Brett Riggs, with local artists—in this case, potters Davy Arch, Betty Maney, and Bernadine George, to name a few—to research techniques and methods of pottery making that had fallen out of use for reasons ranging from environmental changes to assimilation policies.[102] There is also the Revitalization of Traditional Cherokee Artisan Resources (RTCAR) initiative. Due to land development, many of the original supplies used in basketmaking (such as river cane) and other crafts are becoming less abundant. The RTCAR initiative was set in place to ensure the survival of these resources and the methods themselves (the program will eventually expand to cover edible and medicinal plant resources). In reclaiming these methods, the Eastern Band artist-entrepreneurs' repertoires are expanded, thus potentially bolstering their business as well as their skill sets. This outcome is in line with another specific focus of the CPF: "support of entrepreneurship to diversify the regional economy."[103] As such, its support underwrites many of the EBCI's programs for small businesses discussed throughout this book, including the Sequoyah Fund and the downtown revitalization project. These CPF efforts show that for the EBCI, support for community includes a focus on achieving a stable economy through small-business diversity.

But even as casino revenue helped some small businesses, for other Eastern Band business owners, the Cherokee Casino—and, by proxy, the EBCI government itself—was the challenge. Initially, the casino brought more people to Cherokee, but it also corralled the visitors into its own space, for all intents and purposes indirectly discouraging the new visitors from experiencing the rest of Cherokee. As the EBCI's gaming industry grew, some Qualla Boundary small businesses began to suffer from lack of customer traffic.

Issues also arose with regard to potential direct competition between the Native Nation governmental enterprises and private businesses. In the United States, governmental businesses are citizen-service oriented and therefore exist alongside private businesses, with private businesses thriving by offering more complex versions of these services, as in the case of the U.S. Postal Service alongside FedEx and UPS. Native Nation ventures, by comparison, can be noncitizen and for-profit services. As such, they can be in direct competition with small businesses. The casino itself competed with the numerous established hotels and motels that had been in Cherokee for decades.[104] There is also the issue of alcohol sales. During the EBCI debates over alcohol sales and consumption, although it was a citizen vote that kept the Qualla Boundary dry, it also happened to be in the EBCI government's best financial interest to keep tourists drinking only at the casino, with those profits (from alcohol consumption and the associated increase in gambling) going to the EBCI.[105] In March 2018, the *One Feather* announced the launch of the first Eastern Band citizen–owned alcoholic beverage distributorship. The two primary owners will have a warehouse on the Qualla Boundary that will distribute their Seven Clans beer, made off-site in a Canton brewery facility. At the moment, this does not compete with alcohol at the casino, but depending on the outcome of future votes, Seven Clans could also open a brewery on the Qualla Boundary.[106]

The Tribal Gaming Commission, itself including local small-business-owner representation, and the EBCI government have responded to small-business challenges on several fronts. They began by establishing an overflow policy with some of the local and independent hotels and motels. This provides these small businesses with a steady income and gives the casino hotel alternative accommodations for its guests, even in their busiest season. Not everyone was able to benefit from this policy, though, as the amenities have to be on par with what the casino offers (e.g., internet access), but the program alleviated some of the casino-generated competition.[107] In 2000, the Cherokee Transit Service (initially a medical-appointment transport service) began making structural changes by implementing a transit route from the casino to parts of downtown Cherokee (and, now, even to Gatlinburg). This gave visitors, who do not have pedestrian access from the casino to the downtown area as of yet, a direct, convenient, and free way to access the shopping and cultural districts.[108] Even the physical updating of the storefronts currently taking place has its origins in the casino. These updates will provide a cohesive "Cherokee" look, based on the casino's "Cherokee" image, throughout Cherokee tourist areas, thereby drawing people to them. Eventually, the steps taken did have an impact; according to the EBCI economic-development office, retail sales on the Qualla Boundary grew 35 percent from 1997 to 2004.[109] Collectively, then, the increase in visitors, along with the revamping and extension of existing downtown areas, has led to the expansion of the Cherokee market for all tourism businesses.

Taken holistically, the casino has clearly contributed to small-business support on the Qualla Boundary in several ways (e.g., financial aid and expansion of the consumer base); however, it is important to recognize the vital role that small businesses play in the casino's success. Small businesses do for the casino what they do best in general: offer diversity. In terms of supporting the casino, this comes in two forms. The first is direct aid to the casino in the areas of construction and goods and services, including the use of local artists for stonework and—in the case of Nancy and Bruce Martin's business—an armored van service. The second is indirect aid. The casino may bring in 3.6 million tourists per year, but it can only offer a limited amount of entertainment, shopping, and dining. The value of small-business support cannot be underestimated in a rural area that offers little nearby in the way of any of these features. The variety of private restaurants, stores, and attractions undoubtedly increases the number of people willing to visit

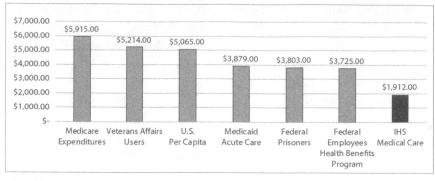

GRAPH 2 Federal health-care spending, annual per capita.

the casino precisely because they can offer family members or friends the opportunity to not be confined to the casino; similarly, these businesses often extend visitor stays in the town of Cherokee. Friends and family members who might not have otherwise taken a casino vacation are willing to come to Cherokee precisely because its small businesses can offer entertainment, such as guided fishing trips; chances to meet Eastern Band artists; and the option to eat less expensive, locally sourced meals. Small businesses can thus heavily contribute to the sustainability of casino-based economies; as we will see, though, that is only a small part of the role they can play in Native Nation economies.

When looking at the question of the benefits of gaming versus those of small businesses, however, there is another broad ideological conflict potentially at play: it could be posited that government enterprises like the casinos bring revenue to the collective, while privately owned businesses bring revenue only to individuals, potentially contributing to increased class divides. While it is true that class divides can and do develop, this is not a given outcome, as this line of thought begins with the assumption that small-business owners generate wealth through their businesses that is beyond other means of income acquisition. The next assumption inherent in this line of thought is that small businesses do not contribute to economic redistribution efforts, which I discuss in the next section. Finally, the choice between the benefits of government-owned enterprises and the benefits of small-business ownership does not need to have an either/or answer, as EBCI efforts demonstrate; government enterprises and the small-business sector can exist together, with the hope of mutually benefiting from each other and ultimately enhancing the well-being of the Nation and its citizens.

Entrepreneurship's Place in Development

> It is an exercise of economic sovereignty when tribal governments and communities decide what types of businesses to allow in Indian Country and what business endeavors a reservation community will support.
>
> —Robert J. Miller, "American Indian Entrepreneurs"

It is clear from the historical records that American Indians have succeeded on every economic stratum from extensive trade routes to agriculture to business ownership, and yet the specter of the financially incapable American Indian still casts a shadow over Native Nations. The United States has undertaken massive acts of economic violence and economic hegemony directed at Native Nations; when the disastrous effects of these efforts were realized, the U.S. government (victim-)blamed American Indians for being financially "incompetent" and continues to do so today, all while severely underfunding programs that are owed by treaties and compacts to Native Nations, as in the case of health care (see graph 2).[110] Research on American Indian citizen entrepreneurship is critical not only because we have so little collective data regarding American Indian small-business owners but also because the collective actions of these individuals help fight this false portrayal of incompetency while also addressing pragmatic issues, such as Dean Howard Smith's "pernicious triad": brain drain, dropouts, and joblessness.[111] In doing so, small businesses support a stable and sustainable economy—a pillar of nation-building—in both measurable and indirect ways.

Along with the diversity and subsequent protection from a range of negative shocks provided by the small-business sector, their nongovernmental ownership status has advantages compared to Native Nation–owned enterprises, including a nimbleness in their ability to restructure and adapt to a variety of changing circumstances, a process that can be time-consuming when a business is owned by a government.[112] In addition, small businesses ease the managerial burden on Native Nation governments, which would otherwise need to create more tribally owned enterprises, hire non-Native contractors, or give incentives to non-Native companies (seen regularly in the casino industry) to support their citizens with job opportunities and services—the latter two of which drain money from the reservation economy.

These general small-business impacts can be broken down into measurable components. Stephen Cornell, Miriam Jorgensen, Ian Wilson Record, and Joan Timeche give eleven impacts that American Indian citizen entrepreneurship has on Native Nations: the multiplier effect, building of community wealth, job creation, increase in the tax base, talent retention, psychological signals to citizens, increased quality of life, support of the Native Nation community, economic diversification, broadening of government-development efforts, and contribution to Native Nation sovereignty.[113] But how do these issues play out on the ground in an economy that was previously based solely on the viability of these small businesses but that has since changed its economic focus to another income stream (gaming)? In evaluating this, three categorical impacts emerge: economic, community, and sovereignty.

Economic Impacts

In 1998, small businesses in rural America accounted for 90 percent (1.2 million) of all businesses and employed nearly two-thirds of all rural workers.[114] Of particular interest to the EBCI, these small businesses had the strongest showing in service industries, including retail, accommodations, social services, and amusement—industries that are the support system for, and backbone of, the already thriving tourism market on the Qualla Boundary.[115] Small businesses also have a particularly strong impact on revenue generation and retention, especially through the multiplier effect and creation of community wealth. The two key components of the multiplier effect are investment and local spending. On the consumer's side, the multiplier effect increases when people are able to spend their money locally. For example, if an entrepreneur starts a restaurant with $100,000, this investment money enters the local economy as new wages for builders and employees and new revenue for local suppliers of building materials, food products, and other resources, which then translates into more income for these employees and suppliers. This income can then be spent locally (groceries, gifts, services), which means that now a third group of people have more income to spend. When money is spent locally, the effects of the initial investment are multiplied, and there is an increase in economic activity and economic growth. The corollary to this concerns the entrepreneurs themselves. Entrepreneurs on reservations (as is true of other local communities) tend to be residents.[116] Because of this, they are more likely to invest their profits locally, not only in the maintenance and expansion of their business but also in overall community services and support. The circulation and retention of these monies is, conversely, reduced when communities use nonlocal corporations.

Small businesses also contribute to government support by increasing the tax base for Native Nations. Before the advent of the casino era on the Qualla Boundary, small-business taxes were the economic foundation of the EBCI. As Abe relates with regard to the initial influx of casino profits, "I mean granted [the EBCI government is] doing better now [since the opening of the casino], but the levy from the businesses supported them for fifty years. Now they act like that levy is just peanuts." Since this conversation, the EBCI, in recognition of the one-industry problem, has begun refocusing more of its efforts on increasing the diversity of the tax base via the encouragement of small-business creation. One way it does this is by keeping its tax rates consistently lower than those of the state of North Carolina, along with providing exemptions for specific cases. The small-business owners I spoke with feel that these taxes are fair, at a minimum, and for many, very attractive.

Job creation is another boon of promoting small business on reservations. Some Native Nation governments cannot create enough jobs alone to combat high unemployment rates; small-business growth can translate to job creation as well as diversity in employment opportunities. Ron echoes this when he talks about his previous business, "So, way up Big Cove there, we employed twenty local people. That's a backbone; it's creating employment."[117] This, again, helps combat the issue of dropouts and brain drain. In an educational context, a type of brain drain can arise when American Indian youths who live on reservations leave to advance their education but then find that they have no adequate employment opportunities back on the reservation (due to either lack of jobs or lack of competitive jobs) and are therefore forced to work off the reservation, taking their knowledge with them. Natalie from Tribal Grounds ran into this issue after she finished her work at Western Carolina University and wanted to return to the Qualla Boundary. She explained, "My job opportunities in this area were none. [They] didn't have any job opportunities at [the EBCI] museums. . . . So it was not possible for me to work as an art educator."[118] Darlene Waycaster (former Cherokee Chamber of Commerce director) related a similar sentiment: "It's better here in Cherokee than the surrounding counties, I think, but a lot of people have to move off, and I think it's still [that way]. And even here, too, in order to start a profession and to get to the point that you can move back, because the salaries are not as high as in the cities, there [are] not that many jobs."[119] EBCI efforts to diversify its national businesses help broaden the types of jobs available on the Qualla Boundary, but there can still only be a limited variety. EBCI initiatives to combat brain drain also include grants to train students in technology information studies as well as school leadership training for Eastern Band children, preparing them for management positions. The Tribal Internship Training Program provides students with internship positions working for the EBCI and preferential hiring for their return after college. (Currently, students can stay on the Qualla Boundary to get an associate's degree, but in the future, the tribe will have its own fully accredited college to further the educational process.) The results of these programs are just beginning to emerge.

The presence of small businesses on reservations augment these efforts in two ways. First, the variety of small businesses (and employment therein) outnumbers the variety of EBCI job offerings. Second, small business are more than just a physical and daily reminder to students that there are diverse opportunities available to them beyond tribal enterprises if they choose to continue their education; they also remind them that when they advance their education, there will be opportunities not just for employment but also for the possibility of starting their own businesses.[120] Teresa from Granny's Kitchen commented, "A [problem] we used to have was that all of the kids who could bring something viable to the tribe used to get out of town. Now, we are at least managing to keep some of them."[121] This small-business job creation not only contributes to economic growth but also impacts the community directly.

Community Impacts

While students drop out of school for many reasons, one of the most frequently suggested causes of dropout among American Indian children is that in economically depressed locations, students see few opportunities to use their education locally. Small businesses help alleviate this issue in two ways. First, small-business ownership can enable citizens to create their own vision of how to make their education work for them. Second, as previously mentioned, a variety of small businesses means that there is diversity in the types of employment available for these students.

These businesses also improve the quality of life for local residents by reducing the need to travel long distances (consequently spending more money on gas, which is priced, for much of the year, higher on the Qualla Boundary than state or national prices due to tourism) just to purchase food, goods, and services. While some progress has been made in making more goods and services available locally, this has been an issue on the Qualla Boundary. EBCI leaders have recently implemented a "weekly shopping trip" transit service to drive citizens to Sylva (half an hour away), which helps lower the cost of shopping-related travel for its citizens.[122] Although this temporarily reduces stress on citizens, a more foundational solution is to increase reservation residents' access to these products and services at home, where the full benefits of local small businesses can be realized.

The local Eastern Band community also benefits from entrepreneurship through the commitment of many business owners to supporting the local area. Direct monetary contributions are one such support. For example, Ron buys ads with the local ball teams and Teresa does the same with local newspapers, as well as with yearbooks, football programs, and calendars. "It's nice to know," she explains, "that the people that you do business with are actually supporting your kids and helping out with the things."[123] I also encountered business owners who did volunteer work for EBCI events. For example, Zena visited the elementary school several times as a motivational speaker. In fact, I found that community and charity work are considered important parts of successful business ownership in Cherokee. As Joel says, "[If I didn't care about the community], why would I be teaching other people what I'm doing? Why take all this experience to start teaching newer generations coming up what I'm doing? Otherwise, well, I could sit back and make the money that I want [for myself]."[124]

Such actions are called "corporate citizenship" by the National Center for American Indian Enterprise Development, which presents the American Indian Business of the Year Award to a business owned and operated by an American Indian who demonstrates good "corporate citizenship" in the community.[125] Although the label "corporate citizenship" is accurate in these instances, it does not capture the fact that these small-business owners on the Qualla Boundary *are* community members. Their contributions are not merely nods to developing good community relations; they have a direct impact on owners' friends, their community's programs, and their land. In these actions, we see the concept of gadugi emerging again. This is also enacted on formal days with set projects (Gadugi Day and Gadugi Earth Day), which some small-business owners additionally support through participation and contributions.

In recognition of these contributions, small businesses on the Qualla Boundary are regularly given publicity and awards when they are seen to be contributing to the greater good through such actions as monetary contributions, volunteering, and longevity. One example is River's Edge Outfitters, a more recently founded business in Cherokee that received the Business of the Year Award, in no small part due to its charitable work in the community.[126] Another example of businesses being recognized for acting for the "greater good" is the Pizza Inn and Dairy Queen signing on to partner with the EBCI Cooperative Extension's 4-H "Hungry to Help Campaign" and EBCI Emergency Management to help raise money for the Japanese Relief Effort. A May 5, 2011, article in the *One Feather* reported, "Leo and Sandra James have been a part of the Cherokee community owning and operating these two establishments for forty-four years. Through a series of different fundraising efforts, the partners have been working hard to make a difference. One hundred percent (100%) of the proceeds of these fundraising efforts will go to the Red Cross to assist Japan in their time of need."[127]

Finally, the impacts of small businesses go far beyond physical ramifications for the economy. The psychological impacts on community are acute, especially for students. In seeing individual community members succeeding, the false notion that one's Indianness is inherently associated with poverty and, as follows, inversely associated with financial success (here, creating and maintaining a stable enterprise) begins to dissolve. As Sean Teuton points out, "Poverty itself is not an American Indian cultural value. Indeed, assuming as much risks leading young tribal people to internalize the dominant culture's frequent insistence that Indigenous people must remain poor in order to be spiritually pure and authentic."[128]

Sovereignty Impacts

The structures of entrepreneurship and small-business ownership directly support Native Nations' actions of political sovereignty. The economic and community impacts illustrate three of these political processes. First, the economic diversity of small businesses aids in reducing Native Nation dependence on outside decision makers, funding, and policy makers; for example, by reducing dependence on one industry, Native Nations are less subject to the whims and demands of external policy makers. Second, they help increase the ability of Native Nations to take over the management of Native Nation resources and services by building a sustainable, stable economy.[129] Third, these benefits are accomplished without the Native Nations being forced into a reduction of sovereignty through state compacts or the necessity of waiving their sovereign immunity to work with external businesses.

Small businesses also contribute to the goal of economic sovereignty, which is to have authority over the economic choices that support a sustainably stable and resilient economy while protecting economic bases. In the case of highly successful, one-industry-dominant economies, as the EBCI's currently is, there is an innate precarity that must be addressed. It is the reliance on this new economic power—which can fuel massive positive change, from increasing citizen services to taking over management of programs once controlled solely by the BIA—that also increases overall vulnerability if that industry fails or even slumps. Diversifying out to more Native Nation enterprises can be one part of the solution, but this course of action has its limitations as well. First, the ownership of these enterprises is concentrated in the same government structures, increasing the management responsibilities of the government. Second, because these enterprises are government owned, they must be approved by several committees, which increases bureaucratic involvement, possibly stagnating efforts to diversify. This is in conjunction with the third limitation, which is increased risk-aversion. This can limit diversification efforts by, for example, focusing on growing only one proven market rather than risking Native Nation funds on new, uncharted projects. Small-business diversity manifests not just in the types of businesses that are created but also in the holistic vision of an economy that operates with the nimbleness, fluidity, and adaptability that is vital to a truly sustainable economy. As Russ Seagle succinctly stated, "The value of entrepreneurship for the tribe is regaining some control."[130]

· · · · · ·

Although it would be impossible to predict the extent of the long-term success of the casinos, in the words of Susan Jenkins (Choctaw citizen and former CPF director), "If that casino blew up tomorrow, they would have some skills they didn't have several years ago."[131] They would also still have their small businesses. The Cherokee Casino has had a profound impact on the Qualla Boundary, from decreasing poverty and poverty-related issues (e.g., youth "acting out") to increasing the practices of sovereignty by the EBCI, such as building and managing their own justice center. It is precisely because these impacts are so significant that the loss of this revenue—a potential threat from multiple directions—could have serious consequences for the Qualla Boundary. One way that this precarity can be offset, as I have argued, is through increased economic diversity. Native Nation enterprises have been successfully diversified, but increasing the number of these enterprises can place increasing strain on the government system, which must now attend to these businesses as well as community-directed services. These endeavors can be additionally weighed down by bureaucratic barriers, curbing entrée into new markets in order to protect government (citizen) assets. Small businesses help alleviate these issues by providing collective diversity that supports the economy, the community, and ultimately Native Nation sovereignty.

For over two hundred years, many Native Nations have been located on forms of reservations while repeatedly battling to retain and regain the practices of their inherent sovereignty.[132] They have keenly felt the sentiment of Woodrow Wilson's 1916 question, "Just what is it that America stands for? If she stands for one thing more than another it is for the sovereignty of self-governing people."[133] Through five eras and five hundred years of lawmaking, they have seen their rights bounced back and forth in the U.S. courts of law and in legislation between policies of sovereignty recognition and those of assimilation and termination.[134] Economically, U.S. governments have enabled and allowed Native Nation commons to be broken and their economic bases to be devastated. As Native Nations continue to take advantage of the strides made during the Self-Determination era, they enter a period of renewal in which they are expanding their rights (e.g., the tribal provisions of the Violence Against Women Act) and winning compensation for misappropriated resources (as in the Cobell case).[135] This is a critical juncture for Native Nations as they stand at the brink of a new era, one that will hopefully continue to move toward increasing recognition of the sovereignty of Native Nations and away from policies of forced assimilation and termination. Remaining on this trajectory will take vigilance and more concerted efforts, as the United States now enters a time when the executive and legislative (and even possibly soon, judicial) branches are largely populated by those who have proven themselves hostile to American Indians (especially rich American Indians) and the practices of Native Nation sovereignty. For Native Nations, who a mere seventy years ago faced the Termination era, this vigilance—and associated deliberate action or inaction—is a skill they continue to hone.

The current momentum of the nation-building movement can only continue if Native Nations increase their economic diversity in order to have a stable, self-sustaining economy to support these efforts. The role of economic stability in these nation-building efforts is vital as Native Nations focus on expanding their practices of sovereignty, reducing their reliance on outside forces, and assuming greater control over their national territories and assets. Small businesses and entrepreneurship practices not only support these qualities of nation-building but also contribute in a variety of ways to their communities while strengthening Native Nation economic enterprises, even through recessionary periods. In fact, the number of small businesses has been seen to increase during recessions, which is supported by my own research on the Qualla Boundary.[136] This success has been bolstered most recently by the EBCI government's efforts to re-prioritize support for entrepreneurship on the Qualla Boundary in the wake of the launch of the Cherokee Casino. These efforts, detailed in chapter 5, bring together many of the pragmatic and logistical threads of economic sovereignty, agency, and the indigenous entrepreneur.

. . . .

Visitors may flock to Cherokee in the fall, but springtime in the mountains has its own magic. Greens, such as ramps, begin to appear, while clear skies allow for the sun to dissipate the slight chill in the air. Visitors trickle back to the Qualla Boundary, and residents venture out more regularly, signaling seasonal small-business owners to open their doors again. I took advantage of this warmth and relative quiet by working outside when I could. One of my regular seats, near both coffee and food, was above the Oconaluftee River, next to the downtown visitor's center. It was also a favorite of many children, who spent hours in the recently built fountain streams (see figure 5.1). It was here, in the midst of the mountains' yearly rebirth, that I read in the *One Feather* that Cherokee would soon have its first and only funeral home, opening to serve the community in July 2009. I was especially interested in sitting down and talking with the owners about why they decided to open this crucial business because my grandfather (a Cherokee Nation citizen) worked in a funeral home as an usher after his formal retirement. During my visits, he would show me around the building, including the casket showcase room filled with chrome, polished wood, and satin. The time spent with him at the funeral home is much of the reason that these spaces have never felt morbid to me—and why I was particularly drawn to Long House Funeral Home.

Long House is located next to the Santa's Land theme park, which is on the way out of town through the mountains on Wolfetown Road (US 19). Housed in a nondescript white building, it is, quite literally, a long house, marked only with a small sign framed in wood by the road (see figure 5.2). I entered the building and was greeted warmly by Bruce Martin Sr., a soft-spoken man with a wealth of business experience, and his wife, Nancy, a petite woman possessing a direct and tenacious business acumen.[1] At their side was their grandson, an adorable, always smiling baby who bounced happily on a door swing while waiting for his dad (Bruce Martin Jr.) to come back from a meeting. The funeral home proudly promotes its identity as an Eastern Band citizen–owned business, offering services specifically geared

FIGURE 5.1
Fountain area with syllabary light post just before spring comes. Photo by author.

toward Cherokee people. They call themselves the "First Funeral Home of the First People" and stated that they are "pleased to now be able to care for our own in our own community." This is significant because finding a funeral home that will respectfully attend to the needs of non-Christian families (such as some Eastern Band citizens) in a region that is heavily Christian (90 percent of the population in some surrounding counties) can be a difficult undertaking during a terrible time.[2] To this end, the Long House website assures, "We understand our unique culture and traditions and can tailor the service to the needs of the surviving family members. . . . We are very sensitive to the impact that discrimination can have and we will not tolerate any practices that might be offensive to any individual or group."

The building that houses the primary funeral home has one main corridor with rooms to the sides that include a service room, a sitting room, and a workshop. The workshop housed the project that inspired the funeral home, which was Nancy's brainchild: Native Clans and Caskets. These

FIGURE 5.2 Sign for Long House Funeral Home. Photo by author.

elegant wood caskets were originally hand carved by a local artist; after he moved from the area, they were made by a mother-and-son team in Georgia. Nancy sewed the linings and finished the caskets herself. To protect her investment, Nancy single-handedly procured a patent for the design of her Native caskets, but unfortunately, she does not have the capital to pursue the patent infringements that have since occurred.

We talked in the sitting room, which was filled with comfy couches and chairs, wooden tables, a bright window at the front, and a large, stone fireplace on the side. I soon learned that the Martins have three businesses in total—the funeral home, the caskets, and a security company that they have had for eighteen years. The security company primarily provides a guard service and armored van for the Cherokee Casino, a sensitive and complex business for which the Martins must untangle a wealth of red tape every day. From keeping up with the bureaucratic minutiae of programs like 8(a) certification, Quality Security certification, and HubZone certification (North Carolina HubZone and also the SBA HubZone) to knowing what the latest refresh is on Schedule 84, they must be able to work quickly and pro-actively to keep their business legally viable for this type of contract work.[3] They must also constantly pursue payment, as security contracts are left unpaid by the federal and state governments for two or more years, and funeral payments (from families struck unexpectedly by the passing of a loved one) can languish for months on end. As Nancy explained, sometimes keeping a stable financial position can seem overwhelming:

> Now, this is a fact. . . . When we were doing government contracts
> (and if you've ever seen one of those contracts . . . there's a big
> attachment from Department of Labor with it), it specifies in there
> how much you must pay for a certain job classification. If you're
> a small business and you don't have health insurance for your
> employees, then there's an additional thing called Health and
> Welfare Benefit. Now, it's [about] $3.39 an hour . . . in addition
> to that pay that you have to pay them. If you have any health
> insurance, you can forget the $3.39. You don't have to give them
> that. Well, we thought, we've got thirty-five people. Maybe that's
> enough, now, we could get Blue Cross/Blue Shield to take a look at
> us and see. They said, "Oh, sure. Send us the names and ages of your
> employees and we'll get a quote back to you." They called back and
> they said $28,000 a month would be what we would have to pay.[4]

Luckily for their customers, the Martins have managed to keep their businesses viable, overcoming bureaucracy and other challenges to continue to offer their much-needed and appreciated services, which would not exist in the local community without them (see figure 5.3). Although the challenges faced by the Martins every day are unique to their businesses, they are not unusual in scope. Capital, collateral, varying and sometimes competing tax laws, hiring preferences, infrastructure, training of employees, and business-education access are issues that many business owners must tackle, but they are especially problematic for American Indian entrepreneurs who want to locate on a reservation. Additionally, the Qualla Boundary has its own specific complexities that small-business owners must contend with. While the EBCI government has historically taken a mostly hands-off approach to these entrepreneurs, with the advent of the casino it has now taken a more prominent role in encouraging and supporting small-business owners on the Qualla Boundary.

The EBCI government recognizes that small-business owners on the Qualla Boundary face very distinctive challenges, and its sovereign status

FIGURE 5.3 Long House Funeral Home—Nancy and Bruce Martin. Photo by author.

allows it to aid in ways particular to Native Nations. As Teresa jokes, "I've got a sign up, or I used to have one back there, that said, 'The only thing that's more overrated than natural childbirth is being self-employed'"—a sentiment that many small-business owners can relate to regarding the frustrations of ownership. As with the issues of representational transformations, the EBCI government has been able to use the success of the casino to create several support structures to aid these individuals in creating sustainable businesses that provide recognized foundational support to the EBCI economy. Former CPF executive director Annette Clapsaddle explained the importance of these support structures: "The tribe must continue to engage in a concerted economic development effort to expand its economy. The Qualla Boundary already offers programs to support small businesses and entrepreneurship, including market demand, capital, talent and community support desired by target businesses. If these attributes are successfully built upon, the tribe will experience sustainable economic growth and prosperity at a higher wage level for its residents and workers."[5]

Just before I began my fieldwork, the key government figures who would also support these measures were being sworn into office, on October 5, 2009.[6] The EBCI Tribal Council was subsequently headed by Principal Chief Michell Hicks and Vice Chief Larry Blythe, along with twelve representatives (each township has two representatives).[7] These council member positions are important to small-business owners because as part of council duties, council members serve on various committees, ranging from business (e.g., approving business licenses) to health to land resources.[8] For specifically business concerns, the EBCI government also has the Office of Planning and Development, which manages economic development efforts, grants, building rental, business development, and geographic information systems (GIS).[9] Many of the EBCI offices that serve small businesses (the Cherokee Business Development Office, the Office of Budget and Finance's Revenue Office, the Office of Planning and Development, the Economic Development Office) work under this division of the EBCI government. Additional independent, government-affiliated entities are the Sequoyah Fund Office, the Cherokee Chamber of Commerce, and the Cherokee Preservation Foundation.[10]

Together, these offices are in place to offer aid to businesses (and potential business owners) on—and surrounding—the Qualla Boundary. The aid they offer generally falls into four categories: financial support, structural support (literally the dilemma of physical space), training, and promotion/marketing. It is only because of its inherent sovereignty that the EBCI can offer this combination of services to encourage the growth of its small-business sector. The community's expectation that the government should and will support its citizens in these ways is also interesting to note. As Valerie Lambert states, Native Nation government duties "include not simply governing and improving the welfare of their people, but also developing and managing their nations' resources for the benefit of their citizens."[11] For the EBCI, these responsibilities include land management (common across Native Nations), its newer management and investment of significant monetary resources, and its more unique responsibility to support the small businesses that supported it for so many years.

In common neoliberal rhetoric,[12] entrepreneurs and businesses are often touted as at their apex when functionally autonomous and unencumbered by regulation—a belief that is countered by the reality of a U.S. financial system that is designed to substantially subsidize the success of large corporations, including banks, to the point of being "too big to fail."[13] For small businesses, these massive levels of government financial-support mechanisms are nearly nonexistent (which also, consequently, restricts their ability to compete with larger corporations), leading to higher risk and a necessarily higher level of autonomy than larger corporations. However, these small-business entrepreneurs do have access to a variety of smaller but valuable support mechanisms, ranging from intergenerational business advantages (as seen in family enterprises) to federal and Native Nation government interventions, which can enhance opportunities and mitigate challenges. It is in these relationships that we see how Native Nations deploy economic sovereignty in a small-business context.

Financial and Structural Help

It should come as no surprise—especially given the timing of my research, carried out during the Great Recession—that finances were the greatest cause of concern and uncertainty for the business owners I spoke with. Although many people in the United States—and especially U.S. small-business owners—were suffering grave financial losses at this time, businesses located on the Qualla Boundary, and indeed on all reservation trust lands, were facing some singular problems. Ron related a conversation: "My neighbor said, 'Why don't you go buy you a new car?' I said, 'Do they take T-shirts for payment? That's where all my money's at.'"[14] Zena contemplated the issue of inventory and capital: "I sold three bean bread grease pitchers this week. We don't have any more. We couldn't order no more. Not yet. We've got to get some money. We've got to earn the money. We just ordered glaze. We just ordered this. We just ordered that, but, oh gosh, you've got to have it to make it."[15]

Zena's personal experience is supported by the Global Entrepreneurship Monitor (GEM), which calculated that a median $17,500 was necessary to start an entrepreneurial venture in 2015; 57 percent of this funding was personally financed by owners. Access to capital is a foundational issue for American Indian small-business owners, as they face significant and distinct challenges compared to non-Native business owners in both the amount and the types of financial services from which they can draw. This relates to a general lack of access to mainstream institutions on reservations, lack of alternative financial institutions, lack of equity resources, lack of adequate financial education, and, one of the most unique issues to American Indian small-business ownership in obtaining the capital they need to start or grow: lack of collateral.[16]

The problems of land ownership and finances are uniquely intertwined for American Indians citizens. This also specifically complicates the dilemma of start-up monies and investment capital for small-business loans due to the trust status of much Native Nation and American Indian land. One unfortunate consequence of this land trust policy, which was designed in part to protect Native Nation land from being dispersed to non-Native parties, is that the land cannot be used as a collateral asset because it legally cannot be taken out of trust status should the loan default. This means that for individual citizens and for Native Nations as a whole, start-up monies are very difficult to raise, even in the best of economies. To help counter this, the EBCI has a series of loan programs, available to its citizens through its economic-development programs, ranging from microloans to larger loans of up to $250,000 for all types of businesses—from nascent endeavors to established businesses that are expanding (see appendixes A and H).[17]

In cases where a loan does not entail collateral, the EBCI can require mandatory training programs from which the recipient must graduate (one such program is the Indianpreneurship course). For smaller loans, the EBCI may accept less standard items as collateral, such as vehicles, personal property, or even casino-dividend distribution pledges. It is also technically possible, in the case of larger loans, for the EBCI to take citizen reservation-based land (possessory holdings) as collateral through an agreement with the BIA. In this case, in the event of a loan default, the EBCI would work with the BIA to recover that land, which the EBCI would then hold until a new qualified buyer is located. This is obviously a more complicated scenario, but it has been done. As Russ Seagle of the Sequoyah Fund conveyed to me, "It's a little trickier and takes longer than if we were able to acquire a deed of trust, but it can be done."[18] This is a clear instance of the EBCI's inherent sovereignty enabling it to aid small-business owners in a way that would be otherwise impossible.

The collateral can also be the businesses itself in the case of physical stores with inventory, as was the case for Tribal Grounds Coffee. During my fieldwork, Tribal Grounds was the only dedicated coffee shop in Cherokee (there is now one inside the Cherokee Casino, a difficult location to get to for those not already in the casino). As such, it had a large customer base of not only tourists—sitting as it was in one of the most prominent cultural districts—but also residents. Although thriving small businesses such as this can weather many larger economic shocks, personal conflicts can often cause great damage. Soon after I left the area, following my primary fieldwork, I learned that the co-owners were separating. Tribal Grounds was one of the casualties. Natalie attempted to run the business on her own, but she was eventually unable to pay the rent for the EBCI-owned space. No one emerged unscathed from this situation; Natalie lost her storefront (although she continues to sell her roasted coffee to stores), and the EBCI was left with an investment that it could not recover. Because Tribal Grounds had received loans from the EBCI (the Sequoyah Fund in particular), the office finally claimed the business and managed it until new owners could be found. Today, the space is once again thriving as the Qualla Java coffee shop, owned by Bobby Raines, a local Eastern Band citizen (a graduate of Cherokee Central School, Haskell Indian Nations University, and Western Carolina University [MBA]), and managed by his wife, Lydia Raines, along with Eliana Martin.

The funding (loans, grants, financing) that the EBCI provides for businesses is sometimes tightly focused to encourage growth in specific areas, as in the case of the Healthy Foods Venture, which provides lending to local businesses focused on offering fresh, healthy, locally produced foods, or the New Economy Fund, which provides capital for green, knowledge-based, or creative-economy businesses. This support system also includes non-lending resources, such as the Cherokee Business Development Center, which gives Eastern Band citizens credit and budget counseling as well as information on credit scores.[19] Business programs on reservations, like the ones the EBCI offices are implementing, have proven effective in increasing the standard of living for all residents. Research by David Benson and colleagues examined the Lakota Fund, an SBA-like loan program on the Pine Ridge reservation that provided microloans, loans up to $20,000, technical assistance, and a business incubator from 1987 to 2006. The results of his regression estimates suggest that the Lakota Fund succeeded in raising the real per capita income of Shannon County residents "consistently and significantly" throughout the study period.[20]

Finally, for the EBCI and other successful gaming Native Nations, there are additional benefits from casino-dividend payments. These EBCI-managed payments are impactful specifically for small businesses because they can serve both as start-up capital and as a way to help finance seasonal expenses. Although the payments are not nearly enough to entirely support any business on the Qualla Boundary, they are enough to supplement a business during the off-season or during a year as difficult as 2009 was; consequently, receiving these dividends can make a profound difference to the longevity of a small business. This aid was further augmented in November 2016, when the EBCI Tribal Council approved a dividend loan program that would allow citizens to borrow up to $500 per month or $2,500 per six-month dividend period, thus increasing the flexibility in availability of these funds. Some young people are also circumventing the loan/collateral issue by using their lump-sum dividend payment to start businesses.[21]

Among the many reasons that Eastern Band citizens—like those recent graduates starting businesses with their lump-sum dividend payment—have chosen to locate their business on the Qualla Boundary is the tax benefit. Because the EBCI is a federally recognized Native Nation, it is not under the jurisdiction of state laws (beyond negotiated exceptions, such as IGRA), including state tax laws.[22] Contrary to "rich Indian" misinformation, portraying American Indians as living tax-free, Native Nation citizens who both live and work on a reservation pay Native Nation and federal taxes.[23] Therefore, citizen residents whose businesses are located within the Qualla Boundary are not subject to state corporate taxes.[24] In order to encourage citizen business owners, the EBCI chooses not to levy a specific corporate tax for citizen business owners on the Qualla Boundary. The EBCI can also offer exemptions to noncitizen businesses, but those exemptions are not yet formalized in any one code. State sales tax also does not apply on the Qualla Boundary, so the EBCI can and does levy its own sales tax, which it attempts to keep lower than that of the state.[25] The EBCI can also offer sales-tax incentives to businesses located on the Qualla Boundary. For example, it does not collect sales tax on artists/crafters, food vendors at the Fall Festival, string bands, or chiefing.[26] Other financial incentives, as we will see, require much more work to obtain than tax relief.

Financial support from Native Nation governments need not always take the form of loans, tax breaks, or incentives; it can also take the form of access to physical space, which can reduce small-business owners' financial outlay. In addition to various forms of direct financial support, the EBCI owns and leases buildings—and space within those buildings—to small businesses. In May 2011, the EBCI opened the Tribal Cannery to encourage small businesses. The cannery provides a shared industrial kitchen for Eastern Band citizens to produce value-added food items (e.g., jams and preserves) for sale or personal use. The large kitchen space and access to industrial canning equipment, however, is much more useful in producing items for sale than for home use, as it allows large-scale production.[27] To help remove a physical space barrier to owning small businesses on the Qualla Boundary, the EBCI began the "Open Office" incubator in the Sequoyah Funds office suite and will be developing a dedicated small-business incubator building. Incubators are generally buildings in which start-up businesses have office space and access to communally shared equipment. These incubators lower the start-up costs for business owners by providing a working area from which businesses can launch. Rather than first accumulating funds and waiting for a permanent location to become available, the incubator allows businesses to start up, bring in some income, and then, once they are well-established, move to a permanent location. On the Qualla Boundary, the incubator model has the additional benefit of allowing businesses to run while they wait for leases to become available. In June 2016, an initial "incubator without walls" was proposed by the Planning Board, which would entail access to much of the same equipment, office space, and coaching, but without a residency requirement. For those small-business owners who wish to do contract work with the EBCI directly, however, there are bureaucratic hurdles that must be negotiated.

Employee Regulation and Management

Joel Queen is one of the most nationally acclaimed contemporary Eastern Band artists, having won both local and national awards, including those coveted at the prestigious Santa Fe Southwestern Association for Indian Arts. One of the days I met with him in January had been particularly difficult. He spoke plainly and with a furrowed brow about his perceptions of working with the bureaucracy of the EBCI government. I asked if his family, well-respected artists themselves, had dealt with the same issues that he does now, and he responded by addressing the impacts of the casino on the workings of the EBCI government: "The modernization of the tribe has brought them a lot of legal issues that nobody's willing to answer yet."[28]

Joel's gallery incorporated in 2005 in partnership with his wife, Kelly, who graduated with a business degree at the same time Joel finished his master's degree in fine arts. The gallery is located just off the Qualla Boundary on the main 441 Highway leading directly to downtown Cherokee (see figure 5.4). Joel opened his first gallery on Main Street in Cherokee when he was just out of high school. It was a tiny room, and, in retrospect, he says that he was probably too young to know "what was going on" businesswise. For his second venture, he decided to locate to an area with fewer leasing hassles and without so much nearby direct competition (his first place was close to the Qualla Arts & Crafts Mutual). The new gallery is a small log-cabin-style building, close to the road and next to a new veterinary facility. Upon entering the building, Joel's office and work studio are on the right, filled with intricately designed pots waiting to be finished and detailed, and paperwork and books lining the walls. To the left is the store, which features Joel's work alongside products by other local and national American Indian artists. The small room houses a variety of crafts, including gemstone settings for jewelry, which Joel has trained himself in over the years. On the walls hang pictures of him at work, digging up clay for his prized black pottery pieces. Clay digging is a grueling and physically damaging

FIGURE 5.4 Joel Queen Gallery. Photo by author.

part of the potter's job; although Joel is a young man—still under forty when I met him—he had had six surgeries already, with many more to come. That day, though, what weighed heaviest on his mind was his dealings with TERO (the Tribal Employment Rights Ordinance), which governs the hiring practices of American Indian–owned businesses.

TERO is a nationwide program that is complicated and sometimes controversial despite its simple mission: "to insure that Indian/Alaska Native people gain their rightful share to employment, training, contracting, subcontracting, and business opportunities on and near reservations and native villages."[29] The TERO ordinance "require[s] that all employers who are engaged in operating a business on reservations give preference to qualified Indians in all aspects of employment, contracting, and other business activities," in order to "increase employment of enrolled members of the EBCI and other Native American tribes, [and] to promote the growth and professionalism of Native-owned businesses with the overall goal of reducing discrimination against Native Americans."[30] This is not a racial preference in hiring; this is a preference based on citizenship in a Native Nation and, therefore, conforms to federal law.[31] TERO is a general guideline that is meant to be customized and administered by each individual Native Nation. There are no standard rules across the board for all Native Nations. For the EBCI, the Tribal Employment Rights Commission (all members are

EBCI council members and citizens) appoints a TERO officer to interpret and enforce its TERO laws.

At its most basic, the EBCI TERO ordinance gives businesses owned by Eastern Band citizens preference over non-Native-owned businesses when applying for EBCI government contracts. For example, Eastern Band–owned businesses have a 5 percent leeway when submitting bids. If their bid is within 5 percent of that of an outside contractor, the bids are viewed as the same, and the Eastern Band business is given a "second chance" at bidding. However, business owners have had decidedly mixed experiences with TERO. Eastern Band citizen Bruce Martin (Long House Funeral Home) said, "It's a really good thing because it's a local thing. So far as I know, they really have been hiring local contractors, which they've never had before. There [were] always outside companies getting it. They've got several companies that [are] doing big business now. . . . If that TERO didn't exist, they'd probably get someone like a big company from Asheville."[32]

But there are obstacles to overcome in order to make TERO truly useful to all of the business categories it chooses to represent, and some business owners were very much against TERO after seeing its disadvantages harm their businesses. First, to qualify for TERO certification, a business must employ a certain percentage of Native Nation citizens, adhere to the Davis-Bacon Act for wages, and be insured and bonded.[33] The catch here is that the competing non-Native businesses do not have to abide by these terms. This means they can offer lower bids because they do not need to have permanent staff or equivalent insurance. For larger contracts, such as construction, the costs of these requirements may not make up a large percentage of the profits; for smaller businesses, though, like restaurants, even a 5 percent additional expenditure can wipe out an entire profit margin. Teresa, from Granny's Kitchen, related an experience she has had when placing bids:

> Anyway, we have to jump through all those hoops. We have to do all the reports. We have to do all this stuff. We go to mandatory meetings, but then when it comes time for the Tribe—for example, the trout derby, picnics, Christmas—we lost those to a guy from Bryson City. He runs a slaughterhouse, but he's built this little thing off to the side to cater [food] and so he doesn't keep a full staff. He only pulls kids [in for temporary work]. So I'm keeping Indian families working. I'm supporting them and I figured up in the last twenty-five years, we've generated about $2 million worth of levee for the tribe, but for that dollar that they saved [accepting the

Bryson City businesses bid], they took I don't know how many away from the people here, and I guarantee you that that man will not spend a dime on the reservation. . . . He's not Indian at all. Nobody else [working with him] is. He's not on TERO. He's not on TERO, and that's what gets me. [I don't mind losing a bid to another business on TERO], but he doesn't have to do anything. He doesn't have to pay to be considered. He doesn't have to fill out all the reports. They don't have to have his tax returns. They don't have to have his proof of insurance. They don't have to have anything from him, but we're the ones that have to do all this, then because of that little 5 percent thing, we lose the bid. . . . I'm not going to ask myself or my kids or my work family to work for nothing. It's not why we're in business. He only calls people in when he needs them. He doesn't have to keep them working all the time like I do. I guarantee you he don't pay any levee to the tribe. . . . There's nothing generated there for Eastern Members and it just drives me nuts. It does.

I'm on my soapbox all the time about that one, and the same thing's happening with a lot of these bigger companies down here at the casino that are taking jobs away from the local people because they've got such deep pockets [they can afford to take the 5 percent hit]. . . . I don't think it's fair to ask these little companies that just have four and five people working for them to compete against these big conglomerates.[34]

TERO is also plagued with bureaucratic red tape that is confusing and (because each Native Nation creates its own system) nonstandardized. For Joel Queen to work within this system, he has to apply to the business committee for a license (and pay a fee), then register for TERO in three different categories (three more fees), and finally apply to get another license to be a vendor for the casino (yet another fee). Things get especially complicated when these TERO categories overlap (for example, what is the dividing line between artistic stonework and stone carvings?). Additionally, he told me, "My company's the one that carries the insurance and everything else that keeps protecting them. . . . Any registered crafter can bid on those jobs, which he pays $20–$50 a year for, and I'm paying $150 for each part of my corporation that I'm registered for." Teresa also had a discouraging experience with TERO regarding recertification fees: "We just had to get re-certified. . . . I let my certification lapse just because I thought it said the fifteenth and it said the fifth and it was a mistake. [I had] never been late before. [They] wouldn't cut me any slack. . . . I had to redo my business plan. I had to redo the safety plan. I had to get more letters of recommendation." This also meant that Granny's had to pay the full initial "one-time" registration fee again, in addition to the yearly fees. The lack of accountability for the TERO committee has been another sticking point for some businesses; when they have a complaint about TERO, who can business owners take that complaint to? At the time of my fieldwork, there was no system hierarchy in place to address grievances. At least one business had, as a last resort, contemplated filing a lawsuit.

The benefit of TERO being only a set of general guidelines is that Native Nations have a lot of freedom to customize its utilization. However, this also means that it can be a slow and difficult process to implement and test on the ground. The frustrations that these businesspeople have encountered are a reflection of the trial-and-error process that EBCI officials are working through in developing an effective bureaucratic system that positively impacts Eastern Band citizens. In 2016, the EBCI government was beginning to implement reforms in the TERO process. New staff was put in place that January and began meeting that month to address issues in transparency and accountability and to start planning ways to disseminate new information and increase the TERO job bank. This included adding workshops and classes (participants completed the first series in April 2016), as well as establishing apprenticeship and industry (hotel, construction) training programs. By September 2016, TERO was formally approved as an independent entity, separate from the EBCI government (a fairly common option chosen by other Native Nations running TERO programs), in order to reduce any perceived political influence. As an independent program, the bulk of its funding now comes from a 1.75 percent fee on contracts over $10,000, with an additional yearly stipend from the EBCI.[35]

The broader subject of employees was also one of the most common topics that came up during my interviews and discussions with business owners. Having been an employer myself, this did not come as a surprise. Hiring your first employee and turning part of your business over to that person is one of the most difficult hurdles for small-business owners. It is also a challenging area to manage, second only to finance and accounting. It is a long and difficult process, from finding an employee to vetting that employee and finally, if all goes well, to transferring some control to that employee. This is true for nearly all businesses, but these problems are especially acute in rural areas where there is a significantly smaller population from which to draw employees.[36] If you are a specialty business, such as a business consulting firm that needs employees with specific certified training, finding these highly specialized employees within commuting distance can be extremely difficult. As Susan Jenkins stated, "We've got to dance with who's in the gym."[37]

Interestingly, the most desirable demographic of employees for many small-business owners here with small workforces (fewer than four employees) are older women. "In their fifties or older, those are the ones who stay," as I was told by one business owner. Another owner related that he thought these women were more dependable. Other owners supported this sentiment, citing that they believed these employees were less likely to have drug or alcohol issues; had fewer family responsibilities, as they were generally empty-nesters; were not planning on leaving for a new career, better position, or college; or were perceived as generally more reliable, since they had presumably already taken care of families. However, this is a narrow demographic pool to draw from, especially as most of the small businesses in my sample were in the category of a "small workforce," having only, on average, two year-round employees.

Even through the worst of the recession, though, most of these business owners kept their workforce on staff—which was no small feat. As Abe vented to me regarding one employee with whom he was having a particularly hard time, "You better be damn thankful that you've got a job right now because I resent every day that you're getting a check and I'm not." Abe's situation of keeping staff employed while not pulling a check himself was not unusual in my findings. To mitigate this large and necessary expense while aiding community members at the same time, some business owners took advantage of EBCI government-employee programs, such as the one that Natalie from Tribal Grounds describes here:

> And [for] one of our employees here now, we used the job bank
> because we have customers that work in that area. Basically it's like
> this little organization that takes useful people, not necessarily
> under eighteen but people that have gotten into legal troubles that
> are working in this program as part of getting up on their feet, basically
> self-help. We took one of them in, and it's a great opportunity because
> the organization pays for their paycheck if you will agree to work
> with them and train them and teach them the skills. And then after
> six months if they want to leave, okay, if they want to stay, they're
> your employee or if you want to keep them they're your employee.
> It's wonderful.[38]

Seasonal businesses, which represent a large portion of the Cherokee economy via tourism and many outdoor work industries, have different employment needs than year-round businesses. It is often difficult for these small businesses to find employees willing to work for only half of the year.[39] The EBCI's programs help ensure that seasonal businesses can fill those needs with qualified workers. In this situation, the impact of the EBCI dividend payments on the workforce of small businesses is substantial because they enable Eastern Band citizens to work part time or seasonally at these businesses and still make ends meet during times between employment. There is also another impact of dividend payments on the workforce: reduction of substance abuse.

Substance abuse has many impacts on rural areas, which can see higher rates in alcohol and non-heroin opiate use than urban areas; one is the decreased number of regionally available and reliable employees.[40] The reduction in substance abuse as a result of EBCI dividend payments was first documented in a 1996 Costello et al. study from Duke University, later published in the *Journal of the American Medical Association*. This study confirms that Eastern Band youths who received dividend payments showed a reduction in substance abuse over time; specifically, this included alcohol, cannabis, nicotine (dependence only), and other drugs (cocaine, amphetamines, inhalants, opioids, hallucinogens, and sedatives).[41] The study tracked Eastern Band youth from 1993 through 2006 (Eastern Band citizens began receiving a share of gaming revenues in 1996) and found a link between the payments and well-being, demonstrating that Eastern Band youth who received the payments were better off as adults than Eastern Band citizens who did not grow up with the revenues (pre-1996). Researchers further found that Eastern Band youth fared "significantly" better as adults than non-Indians in the area.[42]

It should also be noted that positive casino revenue allows for the subsidizing of more structures and programs to combat, prevent, and address the substance abuse that does occur, such as afterschool programs, employment programs, and programs to train and hire police personnel.[43] On the Qualla Boundary, these health programs include the Analenisgi (ᏗᏁᎳᏂᏍᎩ) Substance Abuse and Mental Health Center, the Kanvwotiyi (ᏦᏅᎣᏗᏱᏍ) Snowbird Residential Treatment Center, and the Healthy Cherokee Substance Awareness programs, with additional dedicated programs being planned. Consequently, dividend payments in conjunction with casino-funded programs tangentially aid small businesses by combating a decrease in the number of employees due to rural substance abuse issues. In addition to providing financial support to small-business owners and their employees, employee shortfall issues can be mitigated through indirect efforts, such as training and education. Access to these resources, however, can be a challenge for small businesses located in rural areas.

Training and Promotion

> I went to see him after I got out of college for a job. He said, "Go out there and sweep the pavement." I said, "I got a college education." He said, "I'll go show you how, then."
>
> —Ron Blankenship

How important is training and previous experience to a small-business owner? On the Qualla Boundary, every owner I spoke with had extensive training (formal and informal) before starting their business and would recommend training to anyone considering becoming a new business owner. Many of them lamented gaps in their past or current knowledge that led to significant, unnecessary costs—sometimes to the extent of losing the entire business. These business owners' training fell into three general categories: formal and paid (college, courses, training through work), informal (reading, indirect work training),[44] and family. I have placed "family" in a separate category because while it imparts more knowledge than informal training, as family members are exposed to this experience continuously, it can offer less knowledge than formal training, as many aspects of business ownership may be overlooked, and others are never taught in a regimented way—learners are expected to "pick up" how to work in different positions.

Gaining work experience was, however, easier for those who were from business-owning families. As Abe explained, "When I was old enough to run a cash register, which is at least at the age of eight or nine, I was put in the gift shop." The reliance on paid and unpaid family workers is not unusual in small businesses, and Abe worked for his family until he left for college.[45] He later returned to the Qualla Boundary and continued to work for his family until he started his own business. Ray of Granny's Kitchen also gained experience through "on the ground" training as a youngster (but without the benefit of his family owning the business) after he was hired at a popular local restaurant when he was eleven years old. In this case, he had to work the evening shift so that the health inspector would not catch him. At fourteen, he started working at the former Timber Restaurant for one hundred hours a week making seventy-five cents an hour. Eventually he earned his degree in hotel/motel restaurant management from Asheville-Buncombe Technical Community College in Asheville, North Carolina.[46] He worked his way up to become one of the top-ten food and beverage directors worldwide while working at Holiday Inn, then left Holiday Inn to start Granny's Kitchen with his wife, Teresa. As Ray's case demonstrates, most small-business owners have some combination of all three types of training, with prolonged exposure to insider knowledge as a primary factor in the sustainability of their current businesses.

The most common type of training among business owners whose businesses had passed the five-year mark was formal training. All four of the local colleges (Southwestern Community College, Western Carolina University, Tri-County Community College, and Haywood Community College) offer some type of small-business classes—ranging from accounting to business management for artists—and some have entire small-business centers. These classes are especially popular with owners who had already completed college degrees before starting their businesses. Interestingly, most of these business owners had not majored in business (their major fields of study ranged from hospital administration to art education), but they felt that the broad liberal arts skills they acquired in college contributed to their business success (critical thinking, exposure to diverse perspectives and methodologies, and so on). These successful business owners also had other types of formal training, through either on-the-job training or having taken other (non-college) courses that they said helped them create and run their current business.

Most owners continue to use informal training to keep their business viable: entrepreneurship magazines, books (such as the popular E-Myth series), and information-exchange sessions, such as those sponsored by the Cherokee Chamber of Commerce. When asked about the shuttering of their own previous small businesses as well as others' small-business closures, current business owners cited the lack of basic business and finance-management information and a lack of information on time management as the biggest obstacles. As Ron stated, "And that's another thing about business; I see people [who] . . . want to go into business. [Then] they go into business [and] say, 'Oh, it takes this much time?' They don't know how much is involved. They really need to educate themselves [first]. So they quit."

Calculating your total costs, including your own salary; determining whether or not you need employees; and understanding your rights as a lessee—these are just a handful of the topics that, without enough knowledge, can sink a business before it even opens its doors. But what can a person who does not come from a business family and does not have the means for a college education do when they want to open a business? And how do Native Nations increase the number of businesses that are viable over the long term? Both of these issues are being tackled by the new entrepreneurial programs and small-business programs that the EBCI is offering. The main center for business assistance on the Qualla Boundary is the Cherokee Business Development Center and the Sequoyah Fund. Although they are technically separate entities, many of the two departments' activities overlap, and they were even located in the same office space.[47]

Formal business education and training can be expensive for hopeful small-business owners. To help mitigate this, the EBCI provides financial help from various funding sources for citizens seeking training. This financial help can be in the form of a scholarship, such as the Bill Taylor Scholarship for students pursuing a degree in business administration or a business-related area.[48] EBCI monies can also be used to fund specific training, such as a recent program sponsored by the Sequoyah Fund in which twenty teachers from the Cherokee Central Schools were funded to attend the North Carolina Rural Entrepreneurship through Action Learning (NC REAL) Institute in order to learn how to incorporate entrepreneurship skills development into the Cherokee Central Schools core class curriculum.[49] Sponsoring competitions to encourage business owners to participate in continuing education courses is also popular, such as the Getting Retail Right program, which followed up its efforts with a $5,000 competition for "greatest improvements."[50] These efforts, along with the training opportunities outlined here, have led Cherokee to be designated as a Certified Entrepreneurial Community by the Advantage West Economic Development Group.[51] The Advantage West website says of Cherokee: "Entrepreneurs are welcomed here. . . . There are tax incentives, no state sales tax or property taxes, and excellent resources for starting or relocating a business. Qualla Boundary is a delightful, distinctive place to live and have a business."[52] These groups also sponsor small events, like the one-day Business Opportunity Fair, which provides educational sessions on starting a business. The EBCI also provides direct training, the longest and most comprehensive of which is the Indianpreneurship program.

According to Sequoyah Fund flyers, Indianpreneurship: A Native American Journey into Business is a "business start-up course that teaches all the basics of starting and operating a successful small business. The business course in Cherokee that utilizes the Indianpreneurship program meets once a week for nine weeks and is currently a prerequisite for obtaining a loan from the Sequoyah Fund."[53] This course is designed to give foundational knowledge about business ownership: accounting issues, start-up capital options, business plans, and so on. It serves two main purposes: to prepare inexperienced potential business owners for the surprises that arise when starting and running a business and to serve as a "weeder," as some students may drop out when confronted with the scope of commitments involved in small-business ownership of which they may not have been aware. Both of these processes act to increase the number of successfully stable small businesses by providing potential owners with the initial logistical knowledge of the legal and financial elements required to run a small-business entity.

At the time I took the course, in the fall of 2009, it was also being considered as a prerequisite for obtaining TERO certification, which has since been implemented. The class began by covering mission statements, community analysis, marketing, and advertising. It then progressed to more detailed topics, such as TERO certification, cash-flow projections, book-keeping (pricing and sales forecasting), and operations. This was followed by an examination of larger issues, such as loans, legal considerations, insurance needs, and taxes. Finally, the course wrapped up with the students' presentations of their business plans. Speakers from various departments (including TERO) were brought in to answer questions and give more detailed explanations of their services and requirements. The ever-increasing number of students signing up for the course is a testament to its design, the instructors, and the fortitude of small-business ownership during economic crises. The year before I took the course, the average number of students was six (Russ was the instructor). When I took it in 2009, there were twenty students; in 2011 there were thirty-nine students; and in 2013 it peaked at fifty-two initial enrollees. It has since been turned over to the Enterprise Development department (and is currently taught by Sabrina Arch, EBCI Enterprise Development Specialist, Eastern Band citizen), which teaches it multiple times per year, depending on demand.

Based on my own experience as a small-business owner and a researcher who studies small businesses, I found that the course provided a solid foundation for addressing the realities of starting and sustaining a small business through the always-difficult first few years. However, the on-the-ground version of the course taught in Cherokee was a bit different from what was outlined in the official Indianpreneurship course packet. This was due to the addition by Russ of some elements from the NC REAL training program.[54] The resulting hybrid course used the Indianpreneurship training package for readings and homework and added the REAL handouts for in-class assignments. These materials augmented each other in a cohesive, understandable way. The REAL program addition was found to be so useful, in fact, that in 2015 the EBCI purchased the entire REAL program outright. At the time of this writing, the Native American Development Corporation is designing an American Indian–focused version of REAL for distribution.[55]

Conceptually, the Indianpreneurship packet is an interesting program, especially in its broad marketing. Generally, products marketed to American Indians as a (pan-)whole must walk a fine line. For example, in 2007, Nike announced its Air Native N7 as the first shoe made specifically for "a race or ethnicity," claiming that the "average American Indian" foot—and specifically a diabetic American Indian foot—was wider.[56] It then tacked on fairly subtle imagery (sunrise-to-sunset patterns, feathers) to code that the shoe was intended for American Indian purchase. Nike was widely (though not universally) criticized for both its claim and the generic pan-Indian designs. The N7 line was launched in 2009, and it was not until 2014 that the company consulted with a Native American artist (Peter Boome, Upper Skagit citizen) regarding the shoe embellishments; in 2015, Nike finally hired a Native American artist (Dwayne Manuel, Salt River Pima-Maricopa Indian Community citizen) to autonomously craft the latest shoe embellishments. Nike has also stopped marketing the shoe as racially specific.[57] For the Indianpreneurship course, I was curious to see how a business-training program would market to and advise businesses in addressing the needs of American Indians as a population—that is, across all Native Nations. Would it talk about the legal issues American Indians face on reservations? Would it discuss the issues of familial obligation, noted here and in the broader literature as both a benefit and a hindrance for American Indian business ownership?[58] Would it discuss the economic problems faced specifically by American Indians? Would it give examples of successful American Indian businesspeople and explain how they sustained their businesses? These are all issues confronted by American Indians across the United States. Addressing these overarching problems in a non-Native Nation–specific manner would be feasible for a basic introductory course about starting a business. Finally, I wondered how this program would frame the concept of American Indian entrepreneurship. I kept these questions in mind as I worked my way through the Indianpreneurship program, beginning with the official Indianpreneurship course book itself.

Overall, I found that the book's content was incredibly accurate, useful, and accessible, providing advantageous information to anyone considering starting a business. Furthermore, the book, and the associated program, is the only one put together *by* American Indians *for* American Indians to date. In exploring how this American Indian perspective might manifest, I started with the aesthetics of the course materials. The cover and inside foldout flow chart of the chapters and steps were covered in petroglyphs. The pictures that marked the beginning of each chapter included a canoe maker kneeling by his work in progress in a forest; an elder storyteller with hair in wrapped braids standing in front of a rock wall with carvings; horses in a field; a lonely road trailing off into a pine forest; an older woman (with two younger girls behind) drying salmon by a fire; teepees on a lush lawn; a sunset; shoeprints in the sand under two Indian-head nickels and two antlers; a mountainside that appears to be the face of an Indian man; a large landscape with a lone fly-fisherman casting into a larger river; a fisherman business owner in a guide boat that sports a feather logo; and a modern picture of three program graduates and their teacher standing in front of a heavily used whiteboard. While the text itself did contain discussions of a wide variety of businesses, the course-material images lacked a more diverse visual representation of contemporary American Indian businesspeople, especially those engaging in businesses that would challenge expectations of what constitutes American Indian entrepreneurship. Diverse images could be drawn from the considerable range of American Indian–owned businesses that are succeeding, from software programmers and skateboard designers to American Indian law firms and local gas stations. Next, I turned my attention to the content of the book.

In all business ownership, there are basic logistics that apply no matter where you are, who you are, or what you do—principles such as accounting, inventory and supplies, marketing, and planning. The course excelled at presenting all these elements. The particular challenge I saw for Indian-preneurship was how to make these general concepts specifically relevant to American Indians. To this end, the examples of fictional businesses were always owned by American Indians (the course-material designers did not specifically name Native Nation affiliations, as doing so could presumably make the examples less relevant to American Indian readers from other, possibly radically dissimilar, Native Nations). These businesses ranged from basketmaking, beading (9/11 imagery, specifically), and an "authentic" Indian café to home-maintenance work and an eyeglass retailer. The names of the businesses were both American Indian oriented, such as GreyBear's

Engineering, and generic (Smith's Automotive). The text contained references to casinos and had phrases like, "Good scouting makes good hunting." What was missing, however, was any reference to *situations* specific to American Indians.

American Indians opening a business face unique complexities that go beyond the general principles of business ownership. As discussed, a prime example of this is location and the decision of whether to locate on or off the reservation. To make such a decision, they must be aware of reservation-specific factors, such as tax ramifications, lease pricing and availability, and inventory delivery. They have to know the laws (e.g., if they want to own a restaurant that serves wine, they need to be located on a wet reservation), including citizenship issues (will they be able to pass the business to their children?). And they *absolutely* need to be aware of the services that are available to American Indians: loans through a Native Nation, loans through the U.S. government, training, and professional organizations.[59] Although the course materials discussed some of these ideas from a broad perspective (e.g., loans in general), there was no mention of the particularities of these concepts that can specifically help (or hinder) an American Indian business owner, such as the sixteen federal programs specifically created for American Indian entrepreneurs by 2001.[60]

Not all American Indian business owners find themselves in these circumstances (e.g., not all American Indians have a choice about locating on a reservation or not), but given that this course book was specifically developed for American Indians, it was surprising to see none of these issues directly addressed. For our class that fall, Russ brought in additional resources, outside the Indianpreneurship course materials, to address some of these situations. For instance, Curtis Wildcat (Eastern Band citizen) from the TERO office came in one evening to speak about the details of his office and how to apply for TERO certification. As I found in my discussions with American Indian business owners, sometimes just knowing that help and information is available if you need it can make a considerable difference in having the confidence to begin such a large undertaking.

Indianpreneurship is the longest duration training program that the EBCI offers, but it is far from the only one. During my initial fieldwork, the Sequoyah Fund offered five selections of training classes spaced throughout the year: Start It (important business-planning basics, designed to be taken before starting a new business), Grow It (business policies and practices for the business owner), Tech It (technology skills to grow and improve a business), Improve It (employer and employee skills to improve customer satisfaction, safety, productivity, and employee happiness), and Green It (ways to get involved in the green-business movement).[61] Rather than focusing on more ideological and conceptual concerns, such as business ethics, these classes cover a range of pragmatic topics, from general business operation (like how to use tax software) to training employees in EBCI culture and history (designed primarily for tourist-oriented businesses).

Qualla-T training is a free program, run by the Cherokee Chamber of Commerce, offering employee training that "integrates Cherokee and mountain values and attitudes into your workplace as a basis for providing excellent customer service."[62] Teresa, from Granny's Kitchen, used this half-day program for her employees, served breakfast to all participants (at a nearly 100 percent participation rate), and declared the program "phenomenal."[63] For artists, there are even classes offered by OICA (the Oconaluftee Institute for Cultural Arts, a joint program with Southwestern Community College) on business issues that impact artists, including Copyright and Laws for Artists and Certification in the Building Industry for Cherokee Craft Artists.[64]

With all this training available, though, how much do business owners actually take advantage of? Do they find these courses helpful or even appealing? In general, I found that the business owners who used the training programs did so extensively. It is interesting to note that of the business owners I spoke with who used these training resources, Granny's and Tribal Grounds—the top two businesses at the time in terms of local popularity and daily patronage—did *not* have a strong family background in business ownership but took regular advantage of these programs. The business owners I spoke with who had not taken any courses usually had one of several reasons: they were not aware of the courses, did not have the time, or were reluctant to ask for help. In this last case, the owners' reasoning varied, from Ron, who said that he wanted the sense of accomplishment in succeeding on his own terms, to Abe, who was reluctant to admit that the knowledge he had gained from his family was not enough to help carry his businesses and that he was not doing as well as he could be as a result.

Based on my own business experience, the most difficult hurdle to broadening your training and keeping your business skills up to date is the time factor. This is especially true if you do not yet have employees. Running a business is an intense exercise in time (or lack thereof) management, and it can be especially overwhelming when your business is not doing well— the exact time you need these training services the most. Some of the programs (such as Getting Retail Right) addressed this issue by offering to do an in-house consult for individual businesses. These were only offered occasionally, though, and only to a select number of businesses. Lunch & Learn classes, covering minor topics such as using social media (Facebook, Twitter, or blogging), were also set up to help with the time crunch.

The EBCI also hosts expos and networking opportunities to help with self-promotion. While I lived there, this was mainly in the form of Cherokee Chamber of Commerce (COC) meetings, as the COC was the largest EBCI promoter of small businesses on the Qualla Boundary. The COC office sits in a two-story log cabin on the main tourist drag in Cherokee. On its right, it is flanked by a building whose side is covered in an intricate graffiti-styled mural of American Indian imagery: faces of American Indian men with feathers in their hair, eagles, bears, turtles, foxes, and the mountains (see Figure 5.5). At the time, Darlene Waycaster, a local resident (non–Eastern Band citizen), was executive director of the COC.[65] Originally, the COC began as a group of concerned business owners on the Qualla Boundary called the Heart of Cherokee, formed in conjunction with the Cherokee Preservation Foundation.[66] Eventually, it became so successful that the EBCI government took it over, financed it, and ran it.

The COC plays a major role in how the EBCI is represented to visitors, as it is responsible for designing and producing the yearly tourist travel brochure (distributing approximately forty thousand of them in 2009). This official EBCI promotional brochure contains a calendar, a map, and information about many of the businesses and attractions on the Qualla Boundary. The COC's website also provides listings of local businesses. The COC hosts monthly breakfasts and other special events for local businesses, such as information sessions about issues like greenways. It also offers training courses (the most popular is the free employee-training Qualla-T course) and informational newsletters for local businesses. After the EBCI took over the COC, it retooled the membership policies, widening the level of inclusion and thereby expanding the availability of COC resources not only to Eastern Band citizens or even to Qualla Boundary residents but to all businesses in Swain and Jackson Counties (as the central Qualla Boundary straddles both). The COC also creates promotional programs for businesses. One contest it sponsors is Cherokee Pride, which awards a prize for excellence in customer service; any lodging, restaurant, or tourism-centered business can win the monthly contest, which includes a featured promotion by the COC. The COC also mediates between businesses and the EBCI on issues such as appropriate signage regulations and new district guidelines for business appearances. As Darlene said, "So it's just rethinking

FIGURE 5.5 Cherokee Chamber of Commerce. Photo by author.

[these issues] to where it works for the businesses and the tribe to make Cherokee a better place for everyone."[67]

Beyond those hosted by the COC, there are more EBCI events designed to nurture small businesses on the Qualla Boundary. Within two years of my original fieldwork, the Cherokee Business Summit and Expo—a collaborative effort by the Sequoyah Fund, the Cherokee Business Development Center, and the North Carolina Indian Economic Development Initiative (NCIEDI)—was held at the Cherokee Casino. According to Kimlyn Lambert, an Eastern Band citizen serving on the NCIEDI board, at this summit "we have had a lot of discussions about small business coming to Cherokee, . . . and the need for people to be entrepreneurs and come and do small businesses here such as dry cleaning, etc., that a lot of bigger towns have that we don't have here."[68] These business centers also host such events as the business-plan competition (run by the Sequoyah Fund), which involves students from Western Carolina University, Southwestern Community College, Tri-County Community College, and Haywood Community College.[69] As these events illustrate, EBCI programs for business support do not always end at the Qualla Boundary. Many of the EBCI's programs follow a good-neighbor policy and extend throughout the seven far western counties of North Carolina.[70]

The emphasis on entrepreneurial training also includes programs geared toward educating younger children, such as the small-business entrepreneurial skills and training course Paving Our Own Way, designed for those between eight and twelve years of age, and the Youth Entrepreneurship Camp, for ages ten to fourteen. There are even career fairs for these younger children, consisting of local business owners and designed to "expose elementary students to career information and the occupational choices in their community."[71] For high school students, events like the Cherokee High School Business Plan Competition (open to eleventh- and twelfth-grade students) and the new American Indian Business Leaders (AIBL) organization motivate students to think about starting their own businesses.[72] Although most of these training programs target current and future small-business owners, the training provided also helps create educated employees—one of the most important resources for small-business owners. This K–12 training is not all theory based, however. At the new high school, students get the opportunity to actually run their own business.

In August 2009, I attended the opening ceremonies for the new Cherokee Central Schools building. Its architectural design incorporates Cherokee basket-weave patterns throughout, including the more contemporary "Road to Soco" pattern. It is also the first LEED Silver building of its size on the East Coast.[73] The campus grounds include a large array of facilities, including gardens (composed of 100% native plants), a performing arts center, a large stadium, Cherokee cultural and visual arts studios, SMART Boards in each classroom, Cherokee language rooms, a room with the Ravensclaw site reports (the archaeological reports on the site), and a Cherokee games field. In addition to the students, teachers, and staff, the occasional elk also enjoys walking the new school grounds. Within months of its opening, two separate small-business owners suggested that I look into the T-shirt printing business that Ernie Widenhouse (Eastern Band citizen) helps run for students in the Occupational Course of Study program.[74]

I called Ernie, and he agreed to meet with me and introduce me to the screen-printing business. Ernie met me downstairs the next afternoon to direct me through the labyrinthine school. He had a salt-and-pepper ponytail and a laid-back demeanor that suggested a high level of patience, which seemed especially well suited for working with high school students. He was from the Qualla Boundary and had attended the previous incarnation of Cherokee High School (about a mile away from the new school) and was now heading the business program for youths with disabilities. We talked for an hour about the first business he and the kids tried (a garden) before printing T-shirts and about the transition to the new school that year. When I asked him why he thought running a small business (as a class) was beneficial to students, he explained, "The biggest thing is a good work ethic, but to me the *bigger* thing is actually not what's taught 'in the factory.' The bigger thing is [what we work on in the classroom, which is] more self-advocacy."[75]

While self-advocacy (the skills needed to pursue and attain goals and interests focused on the individual self or community) is a foundational skill stressed in disability studies, it is critical for all students to learn. As Ernie stressed, the concepts apply equally to issues in small-business ownership. Small-business owners need the qualities of self-advocacy and independence to sustain their own businesses as they manage their operations and employees, pursue support networks, and promote their businesses. In the small businesses on the Qualla Boundary, the owners I spoke with train their employees personally, imparting a wide variety of these self-advocacy skills to them. Some even involved their employees at every level of their business, mentoring them and encouraging them to view the business's financial books and participate in decision-making processes.

Before the Indianpreneurship class one day, Russ and I had a chance to talk in his office, which is housed in the Ginger Lynn Welch (GLW) building. This unassuming building lies on a side road, away from the tourists, next to other government buildings, such as Emergency Medical Services and the Boys Club. I spent many hours at GLW, as the Sequoyah Fund, Cherokee business offices, and many of the economic development offices were located there, and many business classes were held in the GLW conference rooms. That day Russ told me a story that illustrates many of the principles he tries to teach during his business-education classes. He described speaking with young employees:

[I said,] "I'm going to teach you everything there is to know about how this business operates." They knew *what* to do. They didn't understand the *why*. So I showed them the profit-and-loss statement. They'd never seen a P&L statement. I showed them how to read it, what it meant. I said, "Here's this line. This is how you affect this line. When you do this, it affects this line this way. When you do that, it affects this line." They went, "Oh, wow!" I showed them what a break-even point was. Showed them why that mattered. They understood everything. They saw my salary. They saw their own pay (I just took their pay and I clumped it all together as "people expense" because I didn't want them to see what each one of them was making), and they went, "That's a big number." I said, "Well, you know why it's a big number? You know the stuff that I take out of your paycheck and send to the government every week?" They said, "Yeah." I said, "I have to match part of that from my pocket and put it in there and send it in." They went, "Really? Wow. I didn't know that." They thought that everything that went into the cash register belonged to me and then I just paid them a little bit out of that. . . . But I said, "Look, here's how we make money. Now if you hold the thing together while I'm gone for a week and you can show that you've made money that week, I'll give you a little bonus." . . . They both made a forty-five dollar bonus the next week when I got back. . . . They were so excited. They said, "Look, we made money! This is great!" *But from then on, the place went through the roof.* Through the roof. Because they treated it like it was their own business. *They were no longer employees; they were part owners, and I continued to pay them a bonus until I sold the business.*[76]

Given the formal training methodologies mentioned in this section, it would be tempting to attribute these programs aimed at young students as a reflection of neoliberal ideologies, thus emphasizing a necessary participation in the premise of unregulated market-driven meritocracy. But the context of the Qualla Boundary, as well as that of Indian Country, must also be taken into account. First, the issues of economic identity and the "politics of perception" combine to portray American Indians as being incompetent or incapable—by nature and culture—of managing money, whether they are wealthy or in poverty. These perceptions must be challenged. Teaching financial skills to children reinforces their capabilities and helps them to personally counter these damaging narratives.[77] Second, it is important to remember that the Qualla Boundary has a historically large presence of small private businesses owned by Eastern Band citizens, and the community takes much pride in the success of this foundational sector. In this context, the availability of small-business training for young students on the Qualla Boundary should not be unexpected. Finally, given the importance of this EBCI sector, owning a small business should be an attainable career goal for Eastern Band citizens who wish to pursue it; offering this training to all at an early age may thus help alleviate class- and family-based stratifications in business ownership.

One final topic that deserves more in-depth study concerns a problem that arose unexpectedly during my fieldwork: the issue of American Indian health as it relates to business ownership. Health problems have consequences for all entrepreneurs, but for American Indians, the intensity of chronic health problems, ranging from diabetes and heart disease to cancer and multiple surgeries (as experienced by Joel as a result of clay digging for his pottery studio), makes it especially difficult for a small business to be run consistently and successfully. Some businesses included in my initial interviews have failed, or have been severely curtailed, as a direct result of health problems, of either the owner or the owner's family. Unfortunately, the state of the federal Indian Health Service (IHS) is such that less money is allocated to American Indians than to any other federally funded group, a problem that intensifies the already poor state of American Indian health outcomes.[78] I spoke with several future business owners who feel that it will be their obligation to pay for additional health insurance for their Eastern Band employees, based on their own personal experiences of being unable to access sufficient health care.[79] To this end, the newly renovated EBCI hospital along with Harrah's contractually owed community donations (e.g., the aforementioned MRI machine) are expected to have a positive impact on overall community health, but it is still too early to assess any changes in health outcomes.

· · · · · ·

As the EBCI attempts to encourage small-business growth in order to stimulate the health of its overall economy, it must address the challenges that these businesses face, both as rural small businesses and as specifically American Indian–owned businesses. The EBCI's inherent sovereignty means that it has the authority to mitigate disadvantages, offer incentives, and bolster the benefits of locating on the Qualla Boundary in order to encourage this growth. Although there is not a resolution in sight for the issue of collateral and trust land, there are ways in which a Native Nation can work with small-business owners to procure loans for the often-significant start-up and growth expenses of business ownership, including using trust land or the business itself as collateral. For the EBCI and other dividend-paying Native Nations, borrowing on such payments is also an option, and one that is less risky for the Native Nation in recovering funds if the business fails. To encourage a wide variety of business endeavors and business owners on a reservation, lowered tax rates and exemptions relative to the surrounding state can be implemented; furthermore, targeted tax laws can be used to attract specifically needed or desired businesses.

The EBCI has also adopted TERO as a means to encourage American Indian business growth and employment on the Qualla Boundary. Although

TERO has been implemented by Native Nations since 1976, there is no singular path to follow for implementation; it is up to each individual Native Nation to create its own ordinances and structures for these guidelines. Its seeming simplicity of purpose—to support American Indian business and employment—belies a much greater complexity, as each Native Nation's needs are unique, and challenges may not surface until a given TERO program has been enacted. The EBCI continues to adapt its TERO program and procedures as these issues arise, focusing now on transparency and independence from the governmental body, much in the way that its casinos operate.

The problems seen in employee recruitment and retention reflect larger issues of operating a business in a rural area, but some of the ways in which these are addressed are very much EBCI based. The EBCI chooses to pay dividends to its citizen-shareholders, which has resulted in an overall betterment of the lives of Eastern Band citizens. These dividend payments also directly affect small-business owners in several ways. First, they enable owners to weather seasonal and market fluctuations. Second, they support employees through issues such as seasonal employment fluctuations and possible health-care costs. Third, these dividends support Eastern Band customers by supplementing their income, thus enabling them to use more local, small-business services when available.[80]

Access to training has also been a concern when considering ways to increase small-business ownership. Even those small-business owners in intergenerational family businesses felt poorly equipped in some ways to undertake ownership themselves, thus pursuing additional training ranging from informal (self-training, such as reading) to formal (college courses) opportunities. The EBCI has recognized this training shortage and now offers a range of options, from short lunch courses to the Indianpreneurship program. Currently, these programs' main focus is on basic issues of small-business operation writ large, without directly addressing issues of rural businesses or reservation- and American Indian–specific aspects of small-business ownership. However, updating and adapting this information (as seen in the EBCI version of the Indianpreneurship course) will likely be seen soon with the 2015 purchase of the REAL program. The introduction of this training to K–12 students may also inherently change this information as students begin to ask more detailed questions throughout their training. The impacts on economic identity for these Eastern Band children and what they demand of their representation, both in private business and publicly, will also be a development to watch.

Through all of these efforts, we see that the EBCI has undertaken a multipronged strategy to encourage small businesses. This includes offering financial aid, creating physical infrastructure and making it more easily accessible, bolstering entrepreneurial knowledge, and marketing small businesses through a variety of methods. These strategies and their results are manifested through the exercise of economic sovereignty, founded in the practices of indigenous autonomy in crafting and implementing economic systems that support—and are supported by—the community. In discussions of future efforts, some have asked what the next steps for the EBCI should be beyond the basic logistics of small-business owners support. As Christy Long (an Eastern Band artist) asked, "What would it look like for the [EBCI] government to support small businesses in a Cherokee way?" Here, there are questions of what EBCI business ethics discussions might look like, addressing how the EBCI should best protect its citizen entrepreneurs (especially in multi-ownership situations), and if the EBCI can put small-business owners' needs before its own (such as by offering graduated lease payments that increase over time, lessening the burden on start-ups). For individuals, a course on Cherokee ethical business practices could be envisioned, drawing from Eastern Band small-business owner guest speakers, who could discuss not only the issues of locating on or off the Qualla Boundary but also Cherokee-specific practices, such as gadugi, that they may see as a part of their work.

Although these questions and the programs discussed in this chapter are mostly specific to the Qualla Boundary, the strategies of the EBCI in encouraging small-business diversity and growth can be applied widely to many communities looking to develop strong, stable economies. This is especially true in the case of a community in which one industry (such as tourism) dominates the economic base, thus leaving that community economically vulnerable and potentially powerless if that industry should fail. Community-centric methods of small-business support and encouragement mitigate such issues and can be key to a thriving economy that has the ability to weather shifting state policies and larger economic shocks, making the promotion and protection of economic sovereignty an imperative for indigenous communities.

Conclusion

Looking Forward

. . . .

Beyond a desire to conceptually and programmatically examine Indianpreneurship, one primary reason that I sat in on the Indianpreneurship training course was to see what this new crop of small-business owners envisioned for the future landscape of small business on the Qualla Boundary. The students included both Eastern Band citizens and noncitizens, with all living on or near the Qualla Boundary—and all wanted to start their businesses locally. During one lesson, Russ collected input from the class on which businesses the Qualla Boundary had and which it lacked. It became clear that what the students believed it lacked at that time, for the most part, were businesses that served local needs: a pharmacy, furniture store, car dealership, bakery, hardware store, and so on. I wondered, given this perceived lack of locally based services, how many of these students would gear their businesses toward locals versus what is seen as the more low-hanging fruit: tourists. In the end, despite the enormity of the tourism industry in Cherokee, the majority of potential future business owners I spoke with in this class were not interested in tourism; they wanted to primarily serve the EBCI community.

Much of what these near Indianpreneurs told me echoed the same concerns about EBCI economy and representation that had emerged throughout my fieldwork. These were primarily issues with the already large (possibly saturated) tourism industry combined with what has been seen as a poor representation of Eastern Band identity within that industry. Ron re-articulated this sentiment when discussing his influences as a fledgling entrepreneur: "And that's why when I opened in '95, I knew [what I wanted in my inventory]. I had seen all these junk stores all my life and I wished they'd go away. I knew what I wanted [and] that's what I got." The stigma attached to opening another "junk store," combined with a perceived inability to compete with other tourist businesses that are entrenched physically, monetarily, and commercially, pushes potential owners away from opening new tourist-focused small businesses. Some also believe—and justifiably so, in many cases—that they cannot compete with families who have been in the tourism industry for generations. When considering what type of new business to create, the interplay of these barriers to starting a tourist-based business on the Qualla Boundary add a level of complexity to the initial decision of which market to serve.

In the final class session of the program, and after working through all the planning and analysis, students were required to make a pitch for their business. Eight of these eleven businesses were not tourist oriented: the Braves Drive-In restaurant, the Kituwah Foundation for traditional medicinal knowledge, a party planner, a laundromat, two landscaping companies, a plumber, and a movie-production studio. The remaining three were geared toward a mixed customer base of tourists and locals. One was a twenty-four-hour restaurant (a niche sorely unfilled throughout western North Carolina), one was a bead artisan, and the last was an art sales website.[1] From the casual discussions that occurred around the tables in the room that evening, it was clear that most people were motivated to start a business based on what they wanted to use personally (a common path to small-business ownership). For one Indianpreneurship student, this was a sports "bar." Because the Qualla Boundary is still a dry reservation (except, as mentioned, in the casino), it could not truly be a bar, but the theme of the restaurant was the key idea for him. During the high school football season, it is a given that when the game is in neighboring Bryson City, many will get dinner at Naber's Drive-In. Naber's, in Bryson City, is where both Eastern Band and Bryson City residents gather to discuss the serious and hotly debated intricacies of high school football before the big games.

This student wanted the equivalent of Naber's for Cherokee. He imagined this being a sports bar in the vein of Buffalo Wild Wings but catering mainly to the community. As he described it, the old men would gather there in the mornings over coffee and discuss the latest football game while surrounded by EBCI sports memorabilia. Later, the high school athletes would come by with coupons designed especially for them, possibly including free-food coupons that coaches could give out as rewards for good practices. The main event would come during home-game nights, when he hoped that everyone, including the surrounding communities, would come for dinner before the game and, possibly, celebrations afterward. In short, he wanted to create a new community tradition in Cherokee. He pictured flat-screen TVs and EBCI sports memorabilia as decoration—like a "Native" Hooters, he said. His preliminary name was the Braves Drive-In (named after the K–12 Cherokee Central Schools Braves). As he gave his business-plan presentation, he rarely looked up from the paper he clutched in both hands, staring so intently that he was slightly hunched over. As he kept reading, however, he got more and more excited and spoke faster, even gesticulating at key points of which he was proud—such as the name. By the time he ended, a smile had spread across his face as everyone nodded in agreement with his idea.

However, not all of the suggestions from these students on what the Qualla Boundary needed were local-centric. Two students, both currently in tourist-based work (one an artist, the other a chef at the Cherokee Casino), did suggest the need for newer and more up-to-date tourist-oriented businesses, either Native Nation or privately owned. This was reiterated by other current tourism-based business owners as they relayed their future visions for the Qualla Boundary. These suggestions, which I heard many times, mainly addressed the need for family entertainment, as opposed to a reliance on the casino tourists alone—a sentiment that was acknowledged formally in a 2009 report commissioned by the Blue Ridge National Heritage Area and Smoky Mountain Host that year, as well as in several reports since.

One-Industry Reliance: Emerging Competition

Since beginning my fieldwork in 2009, the pace of economic transformation on the Qualla Boundary has consistently increased and shows no signs of slowing, bringing challenges as well as gains for EBCI economic-sovereignty practices. The most dramatic change since my initial fieldwork was the construction of a second casino, Harrah's Cherokee Valley River Casino (Valley River), located away from the central hub of Cherokee. The EBCI Tribal Council voted in April 2013, by a margin of 11 to 1, to build this second casino. It then bought and placed into trust the parcel of land farther southwest of the Qualla Boundary in Cherokee County, near Murphy, North Carolina. This county had one of the highest unemployment rates in the state, at 13.5 percent, as of February 2013.[2] This new location is also strategically located within relatively short drives from Atlanta, Knoxville, and Chattanooga. The *One Feather* reported:

> With a construction budget of around $110 million, financed entirely by the EBCI, the casino will be around 60,000 square feet and will have 1,100 gaming machines, 30–40 table games, a food court, and a

300-room hotel. Adele Madden, Harrah's Cherokee director of finance, previously said that the project will generate around $177 million in gaming revenue the first year. The cash flow that would be used for distribution and debt reduction—after the management fee and capital withholding is taken out—would be over $50 million for the first year and close to $58 million in the sixth year. The new casino is expected to create an estimated 900 jobs on-site and will inject up to $39 million in payroll into the surrounding area. It will also bring hundreds of construction jobs to Cherokee County, as well as an additional 500 jobs that will be created in food preparation, food service, office and administration, building maintenance and other service sectors.[3]

This bold, somewhat controversial move (some citizens objected, claiming that they were not given a voice in this national decision) will have many ramifications. The businesses and landowners around the Murphy area seem to believe this will significantly increase the worth of the land, support of their businesses, and overall economic growth in that region, while the county government contends that this will place an undue burden on its existing structures (roads, services) and has tried to negotiate large compensatory payments from the EBCI.[4]

Many questions must be answered when expanding a casino industry, especially one located apart from a central reservation area. Does it help alleviate the precarity of a one-enterprise-dominant economy by physically expanding the market, or will it add to overall economic precarity by continuing to propagate the dominant industry? Will the new casino enable or overshadow broad diversification efforts? It would later be revealed (in 2016) that this newly purchased land would also host the $100 million Mission Critical Data Center, a business that could not locate in Cherokee due to lack of suitable land to host an appropriate building. This data center has the potential to launch a new and substantial industry for the EBCI, providing technology jobs and training not only for its citizens but for those in the region. Yet the question of small-business diversity in this new region remains; how will these new ventures tie in (if it all) with the EBCI's efforts to support small-business owners?[5] Finally, what will be the impacts on the local region economically, environmentally, and in EBCI–local government relationships? These questions demonstrate the importance of economic sovereignty and its exercise. By branching into these new enterprises, the EBCI is exercising its economic sovereignty by growing its current tourism industry, even as it is constricted by state and federal laws (specifically in gaming), while also using this economic sovereignty to expand into a new knowledge industry market—one that is not the target of Native Nation–specific federal and state restrictions and is not subject to the accompanying extractive payments from Native Nations' revenue to the state.

The EBCI expansion into the knowledge industry comes at a time when its gaming enterprises face many potential challenges. One has arisen near the Valley River location: the possibility of competition from another Native Nation. While the EBCI is currently the only federally recognized Native Nation in North Carolina,[6] the Catawba are located only a few hours away in South Carolina. The Catawba were a recognized Native Nation in South Carolina from 1941 to 1959, before they were caught in the Termination era's sweeping net. They were dissolved at the federal level, and their lands were seized in a typical federal display of economic violence. It was not until 1993 that they were again federally recognized (now with significantly less land) via the Catawba Indian Tribe of South Carolina Land Claims Settlement Act. This act specifically excludes the Catawba from using IGRA, clearly demonstrating the threat of even *potential* Native Nation economic power to both the federal and state governments. To reduce this threat, the federal government has literally tied the Catawba's economic sovereignty to their ability to exercise their inherent political sovereignty; here, the federal government is withholding acknowledgment of political sovereignty unless the Catawba agree to reduce their economic sovereignty by eliminating even the possibility of gaming. On the one hand, this means that the Catawba could operate a gaming enterprise without the stipulations that IGRA places on Native Nations. On the other hand, the Catawba do not currently have the option of compacting under IGRA for a gaming enterprise in South Carolina, as gambling (even nonprofit raffles until 2015) is illegal under state law.

Since the time of the settlement act, the Catawba have had many complex legal, political, and economic battles in and with the state of South Carolina, including wrestling with the state's deliberate acts of economic hegemony. One egregious example of this is South Carolina's blocking of the Catawba's settlement right to purchase up to 4,200 acres of land to put into trust, which has stalled the Catawba at 1,006 acres.[7] As these fights with South Carolina continued, the Catawba turned their eyes to nearby North Carolina in 2015. They submitted paperwork to the BIA seeking the purchase of trust land on which to place a casino near Charlotte, North Carolina, and began talks with the Seminole Nation to license their Hard Rock brand, but they face steep odds in this endeavor, including the opposition of 102 out of 120 North Carolina House members.[8]

The EBCI has used its economic sovereignty in negotiating state-compact boundaries that protect its gaming industry from regional North Carolina competition (west of Asheville) to launch new industries to diversify its national-level revenue and to support diversity at a local level by focusing on small-business support. These actions are crucial, as the chance remains that the EBCI will likely face gaming competition in the near future from Georgia, Tennessee, and possibly North Carolina. This situation is not uncommon (as seen in the case of Michigan gaming); it also represents just one facet of the precarity of a one-industry economy and, consequently, the subsequent need for broad multilevel diversity efforts, such as those discussed throughout this book. These efforts must go beyond a focus on developing Native Nation–level enterprises to include the support of small-business efforts.

Multilevel Diversity Efforts and Debt Reliance

The EBCI is clearly aware of the challenges that its gaming enterprise may face and is developing plans for the near future that use and support its economic sovereignty to help mitigate these challenges. It is not the first Native Nation to enter into gaming; consequently, it has had the benefit of closely watching the gaming enterprises of such nations as the Seminoles and Pequots, who had an earlier start (for better or worse). The EBCI has also been able to learn from these forerunners as it tries to shape its own sustainable economy. One part of this plan came in the form of a new 2014 initiative. This initiative's roots could be seen in the endeavors of current and future small-business owners, who have already been crafting changes to the tourism and local markets on the Qualla Boundary. Their visions and directions were deliberated in conversations among many Eastern Band citizens, eventually reaching the EBCI government. The EBCI would ultimately address these ideas and their potential impacts in a report sponsored by the Cherokee Preservation Foundation (see appendix I). In 2014, the EBCI hired two consultants—Ben Sherman of the Oglala Lakota (Sioux) Nation and president of Medicine Root, Inc., and John Weiser of BWB Solutions— to guide and help prepare the forty-one-page report and present it publicly.[9] The report focused on four main areas: real estate, tourism, small-business and entrepreneurial development, and knowledge industry development. As stated on the CPF's website:

Qualla 2020: Diversifying Our Region's Economy

For the Eastern Band of Cherokee Indians (EBCI), economic diversification holds great potential to increase resilience and contribute to achieving and sustaining long-term economic growth and development. While economic diversification is a focus for many tribes across the country, the EBCI is taking notable strides in developing and implementing structures and strategies to support the tribe's key aims of *non-gaming* revenue generation and job creation.

The purpose of the Qualla 2020 Initiative is to diversify the Cherokee economy and reduce its risks so that it can better ensure the wellbeing of the Cherokee population into the future. To do this, the Qualla 2020 Initiative will seek to *mitigate the dependence of the economy on gaming revenues,* and to develop and expand businesses in ways that uphold the core values of the Cherokee people.

Diversification does not occur in a vacuum. There needs to be an enabling environment to make diversification possible, with community input and diverse perspectives being a part of the process. In order to build an economy that is thriving and not dependent on gaming revenues, *the Qualla Boundary will require an entrepreneurial culture.*

Qualla 2020 is a six-month initiative that consists of monthly committee meetings and several follow-up subcommittee meetings on the topics of 8(a) contracting, Small Business Entrepreneurship, Tourism, Real Estate Maximization, and Knowledge Industries.[10]

These meetings were held at the Cherokee Casino and were attended mostly by those associated with the EBCI government, but they also brought in a wide range of concerned Eastern Band citizens, including small-business owners. The topics focused on the future shape of businesses on the Qualla Boundary as the basis for economic diversity, with a heavy emphasis on the role of entrepreneurs and small businesses. The prominence of "entrepreneurial culture" (being used here to emphasize diversity in type and number of small businesses) reflects the importance of the ongoing relationship between the EBCI, Eastern Band citizens, and entrepreneurialism in their community. This emphasis also helps to further dispel ideas of pan-Indian/entrepreneurialism cultural mismatches and singular conceptions of what constitutes indigenous entrepreneurship. It was clear from these presentations that the EBCI government had heard, and agreed with, the Eastern

Band citizens and small-business owners that it was time for a change on the Qualla Boundary—a change that would further invigorate the EBCI's relationship with its small-business owners.

Although the report directly emphasized entrepreneurialism, there were also many large and sweeping changes proposed to the Qualla Boundary more broadly, with grand visions of massive structural overhauls to pave the way for large EBCI tourism projects and major legal changes. These, of course, would all have considerable direct and indirect impacts on Qualla Boundary small businesses. One of the report's proposals suggested a real estate compact between the EBCI and the BIA; this would mean that the EBCI would take over responsibility for real estate from the BIA, as it had already done with its schools, hospital, and new justice center.[11] This real estate compact could be combined with a possible statute change in individual possessory holdings. These changes would provide many benefits—especially in terms of a more efficient real estate management system—and having full control of possessory holdings would also strengthen EBCI sovereignty. The challenge, as always, is the time, money, knowledge, and labor that the EBCI (and other Native Nations) need to outlay in order to take over these and other bureaucratic realms. The EBCI may be financially secure enough to undertake this real estate compact, but it will require a knowledgeable staff and a significant amount of time to make this transition. Overall, the Qualla 2020 initiative proposes some ambitious goals and changes for the EBCI nation that will be exciting to revisit in the decade to come.

Apart from the Qualla 2020 initiative, the EBCI Office of Planning and Development is continually trying to recruit chain stores and restaurants to serve both locals and tourists. These range from regional chain restaurants like Cracker Barrel to local chains like Mast General Store to nationally franchised chains like Ace Hardware, Casual Male, and even a Tangier Outlet Mall.[12] At the time of my fieldwork, most of these stores' expansions into new markets were on hold due to continuing fallout from the recession, and the U.S. economic uncertainties since 2016 continue this trend. I expect that a handful of these projects may move forward in the coming years; what the impact of these national stores will be on the local circulation of money will depend on how many of the new stores are franchises or local chains (which would be owned locally, possibly by Eastern Band citizens) rather than strictly national chains. It also remains to be seen whether these national stores will, as the EBCI expects, draw in additional tourists who wish to dine and shop in the comfort of known entities, even as they vacation in a location specifically pursued for its "exoticness."[13] It is equally possible that tourists will take fewer vacations to Cherokee if it is populated by many familiar American chain stores and restaurants, as it might be seen as too mainstream. There are no clear answers to whether these EBCI-level enterprises and efforts will help or hinder small-business sustainability by increasing competition to small businesses (and thus suppressing new small-business development) or by expanding the overall customer base.

This courting of national chains could also have negative consequences beyond the potential impacts of the tourism industry. While I was in the field, a contentious debate unfolded over the contract between Walmart and the EBCI. According to the *One Feather*, "The Wal-Mart Supercenter was slated to be 120,000 square feet costing the Tribe $25 million to construct and was projected to bring in close to $214 million in increased Tribal levy over a 25-year period. The lease was to be for 20 years with six five-year renewals for a total of 50 years possible. Wal-Mart would have also been responsible for yearly lease payments, averaging $564,000–$720,000, regardless of their decision to close or relocate."[14] It had been announced that negotiations with Walmart were nearly complete and that construction on the proposed site was to begin. Throughout the year I drove past the site—located next to the hospital and across from the new movie theater—and watched as it progressed. It was clear-cut and leveled—and then became oddly quiet.

I asked business owners, Eastern Band citizens, and government employees what they thought of this new venture, and the responses were, as to be expected, mixed. Some welcomed the superstore and claimed that it would have little impact on small businesses; others had already felt negative impacts from a Walmart on previous businesses in other locations.[15] Some felt that their lives would be improved by Walmart's benefits to the tax base and by not having to drive to Sylva (which has its own Walmart) for supplies; others rallied against Walmart's homogenizing influence. Some even predicted that it would fall through entirely. I must admit that I believed this latter situation to be a more cynical scenario.

In the end, the latter prediction was correct. Soon after my initial fieldwork was complete, Walmart pulled out of negotiations and unceremoniously dropped the Cherokee market. Its official statement was that it had made a corporate-wide decision to focus on urban areas.[16] This was a strange turn for a corporation whose initial success was generated directly from the rural market. The reaction from the local residents was again mixed, but also subdued. Walmart was not the first chain to woo the EBCI only to back out. In fact, month after month, reports came in from the economic development office summarizing its talks with various chains, such as Target, about coming to the Qualla Boundary. The answer from the chain stores many times was no. The reason given was usually the legal investment problems of owning a business on the reservation as a noncitizen (e.g., sovereign immunity), while some, like Walmart and Target, stated that they were choosing to focus on urban areas. This reflects a twofold concern: population and accessibility. First, although 3.6 million people visit the Cherokee Casino annually, the Qualla Boundary's permanent population is under 10,000, and there are multiple Walmarts in neighboring towns within a half hour to an hour drive of Cherokee.[17] Second, many of the challenges faced by rural small businesses are also issues for larger corporations, such as ease of accessibility, especially for inventory purposes. Keeping rural areas consistently stocked costs more in travel and time than it does in urban areas. After the Walmart withdrawal, public calls to support small businesses rather than chains increased; for example, Juanita Plummer Wilson stated that the EBCI should quit looking into attracting big-box stores and corporations and asked, "Why not invest into our people here?"[18]

Following a turnover in administration in 2015, however, Walmart negotiations for a full supercenter to be located near the new hospital resumed. A *One Feather* poll asked, "Do you think Walmart is a good fit for Cherokee?" with 43 percent responding yes and 57 percent responding no; the poll also generated three pages of opinions. In support, people cited the gain in levy, increased jobs, and convenient access to many products not currently available in Cherokee. Those against raised issues of poor pay and employee mistreatment, competition to local businesses, poor quality products not made in the United States, the existence of Walmarts in surrounding towns, the potential of it closing after EBCI investment (again), negative impacts on tourism, accusations of price gouging when dividend checks are distributed (reflecting observations conveyed to me by Eastern Band citizens), and a "cultural apocalypse," with many suggesting Target or various grocery stores instead.[19] At the time of this writing, the renewed negotiations are once again on hold.[20]

The EBCI has several directions proposed for future government enterprises. In addition to formally approving the new data center, it is consulting with the Mississippi Band of Choctaw Indians on forming a federal contracting venture. In the realm of tourism, EBCI leaders are in the early idea stages of developing several new parks to combat the seasonal flight of tourists each winter following leaf-changing season. These options include a year-round Cherokee indoor water park (the Adventure Park), a children's discovery center, a new hotel and convention center, and a bowling alley in the Cherokee Casino (already launched in 2017). Collectively, these enterprises are expected to significantly diversify EBCI revenue streams. Eastern Band citizens have contributed many more suggestions to these government-owned options, including a music venue; an IMAX theater, which could include a year-round showing of the EBCI theater drama *Unto These Hills* (currently a summer-only outdoor performance); an animal rehabilitation facility; an EBCI bank; and, finally, the newest business idea on the horizon for many Native Nations: a marijuana farm and dispensary, to be regulated by the EBCI government for Eastern Band medical use only.[21] The newest EBCI diversity efforts have garnered much support in general from Eastern Band citizens but especially from tourism-based small businesses, which will benefit from an extended year-round tourist season.

One of the criticisms leveled against these new EBCI operations, however, is the issue of debt. Eastern Band citizens are rightly concerned with each new project's tab, which can reach multimillions of dollars. For example, the Bowling Entertainment Center alone was projected to cost $13 million. The EBCI administration consistently addresses these issues on the national level, but there is one debt issue that is less discussed: that of individuals' debts. Much of the literature and action items regarding American Indian small-business ownership focuses on securing capital through debt accumulation of some sort. Debt is so ingrained as a normality of U.S. economic existence today that the BIA, under its Division of Economic Development, states that "commerce *is not possible* without the rule of law embodied in strong commercial codes that secure collateral and allow credit to flow freely between persons inside and outside reservations."[22] However, debt has been, and is today, regularly used as a political weapon of suppression and dominance worldwide, and most certainly against American Indian peoples and Native Nations specifically.[23] To not acknowledge this and the inherent threat that debt accumulation continues to pose to indigenous peoples worldwide is to ignore the very factors that contribute to American Indian and Native Nation economic precarity. While American Indians should have the right and ability to access loans and credit as much as any non-Natives, we must explore and offer alternatives to the need for debt accumulation. For the EBCI, the dividend payments (acting as unconditional guaranteed annual income) and lump-sum payments can serve in this capacity. Even if these payments are not enough to cover the costs to start or grow a business, they can reduce debt accumulation. Instead of encouraging American Indian small-business owners to go into debt, risking a further spiral into poverty, we must create financial growth options that support, rather than potentially endanger, American Indian individuals' economic security.

Working for a Sustainable Future

Many models and theories have been developed in the last decade that attempt to answer the urgent question of how we can best support the economic stability and growth (if desired) of the many indigenous nations worldwide that may be deeply in debt and have few resources to pool due to centuries of economic violence and economic hegemony. Much attention is paid to top-down solutions; in the current research, the issues of large-enterprise creation take the lead. This is particularly true in studies of Native Nation economies. The overwhelming majority of research being done on these economies examines Native Nation–owned ventures like casinos. While some of these models have most certainly helped Native Nation leaders make great strides toward achieving the goal of economic power for their nations, this research has historically tended to assume that the most significant agent of large social and economic change is the Native Nation government, leading many to overlook the grassroots population of individual American Indians whose labor continues to drive the economy. A marked increase in researchers foregrounding the experiences of both American Indian laborers and entrepreneurs would begin to emerge in the 2000s and continue through the 2010s.

Similarly, a more individual focus that engages similar economic development issues is present in current international indigenous studies, especially those of Latin American indigenous communities. These studies parallel many of the conflicts occurring in the United States over resource acquisition by the settler-colonial state but with differing tactics toward and by indigenous communities in these attempts.[24] Models of indigenous autonomy in Latin America may lack the more robust, treaty-sanctioned frameworks of political sovereignty that are exercised in the United States and Canada, but recent political movements in Latin America have concentrated on comparable political economy fights through restriction of state government control along with gaining and maintaining autonomous control of resources (e.g., land and water).[25] The defense of diverse livelihoods is a central component in their demands for autonomy.

In Australia, research published since 2015 has begun to focus on indigenous entrepreneurial development, specifically in the tourism realm. This research outlines four sectors where impediments to Aboriginal and Torres Strait Islander tourism businesses manifest, reflecting obstacles that are frequently present for indigenous entrepreneurs internationally: tourism studies in academia (propagation of the cultural-mismatch fallacy, lack of indigenous academics), negative representations in society and media, marginalization within the tourism industry, and lack of voice in settler-colonial governments.[26] My research with the EBCI and its small-business owners draws from international works and interdisciplinary scholars such as these to build a more robust foundation for economic studies of indigenous peoples by contributing to the expansion of economic focus from nation-driven economic power to inclusion of individual impacts—along with their necessary and intimate entanglements. By documenting and exploring the broad range of ways in which American Indian individuals are transforming their reservation economies, this work contributes to contemporary anthropological and interdisciplinary debates in development theory by demonstrating the complex effects of small businesses on reservations and other smaller communities, including the ways in which small businesses can support and strengthen the practices of economic sovereignty in indigenous communities. In doing so, this research adds to the existing bodies of work that dismantle the spectrum of economic stereotypes (from "rich Indian" to "incompetent") of American Indians and indigenous peoples as businesspeople.

The EBCI small-business sector has demonstrated remarkable sustainability over the past century. EBCI leaders and citizens regularly explore ideas to continue this success, such as partnering with the American Indian Alaska Native Tourism Association to focus on international opportunities in American Indian tourism (for example, the especially large market in Europe).[27] The coming decade may bring many changes for citizen business owners, however. Possible increases in chain stores, increasing competition for land, or another possible recession could have deleterious effects on existing and potential businesses. But these challenges may be offset by some hopeful changes, including the large increase in support from the EBCI government and the sheer variety of this support; a possible lengthened tourist season due to additional EBCI development projects; and the increase in Eastern Band young people entering the small-business sector across industries. These are all indicators of the future sustainability

FIGURE C.1 One of Eastern Band artist Jeff Marley's sign installations, seen here (bottom left) at Kituwah Mound. Photo by Jeff Marley, used with permission.

of small businesses on the Qualla Boundary and, by extension, of the overall Qualla Boundary economy as well as the economy of western North Carolina more broadly.

Eastern Band citizens have shown that privately owned American Indian small businesses can have a positive and substantial impact on the development and economic stability of their entire nation. But for American Indians on reservations, the distinct challenges to small-business ownership must be addressed. Because my research testifies to the extensive positive value of small, private businesses to reservations, it is my hope that other Native Nations will include, as the EBCI has recently begun to, a focus on new policies that support local small businesses as a means of strengthening their economies. To accomplish this, Native Nation leaders can take a proactive stance in creating environments that are conducive to small-business ownership; address the pragmatics of training, infrastructure, and financing for American Indians; and stay attuned to potential local issues, such as representation. In order to do so, it is vital to understand economic sovereignty as an aggregate, living action—both in the ways that the small-business sector supports its practice and in how Native Nations use it in crafting the type of stable and sustainably diverse economy that they determine to be most beneficial to their community.

This focus on economic sovereignty also reveals potential vulnerabilities for indigenous communities regarding the ability to manage and control their economic futures. This includes conflicts over autonomy in financial management, the ability to choose economic development paths, the choice of economic systems, and determinations of political–economic entanglements with nonindigenous states. The small-business sector is one resource that indigenous nations, like the EBCI, have successfully drawn from to counter these vulnerabilities. When indigenous nations incorporate the experiences of small-business owners and support the structures of the small-business sector to help address these issues, these nations and their citizens are empowered to create a climate that fortifies their foundational practices of both economic and political sovereignty.

ᏍᎦᏓᎤᏙᎭ

Si Otsedoha

We are still here

Appendix A

Examples of Sequoyah Fund Loans Available at Time of Writing

New Economy Fund provides business loans totaling $50,000–$250,000 for green, knowledge-based, or creative economy businesses located in the seven far-western counties of North Carolina. These funds are available to qualified individuals who have resided in the region for at least two years. SCORE of Asheville will collaborate with the Sequoyah Fund to provide success coaching to these clients. The USDA's Intermediary Relending Program (IRP) in conjunction with the Southwestern Planning Commission's Economic Development Administration (EDA) will provide the capital for this loan product. EBCI enrollment is not required.

Healthy Foods Venture Fund will provide lending prudently and productively in unconventional markets often overlooked by conventional financial institutions. More and more consumers are searching for fresher, healthier, unprocessed, and nutritive foods that will help them stay fit and healthy. An increase in obesity and the incidence of heart disease has resulted in this dramatic change. In response to this market demand and in an effort to bolster local brand development, the Sequoyah Fund will seek investments from the Cherokee Preservation Foundation and the CDFI Fund to support business development in this area. EBCI enrollment is not required.

Downtown Revitalization Fund provides commercial real estate façade renovation loans up to $150,000. Qualifying individuals must own or lease a business located in the Cherokee Business District. EBCI enrollment is not required.

Credit Builder Fund will provide innovative solutions to help build client credit and financial access in order to grow their businesses and/or personal assets. The Credit Builder is a credit-repair loan program coupled with intense one-on-one credit counseling. These consumer loans include a client savings program designed to pay off and remove derogatory comments and past-due bills named on credit reports. The Cherokee Business Center, under the leadership of Gloria Rattler, has committed a full-time staff member to this program. The Sequoyah Fund will seek investments from the Cherokee Preservation Foundation and the CDFI Fund to support this initiative. Anyone living on the Qualla Boundary may quality for this loan.

Business Enterprise Fund provides business retention or expansion loans totaling $50,000–$250,000. Qualifying individuals must be enrolled members of the Eastern Band of Cherokee Indians living on the Qualla Boundary or in the seven far-western counties of North Carolina. See our *Guide to Starting a Business in Cherokee* (PDF).

New Beginnings Fund provides new business start-up loans not exceeding $50,000. Qualifying individuals must be enrolled members of the Eastern Band of

Cherokee Indians living on the Qualla Boundary or in the seven far-western counties of North Carolina. See our *Guide to Starting a Business in Cherokee* (PDF).

Capital Projects Fund provides loans to tribal enterprises/nonprofit organizations. See our *Guide to Starting a Business in Cherokee* (PDF).

Healthy Home Rehabilitation Fund provides consumer loans up to $15,000 for home repairs. New appliances purchased must be Energy Star rated. Qualifying individuals must be enrolled members of the Eastern Band of Cherokee Indians living in the seven far-western counties of North Carolina.

Artisan Studio Fund provides business loans up to $25,000 for the construction of home-based studios. Qualifying individuals must be enrolled members of the Eastern Band of Cherokee Indians living in the seven far-western counties of North Carolina.[1]

Appendix B

Signage Regulations

Merchants and businesses within the Business District of the Qualla Boundary shall display merchandise for sale on the outside of their business premises only if:

(1) Items that are permitted:
   a. A Native American product, art or craft; or
   b. Art, craft or product indigenous to the Appalachian region; or
   c. Is an art, craft or product made by an artisan or craftsman on the premises where the art, craft, or product is displayed; and
   d. The merchant, artisan or craftsman has been issued a business license; and
   e. The display area is kept in a clean, neat and safe condition and appearance for pedestrians and the motoring public; and
   f. Is respectful of traditional Cherokee culture; and

(2) Items that are not permitted:
   a. Anything motorized (4 wheelers, scooters, bikes, etc.);
   b. Airbrushing;
   c. Cardboard boxes or plastic tubs of items;
   d. T-shirts and all other articles of clothing;
   e. Blankets, rugs and towels;
   f. Shoes, hats, belts, purses;
   g. Furniture, lamps and yard statues;
   h. Post cards, pots and bandanas;
   i. Swimwear, tubes and umbrellas;
   j. Bull whips, cow horns and skulls;
   k. Piggy banks, dolls and blow-up characters;
   l. Wind kites and wind chimes;
   m. Flags;
   n. Photographs;

(3) Exempt items are as follows:
   a. Coke machines;
   b. Arcade games;
   c. Rides;
   d. Gumball machines;
   e. Firewood;
   f. Brochure racks;

(4) Merchandise on the sidewalks of Non-Tourist Based Specialty Shops will be determined on a case by case basis. Non-tourist based specialty shops may include hardware stores, pool equipment stores, tubing centers, etc.[1]

Appendix C

Hicks Campaign Ad, 2011

Michell Hicks Campaign Ad, 2011 (Hicks Principal Chief 2011b)

Sustainable Development and Cultural Tourism

If you drove though Cherokee this past weekend, you noticed that the Island Park played host to thousands of families for the annual children's Talking Leaves Trout Derby. I was reminded that events such as this, and natural resources like our waterways and parks, are symbols of the direction our tribe should take for sustainable, eco-friendly, culturally-authentic economic development. Whether it is in the Cultural District of Cherokee, or at ancestral sites in Snowbird, or at historic landmarks in Cherokee County, the Eastern Band has tremendous opportunities to responsibly capitalize on the beauty of our homelands.

Many of us can remember the days, long before gaming, when the streets of Cherokee were packed with visitors excited about what we had to offer. Lately however, many of us are also dismayed to drive by empty store fronts or unkempt retail property sitting vacant. Furthermore, communities such as Snowbird and Cherokee County possess tremendous untapped opportunities for promoting our cultural and natural landscape. We have never explored the depths of their potential to the extent they deserve.

As part of my economic development plan for the next four years, I propose to:

- Awaken the atmosphere of downtown and cultural districts with events and performance artists who invite a dialog with visitors about our culture.
- Insure that tribally-owned lands and buildings are open and accessible for business during the tourism season. This enhances atmosphere and provides both seasonal job opportunities and increased levy revenue for the tribe.
- Create an open access Artists and Craftsman District that encourages walking traffic and maintains cultural integrity with guidelines for the types of products sold. Our artists will not be lost amongst shelves of foreign-made, cheap trinkets. They will have their own space that recognizes their work for the treasure that it is.
- Continue to seek family-oriented attraction opportunities in line with our vision for responsible tourism expansion.
- Explore and implement opportunities for Snowbird and Cherokee County to create their own sustainable attractions that meet the specific needs at their communities.

As a tribal government it is not our role to inhibit or control private business owners. These entities undoubtedly serve an important role for our community. However, we can and will take all necessary steps to insure that tribally-owned businesses and properties are environmentally friendly and culturally authentic.[1]

Appendix D

Enrollment Facts

Enrollment facts submitted by the EBCI Enrollment Office, published in the *Cherokee One Feather*:

October 6, 2009:

Did you know? At one time there were age requirement deadlines for Enrollment. These deadlines were as follows:

- September 11th, 1995–August 1, 1996: A person must have been Enrolled within three years of their date of birth.
- August 2nd, 1996–December 2nd, 1998: A person must have been Enrolled within three years of their date of birth or within one year following their eighteenth birthday.
- December 3rd, 1998–April 7th, 1999: A person must have been Enrolled within the eighteen years of their date of birth.
- April 8th, 1999–August 4th, 1999: A person must have been Enrolled before reaching the age of nineteen.
- August 5th, 1999–Present (2009): There is no deadline for enrollment.[1]

July 1, 2009:

Did you know? As of June 1, 2009, the EBCI had 14,253 Enrolled Members. 7,206 Members are Female; 7,047 Members are Male.[2]

May 28, 2008:

Did you know there have been a total of thirteen Rolls done on the Eastern Band of Cherokee Indians? The first two Rolls were completed prior to the Removal and the final roll is the Revised Roll that new enrollees are placed on today. The thirteen Rolls are:

- 1817 Reservation Roll
- 1817–1835 Emigration Roll
- 1835 Henderson Roll
- 1848 Mulloy Roll
- 1851 Siler Roll
- 1852 Chapman Roll
- 1869 Swetland Roll

- 1882 Hester Roll
- 1907 Council Roll
- 1908 Churchill Roll
- 1909 Guion Miller Roll
- 1924 Baker Roll
- 1957–Present day Revised Roll[3]

September 29, 2011:

Did you know?

The 1924 Baker Roll had 3,148 members. Of those, 104 are still living. Forty-four (44) of the surviving Baker Roll members live on tribal land.

Of the total number of enrolled members, 14,598, there are 407 full blooded members still living.[4]

Currently, there is no age requirement to become a member of the Eastern Band of Cherokee Indians. However, an ordinance was passed in September Council. If ratified, effective Dec. 1, enrollment into the Eastern Band of Cherokee Indians will be restricted to those persons under the age of nineteen.

DNA testing establishing the paternity and maternity of potential applicants is now required for membership into the Eastern Band of Cherokee Indians. The cost for testing through 1 Family Services, located in the Tribal Enrollment Office, is $195 per family unit. Payment is due at the time of testing.[5]

Appendix E

Loss of Membership

    (b) Disenrollments. Disenrollment is defined as revoking a person's membership in the Eastern Band of Cherokee Indians when it is found that said person did not meet the eligibility criteria existing at the time of said person's enrollment. Disenrollment prevents an individual from receiving any monetary benefits, education, housing, possessory holdings or any and all other services offered and provided to enrolled members. The following Disenrollment Procedures are adopted to correct mistakes that resulted when tribal membership was mistakenly approved and to provide a process that would allow a fair hearing in the disenrollment procedure.

(1) Grounds for disenrollment. A Tribal member may be subject to disenrollment if records reveal one or more of the following conditions exist:

    (A) The member was erroneously enrolled (that is, he/she did not meet the eligibility criteria in existence at the time of his/her enrollment).

    (B) The member has accepted benefits of land or money (or if a minor, a parent or guardian has accepted benefits of land or money on the minor's behalf) as an enrolled member of another Indian Tribe after the effective date of this chapter (9-11-1995).

    (C) The member is currently enrolled with another Indian Tribe and has either refused to relinquish membership in the other Tribe or has failed to respond to a notice of the requirement to relinquish membership in the other Tribe.

(2) Procedures for disenrollment. The Enrollment Office shall notify the Enrollment Committee of any member who may be subject to disenrollment. The Enrollment Committee initiates the disenrollment process against any member by authorizing, through a majority vote, the Enrollment Office to:

    a. Provide written notice, by certified mail, return receipt, to the individual to be summoned to appear before the Enrollment Committee. The notice must:

        i. State that the Enrollment Committee has questions regarding the individual's enrollment and state the nature of the questions and what documentation the individual must provide to the Committee to retain his/her membership.

ii. State that the individual has thirty calendar days from the date of receipt of the notice to contact the Enrollment Office and set a date for the individual to appear before the Enrollment Committee.

iii. State that if the individual does not contact the Enrollment Office within the prescribed time period, the individual's non-response will be interpreted as his/her choice to be automatically disenrolled and the individual will be disenrolled at the next meeting of the Enrollment Committee. The date of that meeting will be stated in the letter. No further notice will be given to the individual of his/her disenrollment.

iv. Members on active duty with the military shall have six calendar months to contact the Enrollment Office.

b. The individual has the burden to prove his/her eligibility for enrollment at the time of enrollment.

c. The individual, at his/her own expense, may be represented by legal counsel at the individual's appearance before the Enrollment Committee. The individual, however, must personally appear before the Enrollment Committee and cannot have a legal representative or other agent appear on his/her behalf.

d. If the individual provides evidence that satisfies the Enrollment Committee, by majority vote, the process is terminated and the individual retains his/her membership.

e. If the individual does not provide evidence which satisfies the Enrollment Committee, by majority vote, the individual will be disenrolled effective immediately.

f. The disenrolled individual may file a written appeal of the Enrollment Committee's decision to the Tribal Council within thirty calendar days of the Committee's decision. The written appeal is to be directed to the Tribal Council Chairman and is to request a hearing before the six Tribal Council members who do not comprise the Enrollment Committee. The appeal stays the individual's disenrollment until such time as the appeal is heard and decided.

g. At the appeal hearing, the Tribal Council only reviews the documentation that the Enrollment Committee reviewed and no new evidence or oral argument is allowed to be presented. The Tribal Council may only determine if the Enrollment Committee failed to follow the steps of the disenrollment procedure or was negligent in any way. If the Tribal Council finds, by majority vote, there was error or negligence on the part of the Enrollment Committee, the matter is returned to the Enrollment Committee for reevaluation. If the appeal is successful, the individual's membership is restored. The Tribal Council's decision is final.

h. Any files indicating fraud in the enrollment process shall be forwarded to the Tribal prosecutor for investigation.

(3) Property.
    a. Upon receipt of the list of members whose status is subject to review the Council of the EBCI may impose a temporary stop on all property transfers affecting possessory holdings held by members subject to review. All services, monetary and otherwise, will also be placed on hold and held in escrow until the disenrollment process is completed either by reinstatement of membership or disenrollment.
    b. Once an individual is removed from the Tribe's Roll they shall be deemed to hold a life estate in any possessory holding that was in their name prior to disenrollment.
    c. Such life estate shall revert to the Eastern Band of Cherokee Indians upon expiration.
    d. Alternatively, a disenrolled individual may transfer any of their possessory holding held prior to disenrollment to an enrolled member blood relative.

(4) Policies.
    a. The Enrollment Committee shall have the authority to develop policies and procedures consistent with this ordinance.[1]

Appendix F

Qualifications for Enrollment

The membership of the Eastern Band of Cherokee Indians shall consist of the following:

(a) All persons whose names appear on the roll of the Eastern Band of Cherokee Indians of North Carolina, prepared and approved pursuant to the Act of June 4, 1924 (43 Stat. 376), and the Act of March 4, 1931 (46 Stat. 1518). This is the base roll of the Eastern Band of Cherokee Indians and shall be known as the Baker Roll of 1924. It is the foundation on which all enrollment decisions are made and shall not be subject to challenge or amendment as to the information contained therein. This does not affect the authority set forth in subsection 49-9(b) for disenrollment based on criteria in that section.

(b) All direct lineal descendants of persons identified in section 49-2(a) who were living on August 14, 1963; who possess at least 1/32 degree of Eastern Cherokee blood, who applied for membership prior to August 14, 1963, and have themselves or have parents who have maintained and dwelt in a home at sometime during the period from June 4, 1924, through August 14, 1963, on lands of the Eastern Band of Cherokee Indians in the Counties of Swain, Jackson, Graham, Cherokee and Haywood in North Carolina.

(c) All direct lineal descendants of persons identified in section 49-2(a) who apply for membership after August 14, 1963, and who possess at least 1/16 degree of Eastern Cherokee blood.

(d) All direct lineal descendants of persons identified in § 49-2(a) who apply for membership after December 1, 2011, who possess at least 1/16 degree of Eastern Cherokee Indian blood, and apply for enrollment prior to their nineteenth birthday. This section does not apply to adopted individuals.

(e) All direct lineal descendants of persons identified in § 49-2(a) who have been legally adopted outside the membership of the Eastern Band of Cherokee Indians, who apply for membership after December 1, 2011 and who possess at least 1/16 degree of Eastern Cherokee Indian blood, provided they:

   (1) Were legally adopted as infants;

   (2) Have lived their entire lives in a place sufficiently removed from the Qualla Boundary to preclude their contact with or knowledge of the Tribe; and

(3) Were unaware of their eligibility for membership in the Tribe.

(4) The descendants of individuals identified above, who also satisfy subsections (2) and (3) above and possess at least 1/16 degree of Eastern Cherokee blood, are eligible for membership.

(Ord. No. 284, 8-2-1996; Ord. No. 352, 12-3-1998; Ord. No. 645, 8-5-1999; Ord. No. 787, 9-28-2011; Ord. No. 347, 2-17-2015; Ord. No. 525, 5-27-2015)[1]

Appendix G

EBCI Passport Publicity Announcement

CHEROKEE, N.C.—With the economy the number one concern and tourism the number one economy in Western North Carolina, the Qualla Boundary, the sovereign nation of the Eastern Band of Cherokee Indian, today unveils the Cherokee Passport, which it advises all visitors to the Cherokee Indian Reservation to obtain upon arrival. Beginning Thursday, May 27 at 1:30 P.M., Cherokee border patrol officials will conduct checkpoints to issue and verify passports.

The Qualla Boundary is a sovereign nation, and from the late 1700s to the early 1800s, visitors to the Boundary needed a passport to enter. As a reminder of its sovereignty, the Eastern Band is issuing the passport to visitors to jumpstart the local economy on summer's opening weekend, Memorial Day weekend. Visitors to Cherokee are advised not to wander around Cherokee without a Cherokee Passport.

"Our economy and that of Western North Carolina subsists on tourism," said Robert Jumper, tourism manager for Cherokee Travel and Promotion. "In support of the area's businesses and to help the economy, we have taken a dramatic step to remind visitors that Cherokee is a sovereign nation while providing a pioneering tool full of tourism incentives."

New this year and full of great discounts at more than 20 shops, hotels, restaurants, retailers, attractions and businesses, the Cherokee Passport is a handy guide to all the activities, adventures and attractions in Cherokee, including 101 FREE Things to Do. It includes a detailed map of Cherokee that identifies participating retailers' locations, designates hiking trails and ensures visitors can capture on camera and post to Facebook each of the painted bears throughout town. The passport can be picked up at the Welcome Center and its kiosks, all participating retailers and at participating hoteliers.

Additional coupons and discounts will be posted to www.cherokee-nc.com /passport throughout the year. A trip to Cherokee can fit nearly every budget, and the passport will help visitors stay on budget.

Experience authentic Cherokee culture brought to life in genuine, ancient Cherokee legends, history, tradition, song, dance, ceremony and fascinating period regalia. Cherokee offers activities, packages and itineraries that make visiting an affordable pleasure for all ages and interests. Visit cultural sites and enjoy cultural festivals, camping, tubing, hiking, wading, biking, birding, waterfalls, watermills, a pioneer village, cultural attractions, nostalgic shops and motor lodges, family fun parks, petting zoos, more than 30 miles of untamed trout waters, and Harrah's Cherokee Casino and Hotel. For more information about Cherokee, visit www.cherokee -nc.com.[1]

Appendix H

EBCI Small-Business Assistance Offices

Sequoyah Fund Office: The Sequoyah Fund is an independent, nonprofit American Indian Community Development Financial Institution (CDFI). "Sequoyah Fund's mission is to provide training, technical assistance, and resources to support entrepreneurship, business startup and expansion, and community development in the seven far western counties of North Carolina and on the Qualla Boundary," including commercial lending.[1] Since its inception, the fund has made 397 loans equaling $15,098,071.38; the five categories of loans are Start-Up, Small Business, Home Improvement, Nonprofit, and Loan Servicing. In 2016, twenty-seven loans ($771,921.38) were made on Qualla Boundary and three ($23,150.00) off-Boundary. Because the Sequoyah Fund is a nonprofit, it is unable to borrow from other banks at near-zero interest rates to accommodate increases in lending. As Russ states, "Instead, we must—and we will—diligently pursue all available grant sources offering capital for lending purposes."[2]

Office of Planning and Development: "The Mission of the EBCI Office of Planning and Development is to mobilize available economic resources to enhance the overall quality of life for our people. We strive to grow job opportunities, to improve the business climate and tax base of the Tribe, and to promote a self-sustaining and diverse economy on the Qualla Boundary. The Planning and Development Office oversees the following areas: Economic Development, Tribal Planning, Grants Administration, Building Rental, Business Development, and Geographic Information Systems (GIS)."[3]

Cherokee Business Development Center: The center works in conjunction with the Sequoyah Fund Office, providing counseling and assistance to new and existing business owners in the areas of business plan development, financial projections, loan packaging, retail and development property location, employee background checks, bookkeeping essentials, and assistance in filling out applications. All services are free.[4]

Cherokee Preservation Foundation: "The Cherokee Preservation Foundation was established on November 14, 2000, as part of the Second Amendment to the Tribal-State Compact between the EBCI and the State of North Carolina." "The CPF helps protect, preserve, and enhance the natural resources and aesthetic appearance of Cherokee tribal lands in North Carolina; assists in economic development of the Cherokee community and the seven western most counties in North Carolina in which the EBCI's tribal lands are located (Haywood, Jackson, Swain, Macon, Clay, Graham and Cherokee) through improved public services, recreation and entertainment capabilities, and community economic development; fosters employment opportunities on or near Cherokee tribal lands; and provides funding for the preservation, research, restoration, and/or development of the history, tradition, culture, language, arts, crafts, heritage and overall well-being of the Cherokee people."[5] The CPF has invested over $50 million in the local community since its inception in 2002. The organization gave a total of $5,401,161 to sixty-nine various grantees in 2010 alone.[6]

Cherokee Chamber of Commerce: This nonprofit organization is "dedicated to promoting a healthy business community in and around the town of Cherokee,"[7] offering marketing, merchandising, business management, and financial planning programs.

Greater Cherokee Tourism Council: Formed after my fieldwork in January 2011, "the GCTC's priority will be bringing Cherokee's tourism-related organizations together while working on the common goal of bringing more overnight visitors and tourism dollars to Cherokee. Participation consisted of representatives from the Sequoyah National Golf Club, Ryan Ott, Ryan Lanzen and Chase Sneed, Cherokee Historical Association, Linda Squirrel, The Museum of the Cherokee Indian, Barbara Duncan, EBCI Transit, Kathy Littlejohn, EBCI Fish & Game, Robert Blankenship and EBCI Travel and Promotion, Robert Jumper, Mary Jane Ferguson, Josie Long and the Cherokee Chamber of Commerce, Matthew Pegg, Qualla Arts & Crafts Mutual, Inc. and EBCI Parks & Recreation."[8]

Appendix I

Qualla 2020

Cherokee Core Values (from Vision Qualla, 2005)

- Prayer, Faith, Spirituality
- Group Harmony
- Strong Individual Character
- Sense of Place
- Honoring the Past
- Educating the Children
- Sense of Humor

Goals for Small Business and Entrepreneurs

- Create a single source of relevant information for small businesses
- Strengthen Cherokee Chamber of Commerce
- Create an economic development coalition to support small business
- Build a more vibrant entrepreneurial culture
- Expand businesses through the U.S. Small Business Administration 8(a) and similar programs
- Expand sales by Cherokee artists

Broader Goals

- Implement plan for compacting real estate
- Draft statutes for individual possessory holdings
- Make changes to provide another venue for large attractions/shows in Cherokee, with easy public access and parking
- Identify and attract small-to-midsize knowledge businesses
- Conduct feasibility study for fiber-enabled office building and co-working space[1]

Notes

Introduction

1. I use "EBCI" to refer to the EBCI government or to citizens' collective actions (such as the results of elections); I use "Eastern Band" to designate individual citizens of the EBCI. On occasion, I will refer to "Cherokee citizens" when speaking collectively of citizens from all three federally recognized Cherokee nations.

2. This is a more formal, stilted greeting than would normally be used (a common way of speaking for many beginning language learners).

3. Broadly throughout this work, I situate the use of "economy" and "economic" in a convergence of feminist, development, and peasant economic anthropology constructions. As such, the household is taken to be a vital part of the economy, including the use of unpaid family labor in small businesses, in addition to physical assets such as land and natural resources, while the importance of institutional structures and forces as they relate to individuals' relations with power, property, and privilege have a place of primacy.

4. When studying small businesses, it is often assumed that they are privately owned. When discussing businesses in an American Indian context, however, it is important to clarify which are private and which are owned by a Native Nation, since both are prevalent. For this research with the EBCI, all "small businesses" are privately owned unless specified otherwise.

5. I will refer to the "Qualla Boundary" proper as a whole when discussing the legally defined, place-based physical location of EBCI trust land. I will also at times refer to "Cherokee," the specific town in Yellowhill (not to be confused with the people, "Cherokee citizens"), as the primary location of governmental and tourist activity within the Qualla Boundary.

6. The *Entreprenative* podcast coined this term online; ONABEN (Our Native American Business Network) uses "Indianpreneurship" as the title of its small-business course.

7. This was the syllabary used on the menu, although Sequoyah used "ᏍᏏ4ᏉᎤ" for himself.

8. This issue is complicated by—and is currently debated because of—North Carolina's Blue Ridge law. This provision allows permits for the sale of alcohol to be issued to businesses within 1.5 miles of a Blue Ridge Parkway entrance or exit ramp and was agreed to by the EBCI in 2015.

9. Because my research is with the EBCI—a federally recognized Native Nation—my analyses throughout regarding Native Nations build from a base of federal recognition unless otherwise noted. These theoretical problems and frameworks,

however, can and should be applied more broadly, from issues of state recognition to international indigenous communities.

10. This comparison is difficult to evaluate because measures of unemployment have changed over time, but statisticians generally agree that the magnitudes are on par. Da Costa, "Statistician Says US Joblessness Near Depression Highs."

11. Tickamyer and Duncan, "Poverty and Opportunity Structure in Rural America."

12. Civilian employment–population ratio. United States Bureau of Labor Statistics, "Current Employment Statistics."

13. Respondent asked for anonymous name. Abe, interview with the author, February 2010.

14. National Parks Service, "Travel Increases in Park." Updated statistics and years of record travel in the GSMNP are available online at http://www.nature.nps.gov/stats/view.

15. Service Employees International Union, "Big Bank Profile"; PR Newswire, "Criden & Love."

16. Martin and Martin, interview with the author, October 2009.

17. Respondent asked for anonymous name. Carl, interview with the author, August 2009.

18. Queen, interview with the author, January 2010.

19. Small Business Administration, "Frequently Asked Questions." Data is from 2002 to 2010.

20. Ibid.

21. Small Business Administration, "Minority Business Ownership." This continues a trend seen in the 1990s, in which it is reported that "between 1992 and 1997, the number of Native-owned businesses grew by 84 percent to a total of 197,300 and their receipts increased by 179 percent. In 1997, these businesses generated $34.3 billion in revenues and employed almost 300,000 individuals" (Malkin et al., "Native Entrepreneurship," 10). It is interesting to note that per SBA's regulations, "Native-owned businesses" are defined as "socially and economically disadvantaged," a status (and possible stigma) that gives these businesses access to a range of programs.

22. Kelley et al., *Global Entrepreneurship Monitor.*

23. GEM focuses on "the phase that combines the stage before the start of a new firm (nascent entrepreneurship) and the stage directly after the start of a new firm (owning-managing a new firm). Taken together, this phase is defined as 'early-stage entrepreneurial activity' ('TEA,' continuing to use an earlier acronym of 'total entrepreneurial activity')." Bosma et al., "GEM Manual."

24. Except when used in specific discussions (and provided that their employees number under five hundred), I do not differentiate between small-business owners and entrepreneurs. Among other issues addressed in chapter 1, I find that the standard associations of entrepreneurship with innovation and small businesses with stagnancy is a false dichotomy, as owning and managing any business with its long-term success in mind cannot happen without innovation; thus, maintaining said businesses should not remove one from the category of "innovator." Issues of "in-

novators" versus "maintainers" came to the forefront of work discussions in 2016 with the Maintainers conference. Vinsel, "Maintainers 2016 Papers." Similarly Lundy, Patterson, and O'Neill argue that small businesses in "resource-poor and politically unstable settings" necessarily need to use what would historically be called entrepreneurial practices. Lundy, Patterson, and O'Neill, "Drivers and Deterrents."

25. The multiplier effect is the result of local investment, which keeps more money circulating within the community, which then translates to an even greater increase in a community's income.

26. V. Lambert, *Choctaw Nation*; Dennison, *Colonial Entanglements*; Bruyneel, *Third Space of Sovereignty*.

27. C. Lewis, "Economic Sovereignty in Volatile Times." This use of the concept of economic bases draws from Gudeman, *Anthropology of Economy*.

28. I construct these by drawing from consolidated framings of violence and hegemony as outlined by Michel Foucault, Michael Taussig, and Peter Redfield.

29. McKie, "EBCI Part of Historic Class Action Settlement"; Cobell v. Salazar (Cobell XXII), 573 F.3d 808 (D.C. Cir. 2009).

30. C. Lewis, "Economic Sovereignty in Volatile Times."

31. Although what constitutes these economic resources and the amount of economic resources needed to exercise sovereignty are as varied as the Native Nations themselves. Cattelino, *High Stakes*, 123.

32. Cattelino, "Double Bind," 236; D. H. Smith, *Modern Tribal Development*.

33. Kennedy et al., *American Indian Business*; Gladstone, "All My Relations"; Bressler, Campbell, and Elliott, "A Study of Native American Small Business Ownership: Opportunities for Entrepreneurs"; Garsombke and Garsombke, "Non-Traditional vs. Traditional Entrepreneurs;" Colbourne, "An Understanding of Native American Entrepreneurship."

34. O'Neill, *Working the Navajo Way*; Kamper, *Work of Sovereignty*.

35. Escobar, *Encountering Development*; Colloredo-Mansfeld, *Native Leisure Class*; Chibnik, *Crafting Tradition*; Gudeman, *Anthropology of Economy*; Little, *Mayas in the Marketplace*.

36. Gudeman, *Anthropology of Economy*; Williamson, Imbroscio, and Alperovitz, *Making a Place for Community*.

37. Starnes, *Creating the Land of the Sky*, 145.

38. For more on the roles of Cherokee women, matrilineality, and women's leadership positions historically, see Perdue, *Cherokee Women*.

39. Povinelli, *Economies of Abandonment*; Michaelsen and Johnson, *Border Theory*; Farmer, *Pathologies of Power*.

Chapter One

1. Kent, interview with the author, May 2016.

2. P. J. Deloria, *Indians in Unexpected Places*.

3. Usner, *Indian Work*.

4. Champagne, "Tribal Capitalism and Native Capitalists," 308.

5. Wolf, *Europe and the People without History*, 285.

6. Charles and Harjo, *Gary "Litefoot" Davis Story*. Gary and Carmen Davis are launching their first issue of *Native Business Magazine* (online and in print) in 2018, followed by the associated "Native Business Summit" in 2019. Gary is also the executive director of the Native American Financial Services Association, helping to overcome American Indians lending issues.

7. Harmon, *Rich Indians*, 277; Gercken and Pelletier, Gambling on Authenticity, 45; Champagne, "Tribal Capitalism and Native Capitalists"; Malkin et al., "Native Entrepreneurship"; Jacobsen, "Summary Paper Series."

8. Colloredo-Mansfeld, *Native Leisure Class*, 124 (emphasis added).

9. Sleeper-Smith, *Indian Women and French Men*, 3.

10. Esarey, *Colonialism before Contact*. For another historical archaeology perspective, see also Lance Greene and Mark R. Plane, eds., *American Indians and the Market Economy, 1775–1850*.

11. Miller, "Economic Development in Indian Country."

12. The association of small businesses with American ideals of rugged individualism rose during the Cold War in which they were seen as "bastions of individualism and democracy against the threats of totalitarianism and communism." Blackford, *History of Small Business in America*, 131.

13. Social entrepreneurship, although difficult to define worldwide, often begins with the business mentioning an explicit or implicit social problem-solving mission. Terjesen et al., "2009 Report on Social Entrepreneurship."

14. Hosmer, *American Indians in the Marketplace*, 5.

15. Cattelino, "Double Bind of American Indian Need-Based Sovereignty."

16. Hosmer, *American Indians in the Marketplace*, 153 (emphasis added).

17. Ibid., 219.

18. Ibid., 223.

19. Cattelino, "Casino Roots," 85.

20. Ibid., 86.

21. Finger, *Cherokee Americans*; Finger, *Eastern Band of Cherokees, 1819–1900*.

22. These business owners are not named, but they presumably date back to 1917, when there were six stores on the Qualla Boundary. Finger, *Cherokee Americans*, 7–23. The owners were identified as a white man, a "half-blood" Eastern Band citizen, an Eastern Band citizen, a white man married to an Eastern Band citizen, an Eastern Band citizen partnered in business with a white man, and a white man leasing a building from an Eastern Band citizen, with the businesses ranging from grocery stores to a wagon and harness firm. Ibid., 21.

23. Anderson and Lueck, "Land Tenure and Agricultural Productivity on Indian Reservations"; Beaulieu, "Curly Hair and Big Feet."

24. Peredo et al., "Towards a Theory of Indigenous Entrepreneurship."

25. Dana, "Special Issue: Entrepreneurship among Indigenous Peoples."

26. BeyondBuckskin.com is a retail website for American Indian fashion designers, founded by Jessica Metcalfe (a Turtle Mountain Chippewa). The site features everything from jewelry to clothing; it also includes a blog providing information on related topics, such as what constitutes an "authentic" indigenous product. Met-

calfe, "Is Manitobah Mukluks Indian Enough?" The 1491s, founded by Ryan Red Corn (Osage Nation), are a comedy troupe that produces videos—ranging from comedy skits to PSAs on domestic violence—and travels to perform live. Other members include Dallas Goldtooth (Mdewakanton Dakota-Diné), Migizi Pensoneau (Ponca-Ojibwe), Bobby Wilson (Sisseton-Wahpeton Dakota), and Sterlin Harjo (Seminole-Muscogee). 1491s, "About the 1491s."

27. See Hoover, "From Garden Warriors to Good Seeds"; Hoover, "The River Is in Us"; Yellowtail, "B.Yellowtail."

28. Dana, "Editorial."

29. This is only one criticism leveled at the larger concept of social entrepreneurialism. Others have pointed out significant issues, such as how social entrepreneurialism does not address structural barriers or engage the "truly poor." Moseley, "Limits of New Social Entrepreneurship."

30. Hindle, "Brave Spirits on New Paths," 137.

31. Dana, Dana, and Anderson, "Theory-Based Empirical Study of Entrepreneurship in Iqaluit, Nunavut."

32. Willmott, "Radical Entrepreneurs."

33. The Northwest Area Foundation and Corporation for Enterprise Development report on Native entrepreneurs specifies in its categories, "Entrepreneurs are people who create and grow enterprises. This definition is deliberately widely drawn to encompass *aspiring entrepreneurs* (those who are attracted to the idea of creating an enterprise, including young people), *survival entrepreneurs* (those who resort to enterprise creation to supplement their incomes), *lifestyle entrepreneurs* (those who create enterprises in order to pursue a certain lifestyle or live in a particular community), *growth entrepreneurs* (those who are motivated to develop and expand their businesses to create jobs and wealth), *serial entrepreneurs* (those who go on to create several growth businesses) and *social entrepreneurs* (people who create and grow enterprises or institutions that are primarily for public and community purposes." Malkin et al., "Native Entrepreneurship," 57.

34. Yanagisako, *Producing Culture and Capital*, 7.

35. Pfister, *Individuality Incorporated*, 119.

36. Corntassel and Witmer, *Forced Federalism*; Flaherty, "American Indian Land Rights, Rich Indian Racism, and Newspaper Coverage in New York State, 1988–2008"; Harmon, *Rich Indians*.

37. Wolfe, "Settler Colonialism and the Elimination of the Native." As Pickering discusses in *Lakota Culture, World Economy*, the construction and perpetuation of American Indian economic identity as "in poverty" monetarily benefits many non-Natives, such as through the low-cost leasing of reservation lands to cattle ranchers. Pickering, *Lakota Culture, World Economy*, 126.

38. Harmon, *Rich Indians*, 277; Povinelli, *Economies of Abandonment*.

39. See Harris, "Whiteness as Property," as well as mid-twentieth-century termination policies. A recent example of this was former governor Schwarzenegger's campaign against the sovereignty of California Native Nations based on making them pay their "fair share." This campaign helped elect him and was followed by years of illegal practices against the Indian Gaming and Regulatory Act (IGRA);

these were eventually taken to the U.S. Supreme Court, which ruled in favor of the Native Nations and IGRA. Mazzetti, "How Arnold Schwarzenegger Violated Tribal Sovereignty."

40. Corntassel and Witmer, *Forced Federalism*. See also Flaherty, "American Indian Land Rights," for an excellent analysis of media coverage specifically propagating "rich Indian racism." It is important to note, as Usner details in *Indian Work*, that much of the same rhetorics of authenticity, assimilation, and disappearance can be found historically regarding any work taken up by American Indians beyond what settler-colonial society deems as "legitimate subsistence activities." Usner, *Indian Work*, 13; Starn, *Nightwatch*, 51.

41. Hanson, "Contemporary Globalization and Tribal Sovereignty," 296. This political ideology emerges regularly: "Gianforte Says Indian Reservations Hinder Free Markets."

42. Gilens and Page, "Testing Theories of American Politics."

43. Hanson, "Contemporary Globalization and Tribal Sovereignty," 297.

44. W. Brown, "Neoliberalism and the End of Liberal Democracy."

45. Cattelino, "Double Bind of American Indian Need-Based Sovereignty."

46. O'Neill, *Working the Navajo Way*, 13.

47. Hosmer and O'Neill, *Native Pathways*, 20.

48. O'Neill, *Working the Navajo Way*, 13, 134, 156.

49. Rich, Lossiah, and Driver, ᏆᎥᎫᎩ ᎤᏃ ᎢᏍ (A Very "Wendy" Day).

50. Blankenship, interview with the author, December 2009.

51. Ibid.

52. Yanagisako, *Producing Culture and Capital*, 13.

53. Ibid., 188.

54. As Yanagisako clarifies, "Neither families nor capitalism in Italy are products of Italian culture. Italian culture, after all, is merely a heuristic device. To claim that it produces Italian families and Italian capitalism—both of which encompass a wide range of forms and practices—is to succumb to the fallacy of reification." Yanagisako, *Producing Culture and Capital*, 188.

55. Porter Gaunt, "'Because I Have Been Given Much.'"

56. Lancaster, interview with the author, February 2010.

57. I have not given details of these two families due to serious health issues that arose during and after my fieldwork.

58. Pickering, *Lakota Culture, World Economy*.

59. Smith, interview with the author, December 2009.

60. This store would eventually succumb to the lingering effects of the Great Recession. As fewer wealthy families built houses in the mountains, the need for original art for these homes declined to an unsustainable low.

61. McKie, "Record Park Visitation Continues in 2015."

62. Beard-Moose, *Public Indians, Private Cherokees*. When it looked as if a Walmart would open in Cherokee, one of the most common complaints that I heard was that it was being built on a side road that many locals use to bypass the heavy tourist traffic. This particular road was one of the few that would take you around the tourist's main drag—and its subsequent traffic jams. Having the Walmart there

would essentially reveal the little-used path and literally pave the way for more tourists to foray into the locals' space.

63. Beard-Moose, *Public Indians, Private Cherokees.*

64. See Bruner's "touristic borderzones." Bruner, *Culture on Tour.*

65. Duggan, "Tourism, Cultural Authenticity, and the Native Crafts Cooperative."

66. Respondent asked for anonymous name. Bethany, interview with the author, August 2009.

67. Seagle, interview with the author, October 2009.

68. Baxter, "The 3/50 Project."

69. The math behind this is based on half of the employed population contributing $50 each month, generating a total of $42.6 billion in revenue. This combines with the multiplier effect, resulting in $68 out of every $100 returning to the community versus $43 for national chain stores. Baxter, "The 3/50 Project."

70. Although the Cherokee Chamber of Commerce (COC) seems like a good organization to host this kind of advertisement, it has to serve all businesses; this includes franchises, chains, and large stores as well as small businesses. Therefore, it may be seen as working against other members of the COC if it promotes the "Buy Local" or related movements.

71. Cherokee Business Development Center and the Sequoyah Fund, "Support Small Business Saturday."

72. McKie, "Cherokee to Start Open Air Market."

73. For a "non-capitalocentric" exploration of how mutually interdependent community economies exist alongside, and subversively with, capitalism, see Gibson-Graham, *Postcapitalist Politics.*

74. W. Brown, "Neoliberalism and the End of Liberal Democracy," 59. Although I do not focus here on business practices outside those that are regulated, regular informal and underground market activities occur on the Qualla Boundary, especially in the sale of food products and "flea-market" goods.

Chapter Two

1. King et al., "Why Restaurants Fail."

2. Williamson and Williamson, interview with the author, January 20, 2010.

3. Because the EBCI define its tourism as *heritage tourism*, I will use this term going forward in discussions of the EBCI's industry. Eastern Band of Cherokee Indians, "Eastern Band of Cherokee Indians Economic Development." This heritage tourism focus has remained strong over recent years, as reflected in the 2004 Eastern Band of Cherokee Indian Heritage Development Initiative and the Qualla 2020 initiative.

4. P. C. Smith, *Everything You Know about Indians Is Wrong*, 45.

5. Duggan, "Tourism, Cultural Authenticity, and the Native Crafts Cooperative."

6. Fariello, *Cherokee Basketry*; Fariello, *Cherokee Pottery*; Duggan, "Tourism, Cultural Authenticity, and the Native Crafts Cooperative."

7. Finger, *Cherokee Americans.*

8. Dann, *Language of Tourism*, 218.

9. Anderson, "The Western Film . . . by the numbers!"

10. L. C. Lambert and M. Lambert, *Up from These Hills*, 189.

11. The nearby town of Forks reports that there were 5,000 tourists in 2004 and 73,000 in 2010. Nelson, "The Quileute Reservation copes with tourists brought by 'Twilight'"; B. L. Smith, "The Twilight Saga and the Quileute Indian Tribe."

12. *Cherokee One Feather*, "Poll Facebook Responses"; P. Lambert, "Principal Chief's Report for February 2017."

13. Graff, "Cherokee, North Carolina."

14. See appendix C, Chief Hicks discussing the number of visitors to the downtown area in the past, reminiscing that "many of us can remember the days, long before gaming, when the streets of Cherokee were packed with visitors excited about what we had to offer."

15. MacCannell, *The Tourist*.

16. Handler, "Authenticity."

17. Early anthropologists would be complicit in associating biological measurements with financial competency by claiming to measure whiteness/Indianness. In regard to the scratch test, Smithsonian anthropologists Jenks and Hrdlicka used this measure in an attempt to quantify whiteness/Indianness based on hyperaemia (skin reddening), along with other measurements, such as hair samples, in order to conclude how "competent" a person was to manage land holdings. Beaulieu, "Curly Hair and Big Feet"; D. H. Thomas, *Skull Wars: Kennewick Man, Archaeology, and the Battle for Native American Identity*; Samuels, *Fantasies of Identification*.

18. Handler, "Authenticity," 3.

19. *Implementation of Indian Gaming Regulatory Act: Oversight Hearing Before the Subcommittee on Native American Affairs, Committee on Natural Resources, House of Representatives, 103rd Cong., first session, on implementation of Public Law 100-497, the Indian Gaming Regulatory Act of 1988*.

20. MacCannell, *The Tourist*.

21. Bruner, *Culture on Tour*.

22. O'Brien, *Firsting and Lasting*, xxi.

23. Duggan, "Tourism, Cultural Authenticity, and the Native Crafts Cooperative"; Beard-Moose, *Public Indians, Private Cherokees*.

24. In the case of Migzi, a Ponca-Ojibwe activist, writer, and member of the 1491s American Indian comedy troupe, a trip to Cherokee as a child left a lifelong negative imprint about pan-Indianism after seeing early chiefing in action. Pensoneau, "1491s Q&A."

25. Dombrowski, *Against Culture*, 109.

26. Ibid., 110.

27. Schilling, "Native Actors Walk Off Set of Adam Sandler Movie After Insults to Women, Elders."

28. Finger, *Cherokee Americans*, 163.

29. Another increase of 13 percent in heritage tourism occurred between 1996 and 2003. Travel Industry Association of America, *Historical/Cultural Traveler*.

30. Diamond, Bainbridge, and Hayes, *Reel Injun*.

31. This resistance was not only from the non-Native population—there were also American Indians who resented this movement as pan-Indian and violent. Cobb, *Native Activism in Cold War America*; Means and Wolf, *Where White Men Fear to Tread*.

32. Means and Wolf, *Where White Men Fear to Tread*; Frazier, *On the Rez*; Reinhardt and Kidwell, *Ruling Pine Ridge*.

33. Today, American Indians are still faced with substantially higher rates of violence, such as the case of police murders of American Indians that exceed those, proportionally, of any other U.S. population. Lakota People's Law Project, "Native Lives Matter."

34. Court cases initiated by American Indians advanced a variety of issues during this era including those of economic justice. In one such case, the Supreme Court found in favor of Native Nation economic sovereignty in *McClanahan v. Arizona State Tax Commission* (1973) when it ruled that states cannot tax American Indians who live and work on reservations.

35. Josephy, Nagel, and Johnson, *Red Power*.

36. Such as V. Deloria, *Custer Died for Your Sins*; Thomas and Carolina, *Cherokee Values and World View*; Lewis and Ho, "Social Work with Native Americans."

37. Cobb, *Native Activism in Cold War America*; Means and Wolf, *Where White Men Fear to Tread*.

38. Kirby, Smith, and Wilkins, *New Roadside America*.

39. Colloredo-Mansfeld, *Native Leisure Class*, 197; Bendix, "Tourism and Cultural Displays."

40. Perdue, *The Cherokees*, 94.

41. Coincidentally, Dollywood began in 1961 as Rebel Railroad and reopened as Dollywood in 1986, also reinventing its image to depict a more modern portrayal of mountain culture while distancing itself from confederate symbolism.

42. See P. J. Deloria, *Playing Indian*, as well as MacCannell, *The Tourist*, on tourists' dual motivation of self-discovery (albeit in a more literal sense here) and authenticity.

43. Aversive racism is based on white denial of personal racism while unconsciously harboring negative feelings and thus implicitly acting on those feelings toward people of color. Dovidio, "Aversive Form of Racism." See also Bonilla-Silva, "Racism without Racists."

44. P. J. Deloria, *Playing Indian*.

45. This familial mythology may also feed into the oddly persistent perception by non-Natives of continuous American Indian physical and cultural disappearance. It is relatively common for those who claim unproven descendancy (that is, those who claim some unknown descendancy while also claiming not to be American Indian themselves) to, seemingly paradoxically, also perceive that American Indians are disappearing. In this case, persons who claim descendancy see themselves as the literal embodiment and evidence of this (perception of) disappearance—both physically, in their inability to produce enough "blood" to be American Indian, and culturally, in their lack of any Native Nation–specific practices or connection to community. Although this may not be a conscious connection, the reality of so many

people making these claims to being American Indian (particularly Cherokee)/ not American Indian points to a larger paradigmatic conception of Indianness and its continued existence.

46. Nancy Leong's concept of racial capitalism, "in which a white individual or a predominantly white institution derives social or economic value from associating with individuals with nonwhite racial identities," is also applicable here, being most readily apparent for American Indians in white claims that go beyond mere "associations with" to claims of *being* American Indian. Leong, "Racial Capitalism."

47. Lancaster, interview with the author, February 2010.

48. As Benedict Anderson argues, "Communities are to be distinguished, not by their falsity/genuineness, but by the style in which they are imagined." B. R. Anderson, *Imagined Communities*, 6.

49. Fariello, *Cherokee Pottery*, 121.

50. EBCI Commerce Department, "Public Notice Concerning 'Chiefing'"; Jumper, "Editorial."

51. *Cherokee One Feather*, "Poll: What Is Your Opinion of Chiefing?"

52. Museum of the Cherokee Indian, "Cherokee Friends Kick Off Season."

53. Blankenship, interview with the author, December 2009.

54. Bender, *Signs of Cherokee Culture*.

55. Eastern Band of Cherokee Indians, "Cherokee Preservation Foundation."

56. Museum of the Cherokee Indian, "18th Century Cherokee Clothing Workshops."

57. Foltz, "CPF Announces 19 New Grants Totaling over $2M."

58. J. Anderson, *Time Machines*.

59. "List of Open-Air and Living History Museums in the United States"; ALHFAM, "Living History Sites;" "Association for Living History, Farm and Agricultural Museums" (until 2018 when their conference was hosted in Tahlequah, Oklahoma, the capital of the Cherokee Nation).

60. Cherokee Preservation Foundation, "CPF Announces 19 New Grants Totaling $2.3M."

61. Thompson, Staging "the Drama."

62. Ibid.; EBCI Travel & Promotion, "Greater Cherokee Tourism Council Formed."

63. McKie, "Museum to Host Southeast Tribes Festival."

64. "Give Us Your Thoughts."

65. McKie, "Youth Hold Meet the Candidates Forum."

66. According to the *One Feather*, "The new Park will be culturally-sensitive and correct and Entech [consulting] will work closely with EBCI cultural advisors. . . . They want to be culturally correct in everything that they do. They want to create a class A park." McKie, "World-Renowned Firm to Revamp, Reopen Fun Park."

67. McKie, "Cherokee Fun Park Re-Opens."

68. Ledford, "Commentary." Fishing has been a cornerstone of the tourism industry on the Qualla Boundary (Altman, *Eastern Cherokee Fishing*), with the EBCI hosting large derbies and even raising its own trout (including the golden-colored palomino trout in its trophy waters) to stock the local waters.

69. Office of Economic Development, Downtown Cherokee Revitalization—Design Guidelines (emphasis added).

70. Ibid.

71. Deas, "Final Notice—Sign Ordinance Enforcement"; Eastern Band of Cherokee Indians, Cherokee Code of the Eastern Band of Cherokee Indians, Sec. 136.

72. T. O. P. Office, "Budget Council Results—May 31, 2011."

73. Foltz, "CPF Announces 19 New Grants Totaling over $2M."

74. Hicks, "Paid Political Ad: Sustainable Development and Cultural Tourism."

75. Non-business changes in Cherokee signage have also occurred recently, including street signs written in English and Cherokee syllabary. Bender, *Signs of Cherokee Culture*.

76. Most tourists who come to Cherokee from neighboring residences do so because it is a quick, and cheap, weekend outing.

77. L. C. Lambert and M. Lambert, *Up from These Hills*, 166.

78. McKie, "Youth Hold Meet the Candidates Forum."

79. Cunningham, Solomon, and Muramoto, "Alcohol Use among Native Americans Compared to Whites." "Researchers at the University of Arizona have found that Native Americans abstain from alcohol far more often than do whites, that fewer Native Americans than whites are light or moderate drinkers and that the two groups engage in binge and heavy drinking at pretty much the same rates." Lee, "Study Says the 'Drunken Indian' Is a Myth."

80. *Cherokee One Feather*, "Reader Feedback Sought"; McCoy, "Letter to the Editor"; Ledford, "Letter to the Editor"; Brown, "Letter to the Editor."

81. Arch, "Qualla Arts and Crafts to Host Labor Day Open Air Market."

82. Blankenship, interview with the author, December 2009.

83. Williamson and Williamson, interview with the author, January 2010.

84. Bethany, interview with the author, August 2009.

85. This was part of the Getting Retail Right program, sponsored by the Sequoyah Fund and taught by merchandising consultants Jerry and Laurette Zwickel. Cash prizes were also awarded for "those businesses making the greatest improvements based on what they learned from the program." Seagle, "'Getting Retail Right' Program Wraps Up."

86. Respondent asked for anonymous name. Bob, interview with the author, November 2009.

87. Smith, interview with the author, December 2009.

88. The significance of artists in innovating national and community representation is discussed in depth in Michael Chibnik's book, *Crafting Tradition*.

89. This is one of the aspects of small-business ownership that the Qualla-T program highlights with its incorporation of historical and cultural training into the customer-service program for employees of Cherokee small businesses.

90. Beard-Moose, *Public Indians, Private Cherokees*.

91. Lancaster, interview with the author, February 2010.

92. Bethany, interview with the author, August 2009.

93. The conflict in choosing whether to produce Native-styled art is a long-standing question, addressed in depth on both an individual artist (Morrison and Houser) and a systemic level (the National Museum of the American Indian). P. C. Smith, *Everything You Know about Indians Is Wrong*; Montiel, "Art of George

Morrison and Allan Houser"; Vizenor, "George Morrison"; Martinez, "This Is (Not) Indian Painting."

94. Seagle, "Sequoyah Fund Progress Report 2014."

95. McChesney, "(Art)Writing," 6.

96. For example, there is an entire journal dedicated to this topic: *Journal of Sustainable Tourism*.

Chapter Three

1. Stynes, Hornback, and Propst, "Money Generation Model (MGM2) Reports."

2. At the time of my initial fieldwork, there were over 14,253 enrolled citizens, over 8,092 of whom lived on the reservation. Eastern Band of Cherokee Indians, "Eastern Band of Cherokee Indians Government."

3. Bruyneel, *Third Space of Sovereignty*.

4. Teuton, *Cherokee Stories of the Turtle Island Liars' Club*, 76.

5. Perdue, *Cherokee Nation and the Trail of Tears*, xiii.

6. Ibid., 91.

7. Thornton, *American Indian Holocaust and Survival*.

8. Carroll, *Roots of Our Renewal*.

9. They were composed of the Qualla Indians, living farther into the mountains, and the Cherokee Nation Indians, living near New Echota. Perdue, *Cherokee Nation and the Trail of Tears*, 126.

10. Ibid.

11. L. C. Lambert and Michael Lambert, *Up from These Hills*, xxi, 4–7; Finger, *Eastern Band of Cherokees, 1819–1900*, 41, 83; Perdue, *Cherokee Nation and the Trail of Tears*, 126. The separation between western and eastern Cherokees would be acknowledged by the Supreme Court in 1885. Adams, *Who Belongs?*, 134. At this time, and until the Fourteenth Amendment, states rather than the federal government conferred citizenship, and previous treaties did not guarantee citizenship, thus making it necessary to use a combination of tactics to remain in North Carolina. Furthermore, different groups of Cherokees (the Qualla Indians, the Cherokee Nation citizens in North Carolina, and others) pursued a variety of these strategies to remain in North Carolina. Finger-Smith outlines five strategies that Cherokee people used: in 1819, the treaty separation of the "Citizen Cherokees"; providing certificates of exemption from removal (those who had married white partners); joining Oochella's Band (fugitive); resisting removal (various evasions); and escaping after being removed. Chavez and Finger-Smith, "EBCI Ancestors Remained East for Various Reasons."

12. Perdue, *Cherokee Nation and the Trail of Tears*, 126.

13. Finger, *Eastern Band of Cherokees, 1819–1900*, 188.

14. Ibid., 45, 155.

15. Barker, "Corporation and the Tribe," 256.

16. The Alaska Native Claims Settlement Act of 1971—as opposed to instituting federal recognition as used in the continental United States—created thirteen Alaska Native Regional Corporations (Alaska Native Corporations or ANCSA Corpora-

tions) in which citizens became "shareholders" of stock in their regional or village corporation.

17. Simpson, *Mohawk Interruptus*, 128–29.

18. Finger, *Eastern Band of Cherokees*, 120.

19. Finger, *Cherokee Americans*, 47.

20. Ibid., 118–19.

21. Adams, *Who Belongs?*, 142.

22. Ibid., 153 (emphasis added).

23. Finger, *Eastern Band of Cherokees, 1819–1900*; Adams, *Who Belongs?*

24. Adams, *Who Belongs?*, 160 (emphasis added).

25. Finger, *Cherokee Americans*.

26. Adams, *Who Belongs?*

27. Ibid., 142, 165.

28. Cherokee Nation, Constitution of the Cherokee Nation. In addition, the primary criteria of being able to trace your lineal descent to the Dawes Rolls means that an applicant's parents do not have to be enrolled citizens for an applicant to become a Cherokee Nation citizen.

29. Finger, *Cherokee Americans*; McKie, Final Enrollment Audit Report Submitted. Although the circumstances of the Cherokee Nation differ—greatly, in some cases—from those of the EBCI legally, politically, economically, and culturally regarding citizenship qualifications, in *Blood Politics* Circe Sturm offers a perspective on the settler-colonial state's influences and requirements in the development of Cherokee Nation qualifications (especially as related to constructions of race and racialized laws in the South), as well as what it means to have access, or not, to this citizenship.

30. *Cherokee One Feather*, "Poll: What Do You Feel Gives You Native American Identity."

31. Neely, *Snowbird Cherokees*.

32. As an interesting side note, throughout my fieldwork, Google Maps, known for its extraordinarily detailed mapping of the world via cars and satellite imagery, did not have Cherokee, North Carolina, listed in its database at all. It also had no reference to *any* reservations in the United States, despite their jurisdictional importance, until roughly 2011. By 2012, there was a very faint, light gray designation for reservations, but no text explaining why they were a different color or acknowledging them. In 2015, the reservations were once again erased unless you specifically searched for them, at which point they were marked (with an improved level of accuracy) as a pink space. As of this writing, if you look for and click on the text "Eastern Cherokee Reservation," Google Maps returns a search for the boundary lines as "Eastern Cherokee Reservation, Charleston, NC," but does fairly accurately map the Qualla Boundary, including Murphy and Snowbird.

33. SpaceX is currently developing the Starlink satellite broadband communications system that could provide rural access; plans are for full functionality by 2024. X (formerly Google X) hopes to accomplish a similar goal with its Project Loon high-altitude balloons (no estimated launch date has been given).

34. Hubbs, "BalsamWest FiberNET."

35. Cherokee Broadband, "Got Internet? Cherokee Broadband Can Help."

36. Lewis, "Case of the Wild Onions."

37. McKie, "Youth Hold Meet the Candidates Forum."

38. Eastern Band of Cherokee Indians, Cherokee Code of the Eastern Band of Cherokee Indians.

39. Seagle, interview with the author, October 2009; Seagle, interview with the author, June 2017.

40. McKie, "DOI Proposes Leasing Reform on Indian Lands"; United States Senate Committee on Indian Affairs, "Barrasso Introduces the Interior Improvement Act"; Jumper, "Housing Summit Shines Light on Long Standing Issues."

41. Another scenario is that new business owners may take the first lease that becomes available in order to launch their business but quickly find themselves in a bad leasing situation, which forces them to relocate within the Qualla Boundary (at potentially large cost). This has happened with both Tribal Grounds and Cherokee by Design.

42. Otwell, *Tribe Buying Land for Casino.*

43. Lambert, *Choctaw Nation,* 211.

44. Murphy NC Land, "Great American Land Sale" (emphasis added).

45. Holland, "Place Names in Cherokee County.""

46. It has also been suggested that the trust status of the Qualla Boundary (i.e., prohibitions against non-Native land ownership) keeps the number of locally owned businesses higher than is seen elsewhere in western North Carolina; this is arguably a contributing factor. Starnes, *Creating the Land of the Sky,* 145.

47. In actor network theory, the land could be envisioned as an actor in this network that contains its own transferable cultural capital, thus creating a social capital via the networking of Eastern Band people to land, and tourists to "knowing" the "authentic" land and "authentic" people. Of course, the more dangerous corollary to the marking of the bounded property as indigenous space is that unmarked property is then normalized as nonindigenous space.

48. Richards, "Production and Consumption of European Cultural Tourism" (emphasis added).

49. She adds that this "socio-spatial structure is organized around visual consumption and the products of culture industries." Zukin, "Socio-Spatial Prototypes of a New Organization of Consumption," 39, 45.

50. Colloredo-Mansfeld, *Native Leisure Class,* 196.

51. Economically, they also suffer similarly to the Gatlinburg sprawl businesses, although on a smaller scale, from the fatigue of being far from the downtown area easily accessible by tourists.

52. Richards, "Production and Consumption of European Cultural Tourism."

53. Britton, "Tourism, Capital, and Place," 462.

54. Ibid., 464.

55. Smith, interview with the author, December 2009.

56. Bethany, interview with the author, August 2009.

57. Lewis, "Case of the Wild Onions."

58. Chavez, "Duke Energy Halts Substation Construction near Kituwah Mound."

59. McKie, "Donations Sought for Fire Victims."

60. M. F. Brown, *Who Owns Native Culture?*

61. The issue of price gouging—especially regarding sacred sites—of Native Nations that own economically powerful enterprises, such as casinos, has yet to be fully explored academically but has been noted by Eastern Band citizens. In a letter written to the *One Feather*, Harold Rattler questioned the council's decision to pay the asking "purchase price of deceased tribal members" (here, for the twelve acres of the Tallulah Mound) of $170,000, when the average market price for neighboring land was $5,000 per acre. He states, "Cherokee County–Snowbird Rep. Jones stated that the average price for land in that area was $5000 per acre. Big Rep. McCoy stated that 'everyone thinks we're swimming in money.' This would lead people to believe that 'modern day atrocities' are still being committed against our people by price gouging sacred land. . . . With that being said, 'Was the price too high?'" Rattler, "Tallulah Mound . . . Was the Price Too High?"

62. McKie, "Tribe to Receive 35 Acres near Kituwah in Settlement." These issues of power (fuel) versus the powerful are common occurrences across Indian Country; for an in-depth ethnography of these dilemmas regarding the Diné Nation, see Powell, *Landscapes of Power.*

63. The status of first descendants as non–American Indians was recently affirmed during a murder case in which the defendant (found guilty) was determined "by Superior Court Judge Brad Letts, an EBCI tribal member, that Nobles [a first descendant of the EBCI] did not meet the criteria of being an American Indian." *Cherokee One Feather*, "Nobles Found Guilty in 2012 Murder."

64. Eastern Band of Cherokee Indians, Cherokee Code of the Eastern Band of Cherokee Indians, Sec. 28-2.

65. Abe, interview with the author, February 2010.

66. Finger, *Cherokee Americans*, 174.

67. Eastern Band of Cherokee Indians, Cherokee Code of the Eastern Band of Cherokee Indians, Sec. 115-8.

68. A poll in the *One Feather* also posited another disenrollment cause, asking, "What would be the appropriate action for the Tribe if an EBCI tribal member is convicted of selling, distributing, manufacturing, or trafficking narcotic drugs?" Fifty-two percent of those polled voted for "Disenrollment and Banishment," with another 5 percent voting for "Disenrollment" alone. *Cherokee One Feather*, "Cherokee One Feather* Poll of the Week Results: Convictions."

69. McKie, "First Descendants Lose Life Estate, Land."

70. EBCI Enrollment Office, "Expanded DNA Information for EBCI Enrollment Purposes."

71. EBCI Enrollment Office, "Enrollment Fact!"

72. Eastern Band of Cherokee Indians, Cherokee Code of the Eastern Band of Cherokee Indians, Sec. 49-2.

73. Smith, interview with the author, December 2009.

74. Cherokee Nation, "Our History."

75. The 1990 IACA was built on the earlier 1935 IACA, which never had prosecutions brought under it due to its poor prosecution structure and small penalties: "(49

Stat. 891; 25 U.S.C. 305 et seq.; 18 U.S.C. 1158-59) Any person who shall willfully offer for sale any goods . . . as Indian products or Indian products of a particular Indian tribe or group . . . when such person knows such goods are not Indian products or are not Indian products of the particular Indian tribe or group, shall be guilty of a misdemeanor and be subject to a fine not exceeding $2,000 or imprisonment not exceeding six months, or both such fine and imprisonment."

76. United States Department of Interior, Indian Arts and Crafts Board.

77. M. F. Brown, *Who Owns Native Culture?*

78. United States Department of Interior, Indian Arts and Crafts Board.

79. McKie, "Tribe Establishes Cherokee Identity Protection Committee."

80. Cherokee Tri-Council, "Cherokee Tri-Council Resolutions."

81. Berman, *No Deal!*, xix; McChesney, "(Art)Writing," 2, 6.

82. Lyden, "Seminole Patchwork."

83. O'Neill, *Working the Navajo Way*, 5; Simpson, *Mohawk Interruptus*, 17; Graeber, *Debt*; Piketty, *Capital in the Twenty-First Century*.

84. Duncan, Riggs, and Blue Ridge Heritage Initiative, *Cherokee Heritage Trails Guidebook*; Otwell, "Tribe Buying Land for Casino."

Chapter Four

1. Specifically, they are based on Lt. Henry Timberlake's descriptions of the Cherokee War Dance and Eagle Tail Dance. Museum of the Cherokee Indian, "Education & Outreach."

2. Museum of the Cherokee Indian, "Warriors of AniKituhwa."

3. Goss Agency, "Case Histories and Testimonials of the Goss Agency."

4. McKie, "Cherokee Passports Issued to Visitors." See appendix G for the official press release of this event.

5. Frankel, "Cherokee Advises All Tourists to Carry Cherokee Passport." See also appendix G. A counterpoint to this lack of passports (although it has not been explicitly discussed by the EBCI) is that the refusal of various forms of passports as reified elements of a bureaucratized state (both in creating and obtaining them, as well as refusals of recognition by outside state entities) has also been discussed as a way of asserting indigenous political sovereignty. Simpson, *Mohawk Interruptus*.

6. Biolsi, "Imagined Geographies."

7. For a historical tracing of the development of the rhetoric of "special rights" with regard to the government-to-government relationship between Native Nations and the U.S. federal government tied to indigenous wealth status, see Harmon, *Rich Indians*.

8. Dennison, *Colonial Entanglements*, 131.

9. V. Lambert, *Choctaw Nation*, 259.

10. Bruyneel, *Third Space of Sovereignty*.

11. Keeping in mind that, as Vine Deloria Jr. explains, "The United States never had original sovereignty over Indian people, merely a right to extinguish the title to Indian land." V. Deloria, *Custer Died for Your Sins*, 38.

12. Miner, *Corporation and the Indian*, x.

13. Barker, "Corporation and the Tribe."

14. National Congress of American Indians, *Sovereign Immunity.*

15. Bates Assocs, LLC v. 132 Assocs, LLC, 290 Mich App 52, 64; 799 NW2d 177 (2010).

16. Cedar Band Corporation, "Suh'dutsing Technologies."

17. Mississippi Band of Choctaw Indians, "Businesses"; Malcolm Wiener Center for Social Policy, *State of the Native Nations.*

18. Peroff, *Menominee Drums.*

19. Cattelino, "Double Bind of American Indian Need-Based Sovereignty"; Dennison, *Colonial Entanglements,* 182.

20. Capriccioso, "Tribes among Biggest Campaign Contributors."

21. Ibid.

22. The EBCI were ninth in top donations for 2010 ($360,500); the 2016 voting year significantly altered previous donation patterns, and the EBCI ($294,850) was pushed down to seventeenth as millions ($16,657,067 as opposed to $7,207,724 in 2010) poured into North Carolina above them. OpenSecrets, "North Carolina: Donors."

23. Stull, "Reservation Economic Development in the Era of Self-Determination."

24. Miller, *Reservation "Capitalism."*

25. I prefer to use the term *reclamation,* but I will also use the term *revitalization* when quoting EBCI official documents and discourses.

26. Rickert, "Menominee Seventh Grader Suspended for Saying 'I Love You' in Her Native Language."

27. These instructors were later reinstated after much discussion. In 2018, the EBCI succeeded in helping pass NC House Bill 92, which creates a framework for the EBCI to certify Cherokee language instructors who can then be recognized as state-approved teachers. McKie, "Chief Seeks New Policies Governing Cherokee Language Credits."

28. Ibid.

29. KPEP also has its own community team and manages the Junaluska Museum in Robbinsville.

30. D. H. Smith, *Modern Tribal Development*; Malcolm Wiener Center for Social Policy, *State of the Native Nations.*

31. Escobar, *Encountering Development*; Everett, "Ghost in the Machine"; Gudeman, *Anthropology of Economy*; Williamson, Imbroscio, and Alperovitz, *Making a Place for Community.*

32. Barber, "All Economies Are 'Embedded'"; Burt, *Structural Holes*; Coleman, "Social Capital in the Creation of Human Capital"; Granovetter, "Economic Action and Social Structure"; Putnam, "Prosperous Community"; Long and Roberts, *Miners, Peasants, and Entrepreneurs*; this literature also harkens back to Polanyi, *Great Transformation.*

33. Kar, *Financializing Poverty*; Sen and Majumder, "Narratives of Risk and Poor Rural Women's (Dis)-Engagements with Microcredit-Based Development in Eastern India"; Lont and Hospes, *Livelihood and Microfinance*; Bowles, Gintis, and Wright, *Recasting Egalitarianism*; Hulme, Hanlon, and Barrientos, *Just Give Money to the Poor.*

34. O'Neill, *Working the Navajo Way*, 5; Kamper, *Work of Sovereignty*, 5.

35. McKie, "Experts Help in Discussions on Constitution."

36. Wachacha, "Commentary" (emphasis added).

37. It should be noted that this is a lesson that the United States as a whole continues to struggle with. This influence of business interests on U.S. politics writ large has been an ongoing crisis that continues to especially plague Native Nations, from natural resource battles (such as Standing Rock) to the influence of lobbying (the Jack Abramoff fraud scandal, affecting Native Nations who owned gaming enterprises).

38. Finger, *Eastern Band of Cherokees, 1819–1900*; Cherokee Boys Club, "Cherokee Boys Club, Inc."

39. D. H. Smith, *Modern Tribal Development*.

40. Oakley, "Indian Gaming and the Eastern Band of Cherokee Indians."

41. McKie, "Harrah's, Tribe Re-Up Contract for 7 Years."

42. ICT Staff, "As the Eastern Band of Cherokees Expand Harrah's, Principal Chief Candidates Shift Focus to Diversification."

43. McKie, "Tribe, State Reach Compact Agreement."

44. McKie, "Harrah's Impact to Area Told in UNC Study."

45. Ibid.; Johnson, Kasarda, and Appold, "Assessing the Economic and Non-Economic Impacts of Harrah's Cherokee Casino, North Carolina," ii.

46. Miller, *Reservation "Capitalism,"* 76. Hearing before the House Committee on Interior and Insular Affairs on H.R. 4566, June 19, 1984, 62.

47. Ibid., 77.

48. For more on juridification as it relates to indigenous political economy and activism, see Goodale, "Dark Matter."

49. Inouye, Indian Gaming Regulatory Act.

50. Miller, *Reservation "Capitalism,"* 78.

51. Light and Rand, *Indian Gaming and Tribal Sovereignty*, 56–59, 70, 157; Seminole Tribe of Florida v. Florida, 517 U.S. 44 (1996).

52. These payments are often portrayed as reasonable to those unaware of the sovereign status of Native Nations and who (incorrectly) view Native Nations as a county within a state despite the fact that federally recognized Native Nations have a political and legal status that is independent from their neighboring state. By way of comparison, if North Carolina were to open a casino on the border of South Carolina, North Carolina would not be expected to form a contractual agreement with South Carolina to do so—but Native Nations are required to do just that.

53. See Kamper and Spilde, "Legal Regimenting of Tribal Wealth," for how these restrictions are intimately tied with Native Nation bond restrictions.

54. To be clear, my goal is not to make a case here for or against gaming as an economic-development strategy; rather, I am highlighting the rights of Native Nations to determine for themselves, without states' intervention, what is in their best economic interests.

55. NLRB v. Little River Band of Ottawa Indians Tribal Government, No. 7-CA-51156 (2015).

56. It can also be argued that this reflects the problematics of who the federal government deems worthy of labor protections based on the status of their work

(for-profit versus nonprofit); Kamper, *Work of Sovereignty*; National Labor Relations Board, "Jurisdictional Standards."

57. Cattelino, "Fungibility"; Barlett and Steele, "Indian Casinos"; Stevens, "NIGA Responds to *Time* Article."

58. Blattman, Fiala, and Martinez, "Economic and Social Returns to Cash Transfers"; Costello et al., "Parents' Incomes and Children's Outcomes." See Harmon, *Rich Indians*, particularly Chapter 5, "Osage Oil," for a lengthy discussion on the rhetoric of U.S. paternalistic regulation of Native Nation and American Indian wealth. Although I focus on Native Nations, this neoliberal accusation of money as enabling poverty is commonly used to subvert government welfare programs in general, such as in the "welfare queen" rhetoric.

59. Ha and Ullmer, *Economic Effects of Harrah's Cherokee Casino and Hotel on the Regional Economy of Western North Carolina*; P. Lambert, "Paid Political Ad"; Eastern Band of Cherokee Indians, Cherokee Code, Eastern Band of Cherokee Indians, Sec. 16C-3. Although it was not discussed publicly, in addition to the political rhetoric of the roll audit expunging those who had no legal claim to citizenship, it would also necessarily increase the amount of dividend payments by a maximum of 10 percent per citizen, similar to the situation of the Pechanga in California. Barker, *Native Acts*.

60. Adams, *Who Belongs?*, 139.

61. Cattelino, "Fungibility," 195. For more on the overall picture of the economic impacts of gaming on both Natives and non-Natives, see Spilde and Taylor, "Economic Evidence on the Effects of the Indian Gaming Regulatory Act on Indians and Non-Indians."

62. Barker, "Corporation and the Tribe."

63. Mondragon, "Mondragon Annual Report, 2016."

64. Kosar, "Federal Government Corporations."

65. Small Business Administration, "Tribal Enterprise Business Guide."

66. Gibson-Graham, *Postcapitalist Politics*, xxiv.

67. This figure varies widely over time, but as of January 31, 2011, the Minors' Trust Fund had 4,891 recipient accounts, with each account being worth an average of $67,416.47. McKie, "Minors Fund Discussed in Council Work Session." The lump sum has been as high as $130,000, garnering a $40,000 tax payment in 2016.

68. McKie, "Minors Fund Discussed in Council Work Session."

69. Kays, "Staggered Payments for Cherokee Minors' Fund."

70. Cherokee Preservation Foundation, *Financial Literacy*.

71. InvestNative Project, "Manage Your EBCI Money"; Spruce, "Q&A on the New Manage Your EBCI Money Program."

72. Spruce, "Q&A on the New Manage Your EBCI Money Program."

73. Although I focus on children and young adults here, Eastern Band adults are offered one-on-one counseling and can take finance workshops free of charge. Cherokee Preservation Foundation, "Financial Literacy."

74. SEED, "Stockton Economic Empowerment Demonstration."

75. Aizenman, "How to Fix Poverty."

76. Akee et al., "Young Adult Obesity and Household Income."

77. Costello et al., "Parents' Incomes and Children's Outcomes"; Costello et al., "Association of Family Income Supplements."

78. Velasquez-Manoff, "What Happens When the Poor Receive a Stipend?"

79. Costello et al., "Parents' Incomes and Children's Outcomes," 113.

80. Popular opinion on this issue of alcohol has remained mixed since this initial vote. In 2015, the *One Feather* raised the issue again in a weekly poll, asking, "Are you in favor of alcoholic beverages being available in restaurants or at events on the Qualla Boundary?" The results were 48 percent "Yes"; 30 percent "No, alcohol should not be allowed for sale anywhere on the Qualla Boundary"; 14 percent "No, it should remain only on gaming property"; and 8 percent "No, but in convenience stores sold in sealed bottles or can would be ok." *Cherokee One Feather,* "Are You in Favor of Alcoholic Beverages Being Available in Restaurants or at Events on the Qualla Boundary?" The next year, another poll asked simply, "Would you be in favor of alcohol sales in Cherokee restaurants and special events?" Fifty-four percent responded yes. *Cherokee One Feather,* "Would You Be in Favor of Alcohol Sales in Cherokee Restaurants and Special Events?"

81. The EBCI passage of the liquor allowance for the casino created many legal issues between the state of North Carolina and the EBCI over how and where the EBCI would be allowed to purchase the alcohol (which is heavily regulated in North Carolina). Nearly two years later, an agreement was hammered out allowing the EBCI to buy wholesale from the state. Blankenship, "TABCC Recognized as Sole Regulator of Alcohol for Cherokee Lands."

82. Cunningham, Solomon, and Muramoto, "Alcohol Use among Native Americans Compared to Whites." I followed the dialogues and rhetoric leading up to the decision to allow alcohol throughout my time in Cherokee and was keenly interested in the religious aspect of these discussions. Billboards were posted, letters were written, and articles were published in the *One Feather* newspaper. It was later revealed through a letter written to the newspaper that almost all of the religious rhetoric was being generated by a church from Asheville. Although many Eastern Band citizens are Christian, as was this church, and many were against alcohol on the Qualla Boundary based on their religious beliefs, the idea that an outsider would pass judgment and try to dictate EBCI decisions was blatantly offensive, as Jean C. Holt describes here: "This week, many of us received a pamphlet from Asheville in opposition of the alcohol referendum we will be voting on next week. Once again, people off the Qualla Boundary are telling us we do not have enough intelligence or reasoning to make our own decisions. . . . I thought we had moved past the old caricature portrayed in movies and cartoons of the savage drunk Indian on firewater." Holt, "Guest Commentary."

83. According to the National Indian Gaming Commission, in 2004 the 15 largest gaming facilities accounted for more than 37 percent of all gaming revenues, and the 55 largest accounted for nearly 70 percent. In 2006, 224 out of 561 Native Nations operated such facilities. Malcolm Wiener Center for Social Policy, *State of the Native Nations,* 150.

84. Although extensive studies have not been undertaken with Native Nation casinos, non–Native Nation casino studies have shown that market saturation—for

example, in Atlantic City—is a problem in which "competitive pressures are beginning to reduce the stimulative effects of established casino district." Rephann et al., "Casino Gambling as an Economic Development Strategy." It should be noted that as of 2017, there are twelve Native Nations operating twenty-three casinos in Michigan. The scope of impacts from the 1996 allowance of casinos in Detroit varied across facilities and is difficult to parse out from negative effects of the Great Recession.

85. McKie, "Youth Hold Meet the Candidates Forum."

86. ICT Staff, "As the Eastern Band of Cherokees Expand Harrah's, Principal Chief Candidates Shift Focus to Diversification."

87. Wachacha, "Commentary."

88. Although this increased competition could be highly detrimental (depending on the gaming locations), a situation can be imagined in which tourists, who often bus in groups to Native Nation gaming facilities, would also choose a "tour" of facilities that were closely situated, partially lessening the competitive impacts.

89. Mazzetti, "How Arnold Schwarzenegger Violated Tribal Sovereignty."

90. A newer challenge cropped up in 2011, as the Department of Justice ruled in December of that year that states would now be allowed to regulate online gaming operations in an attempt to generate revenue for the state. Webster, "New DOJ Position on Internet Gaming Creates Both Uncertainty and Opportunities for Tribes."

91. Sheldon, "Atlanta Will Still Have Georgia Gaming Opportunities on Its Mind in 2017."

92. As has been suggested by Eastern Band citizens for many years (supported in 2018 by the Office of Principal Chief), it would also be possible for the EBCI to start their own credit union, as the Seneca and Lakota, among a handful of other Native Nations, have done. Doing so would increase their economic sovereignty in several ways; for example, it could allow them to divest from banks that are hostile to Native Nation rights, such as those that helped fund the Dakota Access Pipeline. For casino-owning Native Nations, however, starting a banking endeavor can reignite the "double-bind" dilemma, as the "rich Indian" attention they already garner often includes overt claims that there are Native Nation–mafia affiliations. This then insinuates that a Native Nation bank would be created for the purpose of laundering money.

93. Hubbs, "BalsamWest FiberNET." The company's mission statement is "to provide open and direct access to advanced telecommunications infrastructure in Western North Carolina, North Georgia and Eastern Tennessee at prices and quality levels enjoyed in major metropolitan areas of the U.S." By 2011, it was worth around $40 million, and the EBCI has around $7 million invested in it. McKie, "BalsamWest FiberNet to Get Funds a Little Early."

94. Eastern Band of Cherokee Indians, "Eastern Band of Cherokee Indians Economic Development."

95. Weiser and Sherman, *Qualla 2020 Final Report.*

96. Hicks, "A Closer Look at Tribal Debt"; Hicks, "Paid Political Ad: Chief Hicks' Comprehensive Plan for Progress."

97. McKie, "DEBT-FREE."

98. McKie, "Minors Fund Discussed in Council Work Session."

99. Eastern Band of Cherokee Indians, "Cherokee Preservation Foundation." The CPF supports environmental initiatives such as impact studies on potential damage caused by increasing traffic and large localized growth. Since 2005, CPF and the Cherokee Cooperative Extension Service have also been sending about fourteen EBCI high school seniors to Costa Rica each year for eco-tours. These tours provide lessons and practical experiences at EARTH University, which teaches the importance of environmental protection, especially in a tourist-heavy economy. The students also meet with other indigenous groups in Costa Rica to share information about their management of these issues.

100. Cherokee Preservation Foundation, "Cherokee Preservation Foundation Announces 24 New Grants." Although the CPF is generally seen as a positive branch of the financial casino arm, some EBCI citizens are resentful of its existence because the state and federal government, via IGRA, mandated its creation. This action not so subtly implies that the federal and state governments believed the EBCI was incapable of managing its own money in a responsible manner. As Mary Wachacha says in the *Cherokee One Feather*, "We were held hostage once before by a previous governor who demanded that 5 million dollars be set aside for cultural and economic preservation and the result of that was the Preservation Foundation." Wachacha, "Commentary."

101. Eastern Band of Cherokee Indians, "Cherokee Preservation Foundation."

102. Lefler, *Under the Rattlesnake*, 58; Riggs, "Cherokee Pottery Revitalization Project."

103. Eastern Band of Cherokee Indians, "Cherokee Preservation Foundation."

104. Lewis, "Betting on Western North Carolina."

105. A referendum vote on whether to allow alcohol sales by the EBCI in EBCI-owned stores on the Qualla Boundary was defeated on May 31, 2018.

106. The name of this brewery and its beers were highly controversial on the Qualla Boundary, prompting the EBCI Tribal Council, after a citizens' petition, to direct their Attorney General to, "establish an ordinance that would regulate the use of cultural, traditional business names that appear derogatory in nature" by fall 2018. Jumper, "Attorney General to Draft a 'Cultural Protection Ordinance.'"

107. Harding, discussion with the author, January 2010.

108. Eastern Band of Cherokee Indians, "Eastern Band of Cherokee Indians Public Transit."

109. Eastern Band of Cherokee Indians, "Eastern Band of Cherokee Indians Economic Development."

110. United States Commission on Civil Rights, "Broken Promises."

111. D. H. Smith, *Modern Tribal Development*.

112. This is an issue acknowledged by the EBCI, which it is hoping to mitigate with the March 2018 passing of Ord. No. 93 creating an LLC headed by the five-person "Kituwah Economic Development" board (three Eastern Band citizens, two citizens of federally recognized Native Nations) that will conduct business on behalf of the EBCI.

113. Cornell et al., "Citizen Entrepreneurship," 199.

114. Small Business Association, "How Important Are Small Businesses to the U.S. Economy?"; Jorgensen, *Rebuilding Native Nations.*

115. Jorgensen, *Rebuilding Native Nations,* 200.

116. Cornell, "Tribal-Citizen Entrepreneurship: What Does It Mean for Indian Country, and How Can Tribes Support It?"

117. Blankenship, interview with the author, December 2009.

118. Smith, interview with the author, December 2009.

119. Waycaster, interview with the author, June 2009.

120. Jorgensen, *Rebuilding Native Nations.*

121. Williamson and Williamson, interview with the author, January 2010.

122. Cherokee Transit, "Wal-Mart Shopping Trip by Cherokee Transit."

123. Williamson and Williamson, interview with the author, January 2010.

124. Queen, interview with the author, January 2010.

125. NCAIED, "RES 2010 to Honor American Indian Business Achievement."

126. McKie, "River's Edge Named Business of the Year."

127. James, "Local Restaurants Help to Raise Money for Japan."

128. Teuton, *Red Land, Red Power,* 207, discussing Duran and Duran, *Native American Postcolonial Psychology,* 35.

129. Jorgensen, *Rebuilding Native Nations.*

130. Seagle, interview with the author, October 2009. C. Lewis, "Economic Sovereignty in Volatile Times."

131. Jenkins, interview with the author, June 2009.

132. The concept of sovereignty that I am referring to here is inherent authority, which for federally recognized Native Nations is currently entangled with the government-to-government relationship of Native Nations to the United States. It is important to acknowledge, though, that not all indigenous peoples in the United States support this form of federally recognized sovereignty. As related in the *One Feather,* "David Inciong is a Native Hawaiian and member of the Hawaiian Independence Action Alliance. He calls the bill [to equate Native Hawaiians' status to that of federally recognized] 'repugnant' and in a recent statement said the bill is 'railroading native Hawaiians into a nefarious U.S. hostage box. . . . We do not desire to be on equal footing with American Indians under the Department of the Interior nor subjected to its paternalistic practices.'" McKie, "Senate Committee Approves Native Hawaiian Bill."

133. Wilson, "Speech."

134. House Concurrent Resolution 108.

135. The reauthorization of the Violence Against Women Act in 2013 (implemented in 2015) by President Obama expanded tribal jurisdiction to non-Natives in cases of domestic violence (including dating violence and violation of protective orders).

136. Arriola, "Small Business Administration Presentation." The EBCI's Office of Budget and Finance's Revenue Office reported a sharp increase in the number of licenses during this time. In 2008, there were 329 on-site businesses on the Qualla Boundary and 161 home-based and off-Boundary vendors, for a total of 490; that increased to about 600 in 2009. It must be noted that the Cherokee Casino was also

beginning its next stage of renovation that year; therefore, some of those applications were for construction companies, including those located off-Boundary. However, those companies might have been owned by Eastern Band citizens and employed Eastern Band citizens for the work; so although they may not have been permanent fixtures on the Qualla Boundary, they certainly had a direct economic impact on it.

Chapter Five

1. In memoriam, Bruce Martin Sr. passed in June 2015; he leaves a lasting legacy of deep kindness and generosity.

2. Association of Religion Data Archives, "Interactive GIS Maps."

3. The 8(a) program bolsters minority enterprises through federal contracts; the HubZone program helps rural businesses; and Schedule 84 lists security, fire, and law enforcement physical protections.

4. Martin and Martin, interview with the author, October 2009.

5. Cherokee Preservation Foundation, "Qualla 2020."

6. McKie, "New Tribal Council Members Take Office."

7. The chief is in the executive branch and serves a four-year term. The council members serve two-year terms in the legislative branch of the EBCI (2010): Yellowhill (Rep. Alan "B." Ensley, Rep. David Wolfe), Big Cove (Rep. Perry Shell, Rep. Teresa McCoy), Birdtown (Rep. Jim Owle, Rep. Gene "Tunney" Crowe Jr.), Wolftown (Rep. Mike Parker, Rep. Dennis Edward "Bill" Taylor), and Painttown (Rep. Tommye Saunooke, Rep. Terri Henry), with Snowbird and Cherokee County communities considered as one township (Rep. Diamond Brown Jr., Rep. Adam Wachacha). Section 23 of the EBCI Charter states, "The Tribal Council is hereby fully authorized and empowered to adopt laws and regulations for the general government of the Tribe, govern the management of real and personal property held by the Tribe, and direct and assign among its members thereof, homes in the Qualla Boundary and other land held by them as a Tribe, and is hereby vested with full power to enforce obedience to such laws and regulations as may be enacted." Current standings for EBCI officials and offices can be found at https://ebci.com.

8. McCoy, "Brief Summary of the Tribal Council and Legislative Branch of the Eastern Band of Cherokee Indians."

9. This office has also been called the EBCI Division of Commerce and the "Tribal Planning Office." Jason Lambert, cited on the 2011 Native American "40 Under 40" list by the National Center for American Indian Enterprise Development (NCAIED) and an Eastern Band citizen, became the EBCI's planning and economic development director in 2010 during my fieldwork.

10. I primarily worked with the Sequoyah Fund (SF) and Cherokee Business Development (CBD) offices because they hosted the most classes and outreach efforts for small businesses and potential small-business owners. Here I met regularly with Russ Seagle (SF senior loan officer and manager of client development), Hope Husky (CBD business development specialist, Eastern Band citizen), and Nell Leatherwood (former executive director, SF) as classes were put together and events were orga-

nized. The other administrators and staff in these offices (all Eastern Band citizens) were Gloria Rattler, CBD director; Jacob Reed, CBD business development specialist; Sherrene Swayney, SF portfolio and finance manager; Kimberly Winchester, CBD business development and resource coordinator; and Lynn Blankenship, CBD office assistant. Sequoyah Fund, "Lending and Training for Business Owners."

11. V. Lambert, *Choctaw Nation*, 104.

12. Chomsky, *Profit over People*.

13. Mattera and Tarczynska, *Uncle Sam's Favorite Corporations*; Ho, "Commentary on Andrew Orta's 'Managing the Margins.'"

14. Blankenship, interview with the author, December 2009.

15. Wolfe and Crowe, interview with the author, October 2009.

16. Malkin et al., "Native Entrepreneurship."

17. Sequoyah Fund, "Lending and Training for Business Owners."

18. Seagle, personal communication, September 2011.

19. Cherokee Preservation Foundation, "Cherokee Preservation Foundation Announces 24 New Grants."

20. Benson et al., "Economic Impact of a Private Sector Micro-financing Scheme in South Dakota."

21. Smoker, "Business Spotlight: The Little People"; Smoker, "Business Spotlight: Two Crowe's Ice Cream."

22. Relatedly, Native Nation citizens and Native Nation enterprises are not legally required to negotiate with states to establish businesses (with the exception of gaming), although they may do so to maintain good relations. Despite this, current battles regarding state-law encroachment onto Native Nation jurisdictions continue to be waged from coast to coast (California, Minnesota, and New York being especially contentious) over issues such as taxes. These tax issues primarily focus on who is being taxed and who is collecting tax revenue; gasoline and cigarettes are the most prominent targets. V. Deloria, *Nations Within*; Bureau of Indian Affairs, "What Is the Relationship between the Tribes and the Individual States?" See also Native American Church of North America v. Navajo Tribal Council, 272 F. 2nd. 131 (1959); Inyo County v. Paiute-Shoshone Indians (U.S. 2003); Maynard v. Narragansett Indian Tribe, 798 F. Supp. 94 (1992); American Indian Agricultural Credit Consortium, Inc. v. Fredericks, 551 F. Supp. 1020 (1982); Wisconsin Potowatomies of Hannahville Indian Community v. Houston, 393 F. Supp. 719.

23. Like the IGRA example, as a resident of, and employee in, North Carolina, you would not pay South Carolina taxes; rather, you would pay North Carolina taxes (which are analogous to the taxes that the EBCI levies) and federal taxes (which, like all U.S. citizens, American Indians pay).

24. In North Carolina, this is currently 6.9 percent corporate tax.

25. This sales tax first began in 1952 with the advent of the Cherokee Tribal Community Services program, which was funded by the new sales tax to pay for public services. Perdue, *The Cherokees*, 92, 112; Treasury, "2011 Levy & Privilege Tax Proposal."

The EBCI is currently in discussion regarding changes to the businesses tax code. In 2015, the EBCI government announced Ordinance No. 556, which would have overhauled much of its tax system. As Cory Blankenship (then EBCI Office of Budget and Finance director), states, "The intent behind the Tax Code is mainly from a business and economic development perspective. There is a lot of gray area when it comes to taxation and where the state has the authority to tax versus where the Tribe has the authority to tax." As noted in the *One Feather*, the current code only has levy, privilege, and lease taxes, while Ordinance No. 556 would establish a Cherokee Tax Commission and add several new taxes for non–Eastern Band persons and businesses operating on EBCI lands. Blankenship continues, "Our position has been that our Tribe is providing all of the governmental services for businesses on the Reservation; however, because some of those businesses are owned by non-Indians, the state can still reach in and tax those businesses." Dual taxation is a possibility in these situations. McKie, "Tribe Considering Overhaul to Tax Code."

26. Food vendors at the Fall Festival, the largest festival for the EBCI, are often families selling homemade foods, such as bean bread, and foods that they have harvested, such as wishi mushrooms.

27. Calhoun, "Tribal Cannery Will Open Monday, May 23."

28. Queen, interview with the author, January 2010.

29. Council for Tribal Employment Rights, "TERO FAQ."

30. Ibid.; EBCI TERO Office, "EBCI TERO Welcomes You."

31. See, for example, Morton v. Mancari, 417 U.S. 535 (1974).

32. Martin and Martin, interview with the author, October 2009.

33. "The Davis-Bacon and Related Acts apply to contractors and subcontractors performing on federally funded or assisted contracts in excess of $2,000 for the construction, alteration, or repair (including painting and decorating) of public buildings or public works. Davis-Bacon Act and Related Act contractors and subcontractors must pay their laborers and mechanics employed under the contract no less than the locally prevailing wages and fringe benefits for corresponding work on similar projects in the area. The Davis-Bacon Act directs the Department of Labor to determine such locally prevailing wage rates" (United States Department of Labor, "Davis-Bacon and Related Acts").

34. Williamson and Williamson, interview with the author, January 2010.

35. McKie, "Council Approves TERO as Independent Entity"; Wildcat, interview with the author, July 2012.

36. The major issues with, and practices of, owning a rural business outside a reservation is a topic that has been covered extensively. See Gladwin et al., "Rural Entrepreneurship." At the time of my fieldwork, employee data for the Qualla Boundary was unavailable from both the EBCI and the U.S. census. That said, one cannot single out the Qualla Boundary for this specific data, as census information is available only by counties. The EBCI are included in five counties, which also include much non–Qualla Boundary land and populations.

37. Jenkins, interview with the author, June 2009. The general issue of access for rural small businesses applies to inventory as well as employees. This includes ramifications of having few distributers locally and various issues related to product deliveries to a rural address (some are not recognized by shipping services), both of which may lead to higher costs for these small businesses.

38. Smith, interview with the author, December 2009.

39. For some larger independent businesses, like Myrtle's, employees are offered the opportunity to train for different positions that are open in the off-season so that they can work year round if they wish.

40. Says Van Gundy, "Rural youth are particularly at risk for substance abuse, and stimulant use among the unemployed is higher in rural America [than in urban areas]" (Van Gundy, "Substance Abuse in Rural and Small Town America").

41. Costello et al., "Association of Family Income Supplements in Adolescence with Development of Psychiatric and Substance Use Disorders in Adulthood among an American Indian Population."

42. McKie, "Harrah's Impact to Area Told in UNC Study"; *Cherokee One Feather,* "Study: Per Cap Linked to Lower Drug Usage."

43. Perdue, *The Cherokees,* 97.

44. This would be working in an environment but not receiving direct training— for example, washing dishes in a restaurant, which does not provide direct managerial training but, when done as an employee, provides indirect training on how to manage other employees.

45. This reliance on unpaid family work has been steadily in decline in both the agricultural—a former primary contributor—and nonagricultural industries since 1948. This is due to such factors as reduced numbers of children per family, reclassification of "farmers' wives" as self-employed, and the classification of both husband and wife as business owners. Bregger, "Measuring Self-Employment in the United States."

46. Waycaster, *Cherokee Chamber of Commerce News.*

47. See appendix H for details on these offices and the particular ways they must operate.

48. Beck, "Bill Taylor Scholarship."

49. Sequoyah Fund, "Lending and Training for Business Owners."

50. Seagle, "'Getting Retail Right' Program Wraps Up." The first- and second-place winners of 2009 were Tribal Grounds Coffee, followed by Cherokee by Design. Sequoyah Fund, "Sequoyah Fund Announces Retail Winners."

51. The two-year, five-step process to be certified includes ensuring that the community is committed to the process; assessing the community's current entrepreneurial landscape; creating a comprehensive strategy for entrepreneurial growth; marshaling the community's entrepreneurial resources; and identifying and nurturing the community's most promising entrepreneurial talents.

52. McKie, "Cherokee Gains Designation as Certified Entrepreneurial Community."

53. Sequoyah Fund, "Lending and Training for Business Owners"; ONABEN, "Indianpreneurship"; ONABEN, *Indianpreneurship: A Native American Journey into Business.*

54. Rural Entrepreneurship through Action Learning (REAL) was created in 1985 and joined the Corporation for Enterprise Development (CFED) in 2004. CFED, which rebranded in 2017 to "Prosperity Now," is a national umbrella nonprofit whose purpose is to alleviate poverty by empowering low- and moderate-income people to build wealth. "North Carolina REAL Enterprises."

55. Seagle, interview with the author, June 2017.

56. "Nike Unveils Shoe Just for American Indians."

57. Keene, "Nike Gets It Right; Brand Collaborates with O'odham Designer." It should also be noted that although Nike continues to claim to support the American Indian community, (1) the target market is American Indians, which means that the proceeds going into the community from these sales are coming directly from the community, after being filtered through the purchase of shoes, and (2) Nike continues to defend selling Washington R*s*s and Chief Wahoo products, despite ongoing protests of the derogatory and racist nature of these mascots.

58. Pickering, *Lakota Culture, World Economy.*

59. The U.S. Small Business Administration has a department dedicated specifically to American Indian businesses: "Office of Native Affairs is committed to help Native American entrepreneurs have full access to the necessary business development and expansion tools available through the Agency's entrepreneurial development, lending and procurement programs" (as written to the *One Feather* by Lynn L. Douthett, SBA North Carolina district director, Nov. 10, 2010).

60. Prosperity Now, "About—Prosperity Now."

61. Sequoyah Fund, "Lending and Training for Business Owners"; Seagle, "Fall Indianpreneurship Class Graduates."

62. As described in its PowerPoint summary, these include Dedication & Loyalty, Group Harmony, Humility, Perseverance & Courage, Reciprocity & Balance, and Respect & Trust. Cherokee Chamber of Commerce, "Qualla-T Customer Service Training."

63. Williamson and Williamson, interview with the author, January 2010.

64. Oconaluftee Institute for Cultural Arts, "Oconaluftee Institute for Cultural Arts Fall Art Schedule"; Moore, "Programs Partner to Help Cherokee Artists."

65. Matthew Pegg is currently the executive director.

66. Waycaster, interview with the author, June 2009.

67. Ibid.

68. McKie, "Bringing Businesses Together."

69. Ibid.

70. Eastern Band of Cherokee Indians, "Cherokee Preservation Foundation."

71. Dingus, "5th Annual CES Career Fair."

72. Cherokee Preservation Foundation, "Cherokee Preservation Foundation Announces 24 New Grants"; Bradley, "CHS Starts American Indian Business Leaders Chapter."

Training and support for American Indian high school and college students received national support in 2015 with the launch of YES! (Youth Entrepreneurship Summit), a joint effort of United National Indian Tribal Youth (UNITY) and the National Center for American Indian Enterprise Development (NCAIED). NCAIED, "Youth Entrepreneurship Summit (YES)." Additionally, one (in progress) study concerning American Indian adolescents is examining the effect of entrepreneurial education on substance use and suicide prevention efforts. Lauren Tingey et al., "Entrepreneurship Education."

73. "LEED, or Leadership in Energy & Environmental Design, is a globally recognized symbol of excellence in green building." The ratings are LEED Certified, LEED Silver, LEED Gold, and LEED Platinum. United States Green Building Council, "About LEED."

74. These are state-adopted standards for children who "function significantly below age and grade level expectations"; it is intended to build "work ready and community college ready skills." These students must also complete in-school service, the school-based enterprise, 360 hours of community service, and 340 hours of actual paid employment. Widenhouse, interview with the author, January 2010; Public Schools of North Carolina, "Occupational Course of Study."

75. Widenhouse, interview with the author, January 2010.

76. Seagle, interview with the author, October 2009 (emphasis added).

77. As with the adult classes, the courses for children are currently pragmatic in nature, teaching only the nuts and bolts of financial management.

78. United States Commission on Civil Rights, "Broken Promises." Lewis, "Frybread Wars."

79. Groenwold, interview with the author, November 23, 2009, Cherokee, N.C. The Affordable Care Act may offer some support to IHS if it remains in place. First, it includes the "permanent reauthorization of the Indian Health Care Improvement Act, which extends current law and authorizes new programs and services within the Indian Health Service" (Indian Health Service, "Indian Health Service—Affordable Care Act"). Second, it can bolster coverage and help to leverage funding. According to an email sent by former acting IHS director Yvette Roubideaux, "A good proportion—approximately 30 percent—of our patients have no health coverage other than IHS. This is the group that may benefit the most from the Affordable Care Act [although American Indians and Alaskan Natives are not required to enroll in ACA]. . . . The Affordable Care Act is about options for additional health coverage in addition to access to the IHS health care system. In fact, we estimate that we could see up to an additional $95 million in third-party collections in FY 2014, mostly from the Medicaid expansion." Roubideaux, "Message from the Director."

80. Lewis, "Economic Sovereignty in Volatile Times."

Conclusion

1. I categorize the website as "mixed" because this individual's intent was to act as an intermediary between local EBCI artists and customers who wanted to buy their work online. In essence, this is both a local service and a tourist enterprise.

2. McKie, "Cherokee County Casino Approved."

3. Ibid.; McKie, "Class II Gaming Eyed in Cherokee County."

4. Otwell, "Tribe Buying Land for Casino."

5. Lewis, "Betting on Western North Carolina."

6. In January 2017, the Department of the Interior reversed previous interpretations of the Lumbee Act of 1956, paving the way for the Lumbee in North Carolina to apply for federal recognition.

7. Senate and House of Representatives of the United States of America in Congress, H.R. 2399, Catawba Indian Land Claims Settlement Act.

8. This casino would fall within the recent EBCI–NC compact allowances of sole Cherokee gaming rights west of I-26 (Asheville). For more on southern globalization trends, see Peacock, *Grounded Globalism*, and Peacock, Watson, and Matthews, *American South in a Global World*.

9. Weiser and Sherman, *Qualla 2020 Final Report*.

10. Cherokee Preservation Foundation, "Qualla 2020" (emphasis added). A more detailed follow-up report by the EBCI Department of Commerce entitled "Eastern Band of Cherokee Indians Comprehensive Economic Development Strategy 2018–2022" was published June 2018.

11. McKie, "Tribe Breaks Ground on New Justice Center"; McKie, "House Approves Tribal Law & Order Act."

12. Duvall, "Cherokee Retail and Business Update."

13. This is especially true of small children (with tired parents) who are picky eaters and leery of new foods. Even Teresa from Granny's Kitchen, whose food is based on comfortable familiarity, related that parents will bring in their kids with McDonald's and Burger King bags in tow to their restaurant.

14. McKie, "Wal-Mart Not Coming to Cherokee."

15. Seagle, interview with the author, October 2009; Carl, interview with the author, August 2009. These were similar to reactions found in V. Lambert, *Choctaw Nation*, 247.

16. Duvall, "Cherokee Retail and Business Update"; McKie, "Wal-Mart Not Coming to Cherokee."

17. 2010 figures. Johnson, Kasarda, and Appold, "Assessing the Economic and Non-Economic Impacts of Harrah's Cherokee Casino, North Carolina."

18. McKie, "Youth Hold Meet the Candidates Forum."

19. *Cherokee One Feather,* "Poll: Do You Think Walmart Is a Good Fit for Cherokee?"

20. Chief Lambert (the first Tribal Gaming Commission executive director, a position he held for twenty years) would be impeached in 2017, putting many negotiations and projects on hold. McKie and Jumper, "Former TGC Commissioners' Lawsuit Dismissed."

21. Anonymous personal communications (EBCI staff) with author, June 2017; *Cherokee One Feather,* "Poll Facebook Responses?"; McKie, "Council Instructs AG to Develop Medical Marijuana Ordinance."

22. Bureau of Indian Affairs, "Building Legal Infrastructure" (emphasis added).

23. This can be seen from instances such as Thomas Jefferson's suggestion to open debt-creating trading posts for American Indians and Graeber's international examination of hegemonic debt.

24. Chibnik, *Crafting Tradition*; Colloredo-Mansfeld, *Native Leisure Class*; Little, *Mayas in the Marketplace*.

25. Starn, *Nightwatch*.

26. Jacobsen, "Aboriginal and Torres Strait Islander Ways of Enterprise Clustering."

27. *Cherokee One Feather,* "EBCI Represented at AIANTA Conference."

Appendix A

1. Sequoyah Fund, "Lending and Training for Business Owners."

Appendix B

1. Eastern Band of Cherokee Indians, Cherokee Code of the Eastern Band of Cherokee Indians, Sec. 136-31.

Appendix C

1. Hicks, "Paid Political Ad: Sustainable Development and Cultural Tourism."

Appendix D

1. EBCI Enrollment Office, "Did You Know?" *Cherokee One Feather*, October 2009.
2. EBCI Enrollment Office, "Did You Know?" *Cherokee One Feather*, July 2009.
3. EBCI Enrollment Office, "Did You Know?" *Cherokee One Feather*, May 2008.
4. EBCI Enrollment Office, "Did You Know?" *Cherokee One Feather*, September 2011.
5. EBCI Enrollment Office, "Expanded DNA Information for EBCI Enrollment Purposes," *Cherokee One Feather*, July 29, 2010.

Appendix E

1. Eastern Band of Cherokee Indians, "Cherokee Code of the Eastern Band of Cherokee Indians, Sec. 49-9."

Appendix F

1. Eastern Band of Cherokee Indians, "Cherokee Code of the Eastern Band of Cherokee Indians, Sec. 49-2.

Appendix G

1. Frankel, "Cherokee Advises All Tourists to Carry Cherokee Passport."

Appendix H

1. Sequoyah Fund, "Lending and Training for Business Owners."
2. Seagle, "Sequoyah Fund—2016 Year-in-Review."
3. Eastern Band of Cherokee Indians. Economic Development.
4. Cherokee Business Development Center and Sequoyah Fund, *Cherokee Business Guide*.
5. Eastern Band of Cherokee Indians, "Cherokee Preservation Foundation."

6. McKie, "CPF Grantees Highlighted at Celebration."

7. Cherokee Business Development Center and Sequoyah Fund, *Cherokee Business Guide*.

8. Ibid.; EBCI Travel and Promotion, "Greater Cherokee Tourism Council Formed."

Appendix I

1. Weiser and Sherman, *Qualla 2020 Final Report*; Cherokee Preservation Foundation, "Qualla 2020."

Bibliography

1491s. "About the 1491s." Accessed April 12, 2017. http://www.1491s.com/who-we -are-1.

Abe. Interview with the author, Cherokee, N.C. Digital recording, February 2010.

Adams, Mikaela. *Who Belongs? Race, Resources, and Tribal Citizenship in the Native South*. New York: Oxford University Press, 2016.

Aizenman, Nurith. "How to Fix Poverty: Why Not Just Give People Money?" NPR .org, August 7, 2017. https://www.npr.org/sections/goatsandsoda/2017/08/07 /541609649/how-to-fix-poverty-why-not-just-give-people-money.

Akee, Randall, Emilia Simeonova, William Copeland, Adrian Angold, and E. Jane Costello. "Young Adult Obesity and Household Income: Effects of Unconditional Cash Transfers." *American Economic Journal: Applied Economics* 5, no. 2 (April 2013): 1–28.

ALHFAM. "Association for Living History, Farm and Agricultural Museums." Accessed November 7, 2016. http://www.alhfam.org.

Altman, Heidi M. *Eastern Cherokee Fishing*. Tuscaloosa: University of Alabama Press, 2006.

Anderson, Benedict R. *Imagined Communities: Reflections on the Origin and Spread of Nationalism*. New York: Verso, 2006.

Anderson, Chuck. "The Western Film . . . by the Numbers!" Old Corral. Accessed July 14, 2018. http://www.b-westerns.com/graphs.htm.

Anderson, Jay. *Time Machines: The World of Living History*. Nashville, Tenn.: American Association for State and Local History, 1984.

Anderson, Terry, and Dean Lueck. "Land Tenure and Agricultural Productivity on Indian Reservations." *Journal of Law and Economics* 35, no. 2 (1992): 425.

Arch, Chrissy. "Qualla Arts and Crafts to Host Labor Day Open Air Market." *Cherokee One Feather*, September 2, 2010.

Arneach, Dawn. "Tribal Member's Cooking Featured in Cookbook and TV." *Cherokee One Feather*, September 15, 2011.

Arriola, Michael. "Small Business Administration Presentation, Cherokee, NC." June 30, 2009.

Association of Religion Data Archives. "Interactive GIS Maps," 2000. http://www .thearda.com/DemographicMap.

Barber, Bernard. "All Economies Are 'Embedded': The Career of a Concept, and Beyond." *Social Research* 62, no. 2 (Summer 1995): 387–413.

Barker, Joanne. "The Corporation and the Tribe." *American Indian Quarterly* 39, no. 3 (2015): 243–70.

———. *Native Acts: Law, Recognition, and Cultural Authenticity.* Durham, N.C.:
Duke University Press, 2011.

Barlett, Donald L., and James B. Steele. "Indian Casinos: Wheel of Misfortune."
Time, December 16, 2002.

Bates Assocs, LLC v. 132 Assocs, LLC, 290 Mich App 52, 64; 799 NW2d 177 (2010).

Baxter, Cinda. "The 3/50 Project." 2009. http://www.the350project.net/home
.html.

Beard-Moose, Christina. *Public Indians, Private Cherokees: Tourism and Tradition
on Tribal Ground.* Tuscaloosa: University of Alabama Press, 2009.

Beaulieu, David L. "Curly Hair and Big Feet: Physical Anthropology and the
Implementation of Land Allotment on the White Earth Chippewa Reservation."
American Indian Quarterly 8, no. 4 (1984): 281–314.

Beck, Frela. "Bill Taylor Scholarship." *Cherokee One Feather*, May 19, 2011.

Bender, Margaret Clelland. *Signs of Cherokee Culture: Sequoyah's Syllabary in
Eastern Cherokee Life.* Chapel Hill: University of North Carolina Press, 2002.

Bendix, Regina. "Tourism and Cultural Displays: Inventing Traditions for Whom?"
Journal of American Folklore 102, no. 404 (June 1989): 131–46.

Benson, David A., Aaron Lies, Albert A. Okunade, and Phanindra V. Wunnava.
"Economic Impact of a Private Sector Micro-financing Scheme in South
Dakota." *Small Business Economics* 36, no. 2 (2011): 157–68.

Berman, Tressa, ed. *No Deal! Indigenous Arts and the Politics of Possession.*
Santa Fe, N.M.: School for Advanced Research Press, 2012.

Bethany. Interview with the author, Cherokee, N.C. Digital recording,
August 2009.

Biolsi, Thomas. "Imagined Geographies: Sovereignty, Indigenous Space, and
American Indian Struggle." *American Ethnologist* 32, no. 2 (2005): 239–59.

Blackford, Mansel G. *A History of Small Business in America.* Chapel Hill:
University of North Carolina Press, 2003.

Blankenship, Bob. "TABCC Recognized as Sole Regulator of Alcohol for Cherokee
Lands." *Cherokee One Feather*, July 21, 2011.

Blankenship, Ron. Interview with the author, Cherokee, N.C. Digital recording,
December 2009.

Blattman, Christopher, Nathan Fiala, and Sebastian Martinez. "The Economic and
Social Returns to Cash Transfers: Evidence from a Ugandan Aid Program."
CEGA Working Paper, 2013.

Bonilla-Silva, Eduardo. *Racism without Racists: Color-Blind Racism and the
Persistence of Racial Inequality in America.* Lanham: Rowman & Littlefield
Publishers, 2006.

Bosma, Niels, Alicia Coduras, Yana Litovsky, and Jeff Seaman. "GEM Manual: A
Report on the Design, Data and Quality Control of the Global Entrepreneurship
Monitor," May 9, 2012.

Bowles, Samuel, Herbert Gintis, and Erik Olin Wright. *Recasting Egalitarianism:
New Rules for Communities, States and Markets.* London: Verso, 1998.

Bradley, Sharon. "CHS Starts American Indian Business Leaders Chapter."
Cherokee One Feather, October 20, 2011.

Bregger, John E. "Measuring Self-Employment in the United States." *Monthly Labor Review,* January 1996, 3–9.

Bressler, Martin S., Kitty Campbell, and Brett Elliott. "A Study of Native American Small Business Ownership: Opportunities for Entrepreneurs." *Research in Business and Economics Journal* 10 (2014): 1–13.

Britton, Steve. "Tourism, Capital, and Place: Towards a Critical Geography of Tourism." *Environment and Planning D: Society and Space* 9 (1991): 451–78.

Brown, Brent "Thunder Rode." "Letter to the Editor: T-Shirt 'Runs with Beer' Is Offensive." *Cherokee One Feather,* August 19, 2009.

Brown, Michael F. (Michael Fobes). *Who Owns Native Culture?* Cambridge, Mass.: Harvard University Press, 2003.

Brown, Wendy. "Neoliberalism and the End of Liberal Democracy." *Theory and Event* 7, no. 1 (2016): 37–59.

Bruner, Edward M. *Culture on Tour: Ethnographies of Travel.* Chicago: University of Chicago Press, 2004.

Bruyneel, Kevin. *The Third Space of Sovereignty: The Postcolonial Politics of U.S.-Indigenous Relations.* Minneapolis: University of Minnesota Press, 2007.

Bureau of Indian Affairs. "Building Legal Infrastructure." Accessed December 22, 2016. https://www.bia.gov/WhoWeAre/AS-IA/IEED/DED/PTETV/index.htm.

———. "What Is the Relationship between the Tribes and the Individual States?" 2012. https://www.bia.gov/FAQs.

Burt, Ronald S. *Structural Holes: The Social Structure of Competition.* Cambridge, Mass.: Harvard University Press, 1992.

Calhoun, Trish. "The Tribal Cannery Will Open Monday, May 23." *Cherokee One Feather,* May 19, 2011.

Capriccioso, Rob. "Tribes among Biggest Campaign Contributors." *Indian Country Media Network,* March 22, 2011.

Carl. Interview with the author, Cherokee, N.C. Digital recording, August 2009.

Carroll, Clint. *Roots of Our Renewal: Ethnobotany and Cherokee Environmental Governance.* Minneapolis: University of Minnesota Press, 2015.

Cattelino, Jessica R. "Casino Roots: The Cultural Production of Twentieth-Century Seminole Economic Development." In *Native Pathways: American Indian Culture and Economic Development in the Twentieth Century,* edited by Brian C. Hosmer and Colleen M. O'Neill, 66–90. Boulder: University Press of Colorado, 2004.

———. "The Double Bind of American Indian Need-Based Sovereignty." *Cultural Anthropology* 25, no. 2 (2010): 235–62.

———. "Fungibility: Florida Seminole Casino Dividends and the Fiscal Politics of Indigeneity." *American Anthropologist* 111, no. 2 (June 2009): 199.

———. *High Stakes: Florida Seminole Gaming and Sovereignty.* Durham, N.C.: Duke University Press, 2008.

Cedar Band Corporation. "Suh'dutsing Technologies." 2017. http://cedarbandcorp.com/suhdutsingtech.

Champagne, Duane. "Tribal Capitalism and Native Capitalists: Multiple Pathways of Native Economy." In *Native Pathways: American Indian Culture and Economic*

Development in the Twentieth Century, edited by Brian C. Hosmer and Colleen M. O'Neill, 308–29. Boulder: University Press of Colorado, 2004.

Charles, Jeremy, and Sterlin Harjo. *Gary "Litefoot" Davis Story*. Osiyo TV, September 3, 2016.

Chavez, Will. "Duke Energy Halts Substation Construction near Kituwah Mound." *Cherokee Phoenix*, April 27, 2010. http://www.cherokeephoenix.org/Article /index/3791.

Chavez, Will, and Anita Finger-Smith. "EBCI Ancestors Remained East for Various Reasons." *Cherokee Phoenix*, March 25, 2016.

Cherokee Boys Club. "About—Cherokee Boys Club," 2018. http://www .cherokeeboysclub.com/

Cherokee Broadband. "Got Internet? Cherokee Broadband Can Help." *Cherokee One Feather*, September 8, 2011.

Cherokee Business Development Center and the Sequoyah Fund. "Support Small Business Saturday." *Cherokee One Feather*, November 25, 2010.

Cherokee Chamber of Commerce. "Qualla-T Customer Service Training," 2010. https://www.cherokeechamber.org.

Cherokee Nation. Constitution of the Cherokee Nation. Article IV., Section 1, 1999. http://www.cherokee.org/Portals/0/Documents/2011/4/308011999-2003-CN -CONSTITUTION.pdf.

———. "Our History," 2015. http://www.cherokee.org/AboutTheNation/History /Facts/OurHistory.aspx.

Cherokee One Feather. "Are You in Favor of Alcoholic Beverages Being Available in Restaurants or at Events on the Qualla Boundary?" *Cherokee One Feather*, November 26, 2015.

———. *"Cherokee One Feather* Poll of the Week Results: Convictions." *Cherokee One Feather*, July 23, 2015.

———. "EBCI Represented at AIANTA Conference." *Cherokee One Feather*, October 7, 2010.

———. "Nobles Found Guilty in 2012 Murder." *Cherokee One Feather*, April 15, 2016. https://theonefeather.com/2016/04/nobles-found-guilty-in-2012 -murder/.

———. "Poll: Do You Think Walmart Is a Good Fit for Cherokee?" *Cherokee One Feather*, June 30, 2016.

———. "Poll Facebook Responses: What Type of Businesses Do You Think Would Be Best for the Tribe to Enter into to Diversify Its Revenue Stream?" *Cherokee One Feather*, July 30, 2015.

———. "Poll: What Do You Feel Gives You Native American Identity?" *Cherokee One Feather*, September 10, 2015.

———. "Poll: What Is Your Opinion of Chiefing?" *Cherokee One Feather*, April 3, 2016.

———. "Reader Feedback Sought: Offensive or No Big Deal?" *Cherokee One Feather*, July 22, 2009.

———. "Study: Per Cap Linked to Lower Drug Usage." *Cherokee One Feather*, June 10, 2010.

———. "Would You Be in Favor of Alcohol Sales in Cherokee Restaurants and Special Events?" *Cherokee One Feather*, May 12, 2016.

Cherokee Preservation Foundation. "Cherokee Preservation Foundation Announces 24 New Grants." *Cherokee One Feather*, March 31, 2011.

———. "CPF Announces 19 New Grants Totaling $2.3M." *Cherokee One Feather*, October 6, 2009.

———. "Financial Literacy," 2012. http://cherokeepreservation.org/what-we-do /economic-development/financial-literacy/.

———. "Qualla 2020: Diversifying Our Region's Economy." Accessed November 4, 2016. http://cherokeepreservation.org/what-we-do/economic-development /economic-diversification-initiatives/qualla-2020/overview/.

Cherokee Transit. "Wal-Mart Shopping Trip by Cherokee Transit." *Cherokee One Feather*, September 22, 2011.

Cherokee Tri-Council. "Cherokee Tri-Council Resolutions." Red Clay, Tenn., September 1, 2015.

Chibnik, Michael. *Crafting Tradition: The Making and Marketing of Oaxacan Wood Carvings*. Austin: University of Texas Press, 2003.

Chomsky, Noam. *Profit over People: Neoliberalism and Global Order*. New York: Seven Stories Press, 1999.

Cobb, Daniel M. *Native Activism in Cold War America: The Struggle for Sovereignty*. Lawrence: University Press of Kansas, 2008.

Cobell v. Salazar (Cobell XXII), 573 F.3d 808 (D.C. Cir. 2009) (2009).

Colbourne, Rick. "An Understanding of Native American Entrepreneurship." *Small Enterprise Research* 24, no. 1 (2017): 49–61.

Coleman, James S. "Social Capital in the Creation of Human Capital." In "Organizations and Institutions: Sociological and Economic Approaches to the Analysis of Social Structure." Supplement, *American Journal of Sociology* 94 (1988): S95–120.

Colloredo-Mansfeld, Rudi. *The Native Leisure Class: Consumption and Cultural Creativity in the Andes*. Chicago: University of Chicago Press, 1999.

Cornell, Stephen. "Tribal-Citizen Entrepreneurship: What Does It Mean for Indian Country, and How Can Tribes Support It?" *Community Dividend*, July 2006. https://www.minneapolisfed.org/publications/community-dividend /tribalcitizen-entrepreneurship-what-does-it-mean-for-indian-country-and -how-can-tribes-support-it.

Cornell, Stephen E., Miriam Ruth Jorgensen, Ian Wilson Record, and Joan Timeche. "Citizen Entrepreneurship: An Underutilized Development Resource." In *Rebuilding Native Nations: Strategies for Governance and Development*, edited by Miriam Jorgensen, 197–222. Tucson: University of Arizona Press, 2007.

Corntassel, Jeff, and Richard C. Witmer II. *Forced Federalism: Contemporary Challenges to Indigenous Nationhood*. Norman: University of Oklahoma Press, 2011.

Costello, E. Jane, William Copeland, Gordon Keeler, Adrian Angold, and Randall K. Q. Akee. "Parents' Incomes and Children's Outcomes: A Quasi-Experiment Using

Transfer Payments from Casino Profits." *American Economic Journal: Applied Economics* 2, no. 1 (January 2010): 86–115.

Costello, E. Jane, Alaattin Erkanli, William Copeland, and Adrian Angold. "Association of Family Income Supplements in Adolescence with Development of Psychiatric and Substance Use Disorders in Adulthood among an American Indian Population." *Journal of the American Medical Association* 303, no. 19 (May 19, 2010): 1954–60.

Council for Tribal Employment Rights. "TERO FAQ." July 31, 2018. http://www.councilfortribalemploymentrights.org/tero-faq.

Cunningham, James K., Teshia A. Solomon, and Myra L. Muramoto. "Alcohol Use among Native Americans Compared to Whites: Examining the Veracity of the 'Native American Elevated Alcohol Consumption' Belief." *Drug and Alcohol Dependence* 160 (March 2016): 65–75.

Da Costa, Pedro Nicolaci. "Statistician Says US Joblessness Near Depression Highs." Reuters, March 9, 2009. http://www.reuters.com/article/2009/03/09/usa-economy-jobs-shadowstats-idUSN0944970920090309.

Dana, Leo Paul. "Editorial." *Journal of Small Business and Entrepreneurship* 18, no. 2 (2005).

———. "Special Issue: Entrepreneurship among Indigenous Peoples." *Journal of Small Business and Entrepreneurship* 18, no. 2 (2005).

Dana, Leo Paul, Teresa E. Dana, and Bob Anderson. "A Theory-Based Empirical Study of Entrepreneurship in Iqaluit, Nunavut." *Journal of Small Business and Entrepreneurship* 18, no. 2 (2005): 143.

Dann, Graham. *The Language of Tourism: A Sociolinguistic Perspective.* Wallingford, Oxon, UK: CAB International, 1996.

Deas, Kim. "Final Notice—Sign Ordinance Enforcement." *Cherokee One Feather,* April 3, 2014.

Deloria, Philip Joseph. *Indians in Unexpected Places.* Lawrence: University Press of Kansas, 2004.

———. *Playing Indian.* New Haven, Conn.: Yale University Press, 1998.

Deloria, Vine, Jr. *Custer Died for Your Sins: An Indian Manifesto.* Norman: University of Oklahoma Press, 1969.

———. *The Nations Within: The Past and Future of American Indian Sovereignty.* Austin: University of Texas Press, 1998.

Dennison, Jean. *Colonial Entanglements: Constituting a Twenty-First-Century Osage Nation.* Chapel Hill: University of North Carolina Press, 2012.

Diamond, Neil, Catherine Bainbridge, and Jeremiah Hayes, dirs. *Reel Injun,* 2009; Montreal: Rezolution Pictures, 2010.

Dingus, Brandi. "5th Annual CES Career Fair." *Cherokee One Feather,* March 18, 2009.

Dombrowski, Kirk. *Against Culture: Development, Politics, and Religion in Indian Alaska.* Lincoln: University of Nebraska Press, 2001.

Dovidio, John F. "The Aversive Form of Racism." In *Prejudice, Discrimination, and Racism,* edited by Samuel L. Gaertner, 61–89. Orlando, Fla.: Academic Press, 1986.

Duggan, Betty J. "Tourism, Cultural Authenticity, and the Native Crafts Cooperative: The Eastern Band Cherokee Experience." In *Tourism and Culture: An Applied Perspective*, edited by Erve Chambers, 31–58. Albany: State University of New York Press, 1997.

Duncan, Barbara R., Brett H. Riggs, and Blue Ridge Heritage Initiative. *Cherokee Heritage Trails Guidebook*. Chapel Hill: Published in association with Museum of the Cherokee Indian by University of North Carolina Press, 2003.

Duran, Eduardo, and Bonnie Duran. *Native American Postcolonial Psychology*. Albany: State University of New York Press, 1995.

Duvall, Micky. "Cherokee Retail and Business Update." *Cherokee One Feather*, April 22, 2010.

Eastern Band of Cherokee Indians. Cherokee Code of the Eastern Band of Cherokee Indians. Tribal Council of the Eastern Band of Cherokee Indians, August 25, 2008. https://www.narf.org/nill/codes/eastern_band_cherokee/.

——. "Cherokee Preservation Foundation," 2005. http://cherokeepreservation.org.

——. "Eastern Band of Cherokee Indians Economic Development," September 1, 2008. http://www.nc-cherokee.com.

——. "Eastern Band of Cherokee Indians Government," 2015. https://nc -cherokee.com.

——. "Eastern Band of Cherokee Indians Public Transit," 2011. http://www .cherokeetransit.com.

——. "Economic Development." Accessed April 30, 2012. http://nc-cherokee .com/economicdevelopment.

EBCI Commerce Department. "Public Notice Concerning 'Chiefing.'" *Cherokee One Feather*, March 1, 2016. https://theonefeather.com/2016/03/public-notice -concerning-chiefing.

EBCI Enrollment Office. "Enrollment Fact!" *Cherokee One Feather*, October 6, 2009.

——. "Expanded DNA Information for EBCI Enrollment Purposes." *Cherokee One Feather*, July 29, 2010.

EBCI TERO Office. "EBCI TERO Welcomes You." July 31, 2018. https://www .ebcitero.com.

EBCI Travel and Promotion. "Greater Cherokee Tourism Council Formed." *Cherokee One Feather*, January 6, 2011.

"Entreprenative Podcast." Entreprenative: Indian Country's Top Entrepreneurs and Native Owned Businesses. Accessed January 24, 2017. http://www.podcasts.com /entreprenative-indian-countrys-top-entrepreneurs-native-owned-businesses.

Esarey, Duane. "Colonialism before Contact: Interrogating Theoretical Limitations of Contact Period Archaeology." Presented at the Southeastern Archaeology Conference, Charlotte, N.C., 2008.

Escobar, Arturo. *Encountering Development: The Making and Unmaking of the Third World*. Princeton, N.J.: Princeton University Press, 1995.

Everett, Margaret. "The Ghost in the Machine: Agency in 'Poststructural' Critiques of Development." *Anthropological Quarterly* 70, no. 3 (July 1997): 137–51.

Fariello, M. A. *Cherokee Basketry: From the Hands of Our Elders*. Charleston, S.C.: History Press, 2009.

———. *Cherokee Pottery: From the Hands of Our Elders*. Charleston, S.C.: History Press, 2011.

Farmer, Paul. *Pathologies of Power: Health, Human Rights, and the New War on the Poor*. Berkeley: University of California Press, 2005.

Finger, John R. *Cherokee Americans: The Eastern Band of Cherokees in the Twentieth Century*. Lincoln: University of Nebraska Press, 1991.

———. *The Eastern Band of Cherokees, 1819–1900*. Knoxville: University of Tennessee Press, 1984.

Flaherty, Anne. "American Indian Land Rights, Rich Indian Racism, and Newspaper Coverage in New York State, 1988–2008." *American Indian Culture and Research Journal* 37, no. 4 (January 2013): 53–84.

Foltz, Nancy. "CPF Announces 19 New Grants Totaling over $2M." *Cherokee One Feather*, October 27, 2011.

Frankel, Jake. "Cherokee Advises All Tourists to Carry Cherokee Passport." Mountain Xpress. Accessed May 2, 2017. http://mountainx.com/news/community-news/cherokee_advises_all_tourists_to_carry_cherokee_passport.

Frazier, Ian. *On the Rez*. New York: Picador, 2001.

Garsombke, Diane J., and Thomas W. Garsombke. "Non-Traditional vs. Traditional Entrepreneurs: Emergence of a Native American Comparative Profile of Characteristics and Barriers." *Academy of Entrepreneurship Journal* 6, no. 1 (2000): 93.

Gercken, Becca, and Julie Pelletier, eds. *Gambling on Authenticity: Gaming, the Noble Savage, and the Not-So-New Indian*. East Lansing: Michigan State University Press, 2017.

"Gianforte Says Indian Reservations Hinder Free Markets." *Billings Gazette*, August 19, 2017. http://billingsgazette.com/news/government-and-politics/gianforte-says-indian-reservations-hinder-free-markets/article_00bac146-8967-591b-b2c0-c658c97b47cf.html.

Gibson-Graham, J. K. *A Postcapitalist Politics*. Minneapolis: University of Minnesota Press, 2006.

Gilens, Martin, and Benjamin I. Page. "Testing Theories of American Politics: Elites, Interest Groups, and Average Citizens." *Perspectives on Politics* 12, no. 3 (September 2014): 564–81.

"Give Us Your Thoughts." *Cherokee One Feather*, July 17, 2017. https://www.facebook.com/tsalaginews/posts/1470187196352866.

Gladstone, Joseph. "All My Relations: An Inquiry into a Spirit of a Native American Philosophy of Business." *The American Indian Quarterly* 42, no. 2 (2018): 191–214.

Gladwin, C. H., B. F. Long, E. M. Babb, L. J. Beaulieu, A. Moseley, D. Mulkey, and D. J. Zimet. "Rural Entrepreneurship: One Key to Rural Revitalization." *American Journal of Agricultural Economics* 71, no. 5 (Proceedings Issue) (December 1989): 1305–14.

Goodale, Mark. "Dark Matter: Toward a Political Economy of Indigenous Rights and Aspirational Politics." *Critique of Anthropology* 36, no. 4 (December 1, 2016): 439–57.

Goss Agency. "Case Histories and Testimonials of the Goss Agency." Tourism Marketing at the Goss Agency. Accessed May 2, 2017. http://culturaltourism .thegossagency.com/case-histories-and-testimonials.

Graeber, Davd. *Debt: The First 5,000 Years*. New York: Melville House, 2012.

Graff, Michael. "Cherokee, North Carolina." *Our State Magazine*, October 2010.

Granovetter, Mark. "Economic Action and Social Structure: The Problem of Embeddedness." *American Journal of Sociology* 91, no. 3 (November 1985): 481–510.

Greene, Lance, and Mark R. Plane, eds. *American Indians and the Market Economy, 1775–1850*. Tuscaloosa: University Alabama Press, 2010.

Groenwold, Alice. Interview with the author, Cherokee, N.C. Digital recording, November 2009.

Gudeman, Stephen. *The Anthropology of Economy: Community, Market, and Culture*. Malden, Mass.: Blackwell, 2001.

Ha, Inhyuck Steve, and James Ullmer. "The Economic Effects of Harrah's Cherokee Casino and Hotel on the Regional Economy of Western North Carolina." *Journal of Economics and Economic Education Research* 8, no. 2 (May 2007): 33–46.

Handler, Richard. "Authenticity." *Anthropology Today* 2, no. 1 (February 1986): 2–4.

Hansen, Terri. *Kill the Land, Kill the People: There Are 532 Superfund Sites in Indian Country!*, June 17, 2014. http://indiancountrytodaymedianetwork.com/2014/06 /17/532-superfund-sites-indian-country-155316.

Hanson, Randel D. "Contemporary Globalization and Tribal Sovereignty." In *A Companion to the Anthropology of American Indians*, edited by Thomas Biolsi. Chichester: Wiley, 2004.

Harding, Lew. Interview with the author, January 2010.

Harmon, Alexandra. *Rich Indians: Native People and the Problem of Wealth in American History*. Chapel Hill: University of North Carolina Press, 2013.

Harris, Cheryl I. "Whiteness as Property." *Harvard Law Review* 106, no. 8 (1993): 1707–91.

Hicks, Michell. "A Closer Look at Tribal Debt." *Cherokee One Feather*, July 21, 2011.

———. "Paid Political Ad: Chief Hicks' Comprehensive Plan for Progress." *Cherokee One Feather*, August 18, 2011.

———. "Paid Political Ad: Sustainable Development and Cultural Tourism." *Cherokee One Feather*, August 11, 2011.

Hindle, Kevin. "Brave Spirits on New Paths: Toward a Globally Relevant Paradigm of Indigenous Entrepreneurship Research." *Journal of Small Business and Entrepreneurship* 18, no. 2 (2005).

Ho, Karen. "Commentary on Andrew Orta's 'Managing the Margins': The Anthropology of Transnational Capitalism, Neoliberalism, and Risk." *American Ethnologist* 41, no. 1 (February 1, 2014): 31–37.

Holland, T. J. "Place Names in Cherokee County." *Cherokee One Feather*, January 29, 2015, sec. Cherokee History.

Holt, Jean C. "Guest Commentary: Tribal Members Can Make up Own Mind on Alcohol Issue." *Cherokee One Feather*, June 3, 2009.

Hoover, Elizabeth. "From Garden Warriors to Good Seeds: Indigenizing the Local Food Movement," 2015. https://gardenwarriorsgoodseeds.com/.

———. The River Is in Us: Fighting Toxics in a Mohawk Community. Minneapolis: University of Minnesota Press, 2017.

Hosmer, Brian C. American Indians in the Marketplace: Persistence and Innovation among the Menominees and Metlakatlans, 1870–1920. Lawrence: University Press of Kansas, 1999.

Hosmer, Brian C., and Colleen M. O'Neill. Native Pathways: American Indian Culture and Economic Development in the Twentieth Century. Boulder: University Press of Colorado, 2004.

House Concurrent Resolution 108. U.S. Statutes at Large. Vol. 67, 1953. http://constitution.org/uslaw/sal/067_statutes_at_large.pdf.

Hubbs, David. "BalsamWest FiberNET." balsamwest, 2017. http://www.balsamwest.net.

Hulme, David, Joseph Hanlon, and Armando Barrientos. Just Give Money to the Poor: The Development Revolution from the Global South. Sterling, Va.: Kumarian Press, 2012.

ICT Staff. "As the Eastern Band of Cherokees Expand Harrah's, Principal Chief Candidates Shift Focus to Diversification." Indian Country Media Network, January 26, 2012.

Indian Health Service. "Affordable Care Act," 2015. http://www.ihs.gov/aca/.

Inouye, Daniel. Indian Gaming Regulatory Act, Pub. L. 100–497, 25 U.S.C. § 2701 et seq. § (1988).

InvestNative Project. "Manage Your EBCI Money," 2011. http://www.investnative.org/ebci.html.

Jacobsen, Damien. "Aboriginal and Torres Strait Islander Ways of Enterprise Clustering." Presented at the Native American and Indigenous Studies Association, Honolulu, Hawaii, May 18, 2016. https://www.nintione.com.au/resources/nol/aboriginal-and-torres-strait-islander-ways-of-enterprise-clustering-2.

———. "Summary Paper Series: Aboriginal and Torres Strait Islander Principles of Enterprise Clustering—Tourism System Linkages." Alice Springs NT Australia: Ninti One, 2015. https://nintione.com.au/resource/Paper06of10_TourismSystemLinkages.pdf.

James, Heather. "Local Restaurants Help to Raise Money for Japan." Cherokee One Feather, May 5, 2011.

Jenkins, Susan. Interview with the author, Cherokee, N.C. Digital recording, June 2009.

Johnson, James H., Jr., John D. Kasarda, and Stephen J. Appold. Assessing the Economic and Non-Economic Impacts of Harrah's Cherokee Casino, North Carolina. Chapel Hill: Frank Hawkins Kenan Institute of Private Enterprise, Kenan-Flagler Business School, University of North Carolina, 2011.

Jorgensen, Miriam Ruth. Rebuilding Native Nations: Strategies for Governance and Development. Tucson: University of Arizona Press, 2007.

Josephy, Alvin M., Joane Nagel, and Troy R. Johnson. Red Power: The American Indians' Fight for Freedom. Lincoln: University of Nebraska Press, 1999.

Jumper, Robert. "Attorney General to Draft a 'Cultural Protection Ordinance,'" *Cherokee One Feather*, April 6, 2018, https://theonefeather.com/2018/04 /attorney-general-to-draft-a-cultural-protection-ordinance.

———. "The Best Things in Life Are Free and in Cherokee." *Cherokee One Feather*, June 2, 2016. https://theonefeather.com/2016/06/editorial-the-best-things-in -life-are-free-and-in-cherokee.

———. "Diversify." *Cherokee One Feather*, November 12, 2015, sec. Opinion.

———. "Housing Summit Shines Light on Long Standing Issues." *Cherokee One Feather*, June 20, 2017. https://theonefeather.com/2017/06/housing-summit -shines-light-on-long-standing-issues.

Kamper, David. *The Work of Sovereignty: Tribal Labor Relations and Self-Determination at the Navajo Nation.* Santa Fe: School for Advanced Research Press, 2010.

Kamper, David, and Katherine A. Spilde. "The Legal Regimenting of Tribal Wealth: How Federal Courts and Agencies Seek to Normalize Tribal Governmental Revenue and Capital." *American Indian Culture and Research Journal* 40, no. 2 (2016): 1–29.

Kar, Sohini. *Financializing Poverty: Labor and Risk in Indian Microfinance.* Stanford, Calif: Stanford University Press, 2018.

Kays, Holly. "Staggered Payments for Cherokee Minors' Fund." *Smoky Mountain News*, June 29, 2016. http://www.smokymountainnews.com/news/item/17914 -staggered-payments-for-cherokee-minors-fund.

Keene, Adrienne. "Nike Gets It Right; Brand Collaborates with O'odham Designer." *Indian Country Media Network* (blog), February 5, 2015. https:// indiancountrymedianetwork.com/culture/arts-entertainment/keene-nike-gets -it-right-brand-collaborates-with-oodham-designer/.

Kelley, Donna J., Abdul Ali, Candida Brush, Andrew C. Corbett, Caroline Daniels, Phillip H. Kim, Thomas S. Lyons, Mahdi Majbouri, and Edward G. Rogoff. *Global Entrepreneurship Monitor: 2015 United States Report.* Wellesley, Mass.: Babson College, 2015.

Kennedy, Deanna M., Charles F. Harrington, Amy Klemm Verbos, Daniel Stewart, Joseph Scott Gladstone, and Gavin Clarkson, eds. *American Indian Business: Principles and Practices.* Seattle: University of Washington Press, 2017.

Kent, Todd. Interview with the author, Cherokee, N.C. Digital recording, May 2016.

King, Tiffany, David Njite, H. G. Parsa, and John T. Self. "Why Restaurants Fail." *Cornell Hospitality Quarterly* 46, no. 3 (August 2005): 304–22.

Kirby, Doug, Ken Smith, and Mike Wilkins. *The New Roadside America: The Modern Traveler's Guide to the Wild and Wonderful World of America's Tourist Attractions.* New York: Simon & Schuster, 1992.

Kosar, Kevin R. "Federal Government Corporations: An Overview." CRS Report for Congress. Congressional Research Service, June 8, 2011. https://fas.org/sgp /crs/misc/RL30365.pdf.

Lakota People's Law Project. "Native Lives Matter," 2015. http://lakotalaw.org /special-reports/native-lives-matter.

Lambert Jr., Leonard Carson, and Michael Lambert. *Up from These Hills: Memories of a Cherokee Boyhood.* Lincoln: University of Nebraska Press, 2011.

Lambert, Patrick. "Paid Political Ad: Per Capita Payments Under the Past 4 Years of Hicks Administration." *Cherokee One Feather,* August 25, 2011.

———. "Principal Chief's Report for February 2017." *Cherokee One Feather,* February 27, 2017. https://theonefeather.com/2017/02/principal-chiefs-report -for-february-2017.

Lambert, Valerie. *Choctaw Nation: A Story of American Indian Resurgence.* Lincoln: University of Nebraska Press, 2007.

Lancaster, Pooh. Interview with the author, Cherokee, N.C. Digital recording, February 2010.

Ledford, William J. "Commentary: Government Transparency and Other News Issues." *Cherokee One Feather,* May 5, 2016.

———. "Letter to the Editor: Finds T-Shirt Offensive." *Cherokee One Feather,* August 12, 2009.

Lee, Tanya H. "Study Says the 'Drunken Indian' Is a Myth." Indian Country Today Media Network.com, February 24, 2016. http://indiancountry todaymedianetwork.com/2016/02/24/study-says-drunken-indian-myth -163446.

Lefler, Lisa J. *Under the Rattlesnake: Cherokee Health and Resiliency.* Tuscaloosa: University of Alabama Press, 2009.

Leong, Nancy. "Racial Capitalism." SSRN Scholarly Paper. Rochester, N.Y.: Social Science Research Network, February 21, 2012.

Lewis, Courtney. "Betting on Western North Carolina: Harrah's Cherokee Casino Resort's Regional Impacts." *Journal of Appalachian Studies* 23, no. 1 (2017): 29–52.

———. "The Case of the Wild Onions: The Impact of Ramps on Cherokee Rights." *Southern Cultures* 18, no. 2 (2012): 104–17.

———. "Economic Sovereignty in Volatile Times: Eastern Band of Cherokee Indians' Intersectionalities Supporting Economic Stability." *Research in Economic Anthropology* 38 (2018).

———. "Frybread Wars: Biopolitics and the Consequences of Selective United States Healthcare Practices for American Indians." *Food, Culture & Society* 21, no. 4 (2018).

Lewis, Ronald G., and Man Keung Ho. "Social Work with Native Americans." *Social Work* 20, no. 5 (September 1, 1975): 379–82.

Light, Steven Andrew, and Kathryn R. L. Rand. *Indian Gaming and Tribal Sovereignty: The Casino Compromise.* Lawrence: University Press of Kansas, 2005.

"List of Open-Air and Living History Museums in the United States." Wikipedia. Accessed November 6, 2016. https://en.wikipedia.org/w/index.php?title=List _of_open-air_and_living_history_museums_in_the_United_States&oldid =748142636.

Little, Walter E. *Mayas in the Marketplace: Tourism, Globalization, and Cultural Identity.* Austin: University of Texas Press, 2004.

"Living History Sites." Accessed November 7, 2016. http://livinghistorysites.com/.

Long, Norman, and Bryan R. Roberts. *Miners, Peasants, and Entrepreneurs: Regional Development in the Central Highlands of Peru.* Cambridge: Cambridge University Press, 1984.

Lont, Hotze, and Otto Hospes, eds. *Livelihood and Microfinance: Anthropological and Sociological Perspectives on Savings and Debt.* Delft: Eburon, 2004.

Lundy, Brandon D., Mark Patterson, and Alex O'Neill. "Drivers and Deterrents of Entrepreneurial Enterprise in the Risk-Prone Global South." *Economic Anthropology* 4, no. 1 (January 1, 2017): 65–81.

Lyden, Jacki. "Seminole Patchwork: Admiration and Appropriation." NPR.org. Accessed December 22, 2017. https://www.npr.org/sections/codeswitch/2017 /02/18/510241789/seminole-patchwork-admiration-and-appropriation.

MacCannell, Dean. *The Tourist: A New Theory of the Leisure Class.* Berkeley: University of California Press, 1976.

Malcolm Wiener Center for Social Policy. *The State of the Native Nations: Conditions under U.S. Policies of Self-Determination.* New York: Oxford University Press, 2008.

Malkin, Jennifer, Brian Dabson, Kim Pate, and Amy Mathews. "Native Entrepreneurship: Challenges and Opportunities for Rural Communities." Northwest Area Foundation and CFED, December 2004.

Martin, Bill, and Nancy Martin. Interview with the author, Cherokee, N.C. Digital recording, October 2009.

Martinez, David. "This Is (Not) Indian Painting." *American Indian Quarterly* 39, no. 1 (January 2015): 25–51.

Mattera, Philip, and Kasia Tarczynska. *Uncle Sam's Favorite Corporations: Identifying the Large Companies That Dominate Federal Subsidies.* Washington, D.C.: Good Jobs First, March 2015. http://www.goodjobsfirst.org/sites/default /files/docs/pdf/UncleSamsFavoriteCorporations.pdf.

Mazzetti, Bo. "How Arnold Schwarzenegger Violated Tribal Sovereignty." Indian Country Today Media Network, September 11, 2011. http:// indiancountrytodaymedianetwork.com/2011/09/21/how-arnold -schwarzenegger-violated-tribal-sovereignty.

McChesney, Lea S. "(Art)Writing: A New Cultural Frame for Native American Art." In *No Deal! Indigenous Arts and the Politics of Possession,* edited by Tressa Berman, 2–31. Santa Fe, N.M.: School for Advanced Research Press, 2012.

McCoy, Rosie R. "Brief Summary of the Tribal Council and Legislative Branch of the Eastern Band of Cherokee Indians," 2012. http://nc-cherokee.com /council.

———. "Letter to the Editor: Response to T-Shirt." *Cherokee One Feather,* July 29, 2009.

McKie, Scott. "BalsamWest FiberNet to Get Funds a Little Early." *Cherokee One Feather,* October 20, 2011.

———. "Bringing Businesses Together 1st Annual Cherokee Business Summit & Expo Held at Casino." *Cherokee One Feather,* August 4, 2011.

———. "Cherokee County Casino Approved." *Cherokee One Feather*, April 1, 2015.

———. "Cherokee Fun Park Re-Opens." *Cherokee One Feather*, June 2, 2011.

———. "Cherokee Gains Designation as Certified Entrepreneurial Community." *Cherokee One Feather*, April 26, 2011.

———. "Cherokee Passports Issued to Visitors." *Cherokee One Feather*, June 3, 2010.

———. "Cherokee to Start Open Air Market." *Cherokee One Feather*, June 3, 2010.

———. "Chief Seeks New Policies Governing Cherokee Language Credits." *Cherokee One Feather*, March 21, 2016. https://theonefeather.com/2016/03 /chief-seeks-new-policies-governing-cherokee-language-credits.

———. "Class II Gaming Eyed in Cherokee County." *Cherokee One Feather*, March 25, 2010.

———. "Council Approves TERO as Independent Entity." *Cherokee One Feather*, August 5, 2016.

———. "Council Instructs AG to Develop Medical Marijuana Ordinance." *Cherokee One Feather*, May 6, 2016. https://theonefeather.com/2016/05/council -instructs-ag-to-develop-medical-marijuana-ordinance.

———. "DEBT-FREE: Tribe Pays off Hospital, Waste Water Treatment Plant Loans." *Cherokee One Feather*, May 11, 2016. https://theonefeather.com/2016/05 /debt-free-tribe-pays-off-hospital-waste-water-treatment-plant-loans.

———. "DOI Proposes Leasing Reform on Indian Lands." *Cherokee One Feather*, December 1, 2011.

———. "Donations Sought for Fire Victims." *Cherokee One Feather*, February 4, 2010.

———. "EBCI Part of Historic Class Action Settlement." *Cherokee One Feather*, October 22, 2015. https://theonefeather.com/2015/10/ebci-part-of-historic-class -action-settlement.

———. "Experts Help in Discussions on Constitution." *Cherokee One Feather*, August 18, 2011.

———. "Final Enrollment Audit Report Submitted." *Cherokee One Feather*, October 20, 2009.

———. "First Descendants Lose Life Estate, Land." *Cherokee One Feather*, August 4, 2011.

———. "Harrah's Impact to Area Told in UNC Study." *Cherokee One Feather*, July 28, 2011.

———. "Harrah's, Tribe Re-Up Contract for 7 Years." *Cherokee One Feather*, May 26, 2011.

———. "Historic Meeting Held at Red Clay." *Cherokee One Feather*, September 10, 2015.

———. "House Approves Tribal Law & Order Act." *Cherokee One Feather*, July 29, 2009.

———. "Minors Fund Discussed in Council Work Session." *Cherokee One Feather*, February 3, 2011.

————. "Museum to Host Southeast Tribes Festival." *Cherokee One Feather*, September 15, 2011.

————. "New Tribal Council Members Take Office." *Cherokee One Feather*, October 6, 2009.

————. "Record Park Visitation Continues in 2015." *Cherokee One Feather*, February 26, 2015.

————. "River's Edge Named Business of the Year." *Cherokee One Feather*, January 20, 2011.

————. "Senate Committee Approves Native Hawaiian Bill." *Cherokee One Feather*, May 12, 2011. http://theonefeather.com/2011/05/senate-committee -approves-native-hawaiian-bill-2.

————. "Tribe Breaks Ground on New Justice Center." *Cherokee One Feather*, August 11, 2011.

————. "Tribe Considering Overhaul to Tax Code." *Cherokee One Feather*, July 23, 2015.

————. "Tribe Establishes Cherokee Identity Protection Committee." *Cherokee One Feather*, October 20, 2011.

————. "Tribe, State Reach Compact Agreement." *Cherokee One Feather*, December 1, 2011.

————. "Tribe to Receive 35 Acres near Kituwah in Settlement." *Cherokee One Feather*, September 30, 2016. https://theonefeather.com/2016/09/tribe-to -receive-35-acres-near-kituwah-in-settlement.

————. "Wal-Mart Not Coming to Cherokee." *Cherokee One Feather*, May 6, 2010.

————. "World-Renowned Firm to Revamp, Reopen Fun Park." *Cherokee One Feather*, January 28, 2010.

————. "Youth Hold Meet the Candidates Forum." *Cherokee One Feather*, May 26, 2011.

McKie, Scott, and Robert Jumper. "Former TGC Commissioners' Lawsuit Dismissed." *Cherokee One Feather*, May 13, 2016. https://theonefeather.com /2016/05/former-tgc-commissioners-lawsuit-dismissed.

Means, Russell, and Marvin J. Wolf. *Where White Men Fear to Tread: The Autobiography of Russell Means.* New York: St. Martin's Griffin, 1995.

Metcalfe, Jessica R. "Is Manitobah Mukluks Indian Enough?" February 5, 2013. http://www.beyondbuckskin.com/2013/02/is-manitobah-mukluks-indian -enough.html.

Michaelsen, Scott, and David E. Johnson, eds. *Border Theory: The Limits of Cultural Politics.* Minneapolis: University of Minnesota Press, 1997.

Miller, Robert J. "American Indian Entrepreneurs: Unique Challenges, Unlimited Potential." Lewis & Clark Law School Legal Research Paper No. 2008-20, Arizona State University, 2008.

————. "Economic Development in Indian Country: Will Capitalism or Socialism Succeed?" *Oregon Law Review* 80, no. 3 (July 1, 2002).

————. *Reservation "Capitalism": Economic Development in Indian Country.* Santa Barbara, Calif.: Praeger, 2012.

Miner, H. Craig. *The Corporation and the Indian: Tribal Sovereignty and Industrial Civilization in Indian Territory, 1865–1907*. Columbia: University of Missouri Press, 1976.

Mississippi Band of Choctaw Indians. "Businesses." Accessed August 4, 2015. http://www.choctaw.org/businesses/index.html.

Mondragon. "Mondragon Annual Report—2016." Accessed July 16, 2018. https://www.mondragon-corporation.com/en/about-us.

Montiel, Anya. "The Art of George Morrison and Allan Houser: The Development and Impact of Native Modernism." *American Indian Quarterly* 29, no. 3/4 (June 2005): 478–90.

Moore, Jenny. "Programs Partner to Help Cherokee Artists." *Cherokee One Feather*, February 24, 2011.

Moseley, William. "The Limits of New Social Entrepreneurship." *Al Jazeera*, December 22, 2014. http://www.aljazeera.com/indepth/opinion/2014/12/limits-new-social-entrepreneu-20141221113250395741.html.

Murphy NC Land. "Great American Land Sale," September 2, 2010. http://www.murphyncland.com/.

Museum of the Cherokee Indian. "18th Century Cherokee Clothing Workshops." *Cherokee One Feather*, August 25, 2011.

———. "Cherokee Friends Kick Off Season." *Cherokee One Feather*, May 18, 2015. https://theonefeather.com/2015/05/cherokee-friends-kick-off-season.

———. "Education & Outreach," August 25, 2012. http://www.cherokeemuseum.org.

———. "The Warriors of AniKituhwa." Accessed April 24, 2017. http://www.cherokeemuseum.org/learn/the-warriors-of-anikituhwa.

National Center for American Indian Enterprise Development. "RES 2010 to Honor American Indian Business Achievement," February 18, 2010. http://res.ncaied.org.

———. "Youth Entrepreneurship Summit (YES)." National Center for American Indian Enterprise Development, August 4, 2015. http://res.ncaied.org/youth-entrepreneurship-summit-yes.

National Congress of American Indians. "Sovereign Immunity," 2012. http://www.ncai.org/policy-issues.

National Labor Relations Board. "Jurisdictional Standards." Accessed April 25, 2017. https://www.nlrb.gov/rights-we-protect/jurisdictional-standards.

National Parks Service. "Travel Increases in Park." *Cherokee One Feather*, March 24, 2011.

Neely, Sharlotte. *Snowbird Cherokees: People of Persistence*. Athens: University of Georgia Press, 1991.

Nelson, Bryn. "The Quileute Reservation Copes with Tourists Brought by 'Twilight,'" July 2, 2012. https://www.hcn.org/issues/44.11/the-quileute-reservation-copes-with-tourists-brought-by-twilight.

"Nike Unveils Shoe Just for American Indians," September 26, 2007. http://www.nbcnews.com/id/20980046/ns/business-sports_biz/t/nike-unveils-shoe-just-american-indians.

"North Carolina REAL Enterprises," 2008. http://www.learnnc.org/lp
/organizations/73.

Oakley, Christopher Arris. "Indian Gaming and the Eastern Band of Cherokee
Indians." *North Carolina Historical Review* 78, no. 2 (2001): 133–55.

O'Brien, Jean M. *Firsting and Lasting: Writing Indians out of Existence in New
England.* Minneapolis: University of Minnesota Press, 2010.

Oconaluftee Institute for Cultural Arts. "Oconaluftee Institute for Cultural Arts
Fall Art Schedule." *Cherokee One Feather,* September 9, 2010.

Office of Economic Development. Downtown Cherokee Revitalization—Design
Guidelines, 2009.

Office of the Treasury. 2011 Levy and Privilege Tax Proposal. Eastern Band of
Cherokee Indians, 2011.

ONABEN. "Indianpreneurship." 2011. http://www.onaben.org/indianpreneurship.

———. *Indianpreneurship: A Native American Journey into Business,* 2005.

O'Neill, Colleen. *Working the Navajo Way: Labor and Culture in the Twentieth
Century.* Lawrence: University Press of Kansas, 2005.

OpenSecrets. "North Carolina: Donors," 2016. http://www.opensecrets.org/states
/donors.php?state=NC.

Otwell, Dwight. *Tribe Buying Land for Casino.* May 11, 2010. http://www
.thecherokeescout.com/articles/2010/05/11/news
/doc4be9b95e05d95980267420.txt.

Peacock, James L. *Grounded Globalism: How the U.S. South Embraces the World.*
Athens: University of Georgia Press, 2007. http://search.lib.unc.edu.libproxy
.lib.unc.edu?R=UNCb6617462.

Peacock, James L., Harry Watson, and Carrie Matthews, eds. *The American South
in a Global World.* Chapel Hill: University of North Carolina Press, 2005.

Pensoneau, Migizi. "1491s Q&A." Presented at the Native American Indigenous
Studies Conference, Washington D.C., 2015.

Peredo, Ana Maria, Robert B. Anderson, Craig S. Galbraith, Benson Honig, and Leo
Paul Dana. "Towards a Theory of Indigenous Entrepreneurship." *International
Journal of Entrepreneurship and Small Business* 1, no. 1/2 (2004): 1–20.

Perdue, Theda. *The Cherokee Nation and the Trail of Tears.* New York: Viking, 2007.

———. *The Cherokees.* Philadelphia, Penn.: Chelsea House, 2005.

———. *Cherokee Women: Gender and Culture Change, 1700–1835.* Lincoln:
University of Nebraska Press, 1998.

Peroff, Nicholas C. *Menominee Drums: Tribal Termination and Restoration,
1954–1974.* Norman: University of Oklahoma Press, 1982.

Pfister, Joel. *Individuality Incorporated: Indians and the Multicultural Modern.*
Durham, N.C.: Duke University Press Books, 2004.

Pickering, Kathleen Ann. *Lakota Culture, World Economy.* Lincoln: University of
Nebraska Press, 2004.

Piketty, Thomas. *Capital in the Twenty-First Century.* Translated by Arthur
Goldhammer. Cambridge, Mass.: Belknap Press: An Imprint of Harvard
University Press, 2014.

Polanyi, Karl. *The Great Transformation: The Political and Economic Origins of Our Time*. Boston, Mass.: Beacon Press, 1944.

Porter Gaunt, LaRene. "'Because I Have Been Given Much,'" December 1997. https://www.lds.org/ensign/1997/12/because-i-have-been-given-much?lang=eng.

Povinelli, Elizabeth A. *Economies of Abandonment: Social Belonging and Endurance in Late Liberalism*. Durham, N.C.: Duke University Press Books, 2011.

Powell, Dana E. *Landscapes of Power: Politics of Energy in the Navajo Nation*. Durham, N.C.: Duke University Press Books, 2018.

Prosperity Now. "About—Prosperity Now." Accessed July 17, 2018. https://prosperitynow.org/.

PR Newswire. "Criden & Love, P.A. Announces Amended Class Action Lawsuit Against Bank of America Corporation," March 25, 2011. https://www.prnewswire.com/news-releases/criden--love-pa-announces-amended-class-action-lawsuit-against-bank-of-america-corporation-nyse-bac---modifying-class-period-118675649.html.

Public Schools of North Carolina. "Occupational Course of Study." Accessed December 16, 2016. http://ec.ncpublicschools.gov/disability-resources/intellectual-disabilities/occupational-course-of-study.

Putnam, R. D. "The Prosperous Community: Social Capital and Economic Growth." *American Prospect* 45, no. 13 (1993): 35.

Queen, Joel. Interview with the author, Cherokee, N.C. Digital recording, January 2010.

Rattler, Harold R. "Tallulah Mound . . . Was the Price Too High?" *Cherokee One Feather*, November 12, 2015, sec. Letters.

Reinhardt, Akim D., and Clara Sue Kidwell. *Ruling Pine Ridge: Oglala Lakota Politics from the IRA to Wounded Knee*. Lubbock: Texas Tech University Press, 2009.

Rephann, Terance J., Margaret Dalton, Anthony Stair, and Andrew Isserman. "Casino Gambling as an Economic Development Strategy." *Tourism Economics* 3, no. 2 (1997): 161–83.

Rich, Billie Jo, Bo Lossiah, and Myrtle Driver. ᎣᎥᎦᎩ ᎣᏃᏍᏛ ᏔᏍ *(A Very "Wendy" Day)*. Cherokee, N.C.: Eastern Band of Cherokee Indians, 2010.

Richards, Greg. "Production and Consumption of European Cultural Tourism." *Annals of Tourism Research* 23, no. 2 (1996): 261–83.

Rickert, Levi. "Menominee Seventh Grader Suspended for Saying 'I Love You' in Her Native Language," *The Red Phoenix*, February 3, 2012.

Riggs, Brett. "Cherokee Pottery Revitalization Project," 2002. http://rla.unc.edu/Research/CherPot.html.

Roubideaux, Yvette. "Message from the Director: Affordable Care Act Update," September 9, 2013.

Samuels, Ellen. *Fantasies of Identification: Disability, Gender, Race*. New York: NYU Press, 2014.

Samuelson, Paul A. "Social Indifference Curves." *Quarterly Journal of Economics* 70, no. 1 (1956): 1–22.

Schilling, Vincent. "Native Actors Walk Off Set of Adam Sandler Movie After Insults to Women, Elders." *Indian Country Today,* April 23, 2015.

Seagle, Russell. "Fall Indianpreneurship Class Graduates." *Cherokee One Feather,* December 1, 2009.

———. "'Getting Retail Right' Program Wraps Up." *Cherokee One Feather,* July 15, 2009.

———. Interview with the author, Cherokee, N.C. Digital recording, October 2009.

———. Interview with the author, Cherokee, N.C. Digital recording, June 2017.

———. Personal communication. September 13, 2011.

———. "Sequoyah Fund Progress Report 2016." Accessed July 14, 2018. https://www.sequoyahfund.org/wp-content/uploads/2018/02/2016-Annual-Report-1.pdf.

SEED. "Stockton Economic Empowerment Demonstration," 2017. https://www.stocktondemonstration.org.

Sen, Debarati, and Sarasij Majumder. "Narratives of Risk and Poor Rural Women's (Dis)-Engagements with Microcredit-Based Development in Eastern India." *Critique of Anthropology* 35, no. 2 (June 1, 2015): 121–41.

Senate and House of Representatives of the United States of America in Congress. Catawba Indian Land Claims Settlement Act, "H.R. 2399, October 12, 1993.

Sequoyah Fund. "Lending and Training for Business Owners," 2011. https://www.sequoyahfund.org/business-owner.html.

———. "Sequoyah Fund Announces Retail Winners." *Cherokee One Feather,* September 2, 2009.

Service Employees International Union. "Big Bank Profile: Bank of America," 2012. http://www.seiu.org.

Sheldon, David. "Atlanta Will Still Have Georgia Gaming Opportunities on Its Mind in 2017." Casino.org, December 15, 2016. https://www.casino.org/news/atlanta-will-still-have-georgia-gaming-opportunities-on-its-mind-in-2017.

Simpson, Audra. *Mohawk Interruptus: Political Life across the Borders of Settler States.* Durham, N.C.: Duke University Press Books, 2014.

Sleeper-Smith, Susan. *Indian Women and French Men: Rethinking Cultural Encounter in the Western Great Lakes.* Amherst: University of Massachusetts Press, 2001.

Small Business Administration. "Frequently Asked Questions about Small Business," 2012. https://www.sba.gov/advocacy/frequently-asked-questions-about-small-business.

———. "Minority Business Ownership: Data from the 2012 Survey of Business Owners." September 14, 2016. https://www.sba.gov/sites/default/files/advocacy/Minority-Owned-Businesses-in-the-US.pdf.

———. "Tribal Enterprise Business Guide: 8(a) Business Development Program," August 2013. https://www.sba.gov/sites/default/files/Tribal%20Ent%20—%20workbook%20P.pdf.

Small Business Association. "How Important Are Small Businesses to the U.S. Economy?" 2007. https://www.sba.gov/tools/sba-learning-center/search/training.

Smith, Barbara Leigh. "The Twilight Saga and the Quileute Indian Tribe: Opportunity or Cultural Exploitation?" Evergreen State College, July 5, 2011. http://nativecases.evergreen.edu/collection/cases/twilight.

Smith, Bob. Interview with the author, Cherokee, N.C. Digital recording, November 2009.

Smith, Dean Howard. *Modern Tribal Development: Paths to Self-Sufficiency and Cultural Integrity in Indian Country*. Vol. 4. Walnut Creek, Calif.: AltaMira Press, 2000.

Smith, Natalie. Interview with the author, Cherokee, N.C. Digital recording, December 2009.

Smith, Paul Chaat. *Everything You Know about Indians Is Wrong*. Minneapolis: University of Minnesota Press, 2009.

Smoker, Amble. "Business Spotlight: The Little People." *Cherokee One Feather*, June 25, 2015.

———. "Business Spotlight: Two Crowe's Ice Cream." *Cherokee One Feather*, July 9, 2015.

Spilde, Katherine A., and Jonathan B. Taylor. "Economic Evidence on the Effects of the Indian Gaming Regulatory Act on Indians and Non-Indians." *UNLV Gaming Research and Review Journal* 17, no. 1 (2013): 13.

Spruce, Shawn. "Q&A on the New Manage Your EBCI Money Program." *Cherokee One Feather*, November 4, 2011.

Starn, Orin. *Nightwatch: The Politics of Protest in the Andes*. Durham, N.C.: Duke University Press, 1999.

Starnes, Richard D. *Creating the Land of the Sky: Tourism and Society in Western North Carolina*. Tuscaloosa: University of Alabama Press, 2010.

Stevens, Ernest L., Jr. "NIGA Responds to *Time* Article," December 10, 2002. http://archive.li/r5WB1.

Stoll, David. *El Norte or Bust! How Migration Fever and Microcredit Produced a Financial Crash in a Latin American Town*. Lanham, Md.: Rowman & Littlefield, 2012.

Stull, Donald D. "Reservation Economic Development in the Era of Self-Determination." *American Anthropologist* 92, no. 1 (March 1990): 206–10.

Sturm, Circe. *Blood Politics: Race, Culture, and Identity in the Cherokee Nation of Oklahoma*. Berkeley: University of California Press, 2002.

Stynes, Daniel, Ken Hornback, and Dennis Propst. "Money Generation Model (MGM2) Reports." National Parks Service, 2010. http://www.nature.nps.gov /socialscience/products.cfm.

Sulaiman, Munshi, Nathanael Goldberg, Dean Karlan, and Aude de Montesquiou. "Eliminating Extreme Poverty: Comparing the Cost-Effectiveness of Livelihood, Cash Transfer, and Graduation Approaches." CGAP, 2016. http://www.cgap.org /sites/default/files/Forum-Eliminating-Extreme-Poverty-Dec-2016.pdf.

T.O.P. Office. "Budget Council Results—May 31, 2011." *Cherokee One Feather*, June 16, 2011.

Terjesen, Siri, Jan Lepoutre, Rachida Justo, and Niels Bosma. "2009 Report on Social Entrepreneurship." Global Entrepreneurship Monitor, 2009.

Teuton, Christopher B. *Cherokee Stories of the Turtle Island Liars' Club*. Chapel Hill: University of North Carolina Press, 2012.

Teuton, Sean. *Red Land, Red Power: Grounding Knowledge in the American Indian Novel*. Durham, N.C.: Duke University Press Books, 2008.

Thomas, David Hurst. *Skull Wars: Kennewick Man, Archaeology, and the Battle for Native American Identity*. New York: Basic Books, 2000.

Thomas, Robert K. *Cherokee Values and World View*. Chapel Hill: University of North Carolina Press, 1958.

Thompson, Matthew. "Staging 'the Drama': The Continuing Importance of Cultural Tourism in the Gaming Era." Doctoral diss., University of North Carolina, 2009.

Thornton, Russell. *American Indian Holocaust and Survival: A Population History since 1492*. Norman: University of Oklahoma Press, 1987.

Tickamyer, Ann R., and Cynthia M. Duncan. "Poverty and Opportunity Structure in Rural America." *Annual Review of Sociology* 16, no. 1 (August 1990): 67–86.

Tingey, Lauren, Francene Larzelere-Hinton, Novalene Goklish, Allison Ingalls, Todd Craft, Feather Sprengeler, Courtney McGuire, and Allison Barlow. "Entrepreneurship Education: A Strength-Based Approach to Substance Use and Suicide Prevention for American Indian Adolescents." *American Indian and Alaska Native Mental Health Research: The Journal of the National Center* 23, no. 3 (September 2016): 248–70.

Travel Industry Association of America. *The Historical/Cultural Traveler*. Washington, D.C.: Travel Industry Association, 2003.

United States Bureau of Labor Statistics. "Current Employment Statistics." Accessed April 6, 2017. https://www.bls.gov/ces/.

United States Commission on Civil Rights. "Broken Promises: Revaluating the Native American Health Care System." Washington, D.C.: U.S. Commission on Civil Rights, 2004. http://www.usccr.gov/pubs/nahealth/nabroken.pdf.

United States Department of Interior. Indian Arts and Crafts Board: The Indian Arts and Crafts Act of 1990. September 2, 2010.

United States Department of Labor. "Davis-Bacon and Related Acts: WH Publication 1246." Accessed August 3, 2015. https://www.dol.gov/whd/govcontracts/dbra.htm.

United States Green Building Council. "About LEED." Accessed July 17, 2018. https://new.usgbc.org/leed.

United States Senate Committee on Indian Affairs. "Barrasso Introduces the Interior Improvement Act," July 29, 2015. http://www.indian.senate.gov/news/press-release/barrasso-introduces-interior-improvement-act.

Usner, Daniel H. *Indian Work: Language and Livelihood in Native American History*. Cambridge, Mass.: Harvard University Press, 2009.

Van Gundy, Karen. "Substance Abuse in Rural and Small Town America." Carsey Institute, June 15, 2006. http://www.carseyinstitute.unh.edu/publications/Report_SubstanceAbuse.pdf.

Velasquez-Manoff, Moises. "What Happens When the Poor Receive a Stipend?" *New York Times*, January 18, 2014. http://opinionator.blogs.nytimes.com/2014 /01/18/what-happens-when-the-poor-receive-a-stipend.

Vinsel, Lee. "Maintainers 2016 Papers." The Maintainers. Accessed January 11, 2017. http://themaintainers.org/program.

Vizenor, Gerald. "George Morrison: Anishinaabe Expressionist Artist." *American Indian Quarterly* 30, no. 3/4 (June 2006): 646–60.

Wachacha, Mary. "Commentary." *Cherokee One Feather*, September 8, 2011.

Waycaster, Darlene. *Cherokee Chamber of Commerce News.* Vol. C, 2009.

———. Interview with the author, Cherokee, N.C. Digital recording, June 2009.

Webster, Joseph H. "New DOJ Position on Internet Gaming Creates Both Uncertainty and Opportunities for Tribes." Indian Country Today Media Network. January 3, 2012. https://indiancountrymedianetwork.com/news/new -doj-position-on-internet-gaming-creates-both-uncertainty-and-opportunities -for-tribes.

Weiser, John, and Ben Sherman. *Qualla 2020 Final Report*, August 2014.

Widenhouse, Ernie. Interview with the author, Cherokee, N.C. Digital recording, January 2010.

Wildcat, Curtis. Interview with the author, Cherokee, N.C. Digital recording, July 2012.

Williamson, Teresa, and Ray Williamson. Interview with the author, Cherokee, N.C. Digital Recording, January 2010.

Williamson, Thad, David L. Imbroscio, and Gar Alperovitz. *Making a Place for Community: Local Democracy in a Global Era.* New York: Routledge, 2002.

Willmott, Cory. "Radical Entrepreneurs: First Nations Designers—Approaches to Community Economic Development." *Anthropology of Work Review* 35, no. 2 (2014): 95.

Wilson, Woodrow. "Speech." Pittsburg, Pa., January 29, 1916.

Wolf, Eric R. *Europe and the People without History.* Berkeley, Calif.: University of California Press, 1982.

Wolfe, Patrick. "Settler Colonialism and the Elimination of the Native." *Journal of Genocide Research* 8, no. 4 (2006): 387–409.

Wolfe, Zena, and Charla Crowe. Interview with the author, Cherokee, N.C. Digital recording, October 2009.

Yanagisako, Sylvia Junko. *Producing Culture and Capital: Family Firms in Italy.* Princeton, N.J.: Princeton University Press, 2002.

Yellowtail, Bethany. "B.Yellowtail," 2017. https://www.byellowtail.com.

Zukin, Sharon. "Socio-Spacial Prototypes of a New Organization of Consumption: The Role of Real Cultural Capital." *Sociology* 24, no. 1 (1990): 37.

Index

Note: Italic page numbers refer to illustrations.

American Indian small businesses: and artists, 1, 10, 11, 23, 26, 32, 37, 40, 42, 51, 60–63, 71–72, 75–79, 107–12, 138, 140, 152, 159, 160, 163, 168, 171, 174, 182, 185, 229n93, 247n1; collective diversity of, 2–3, 4, 10, 20, 21–23, 115, 138, 140, 141–42, 147, 148, 182, 186, 189–90, 193, 197; and community support activities, 2, 42, 75, 76, 77–78, 144–46, 182; and political economy, 2, 219n3; and representations, 2, 19, 80; and family-business ownership, 4, 18–19, 31, 32–37, 45, 91, 103, 167, 169, 171, 173, 174, 181, 245n45; land, legal, and representational boundaries affecting, 4; Native Nation-ownership, 4, 219n4; collective actions of, 5, 12–13; familial arrangement of business integration, 5–6; Cherokee Casino's impact on, 6, 45, 47, 65–66, 138–40, 160; and leasing spaces, 6–7; private ownership, 7, 9, 179, 219n4; EBCI support for, 9, 18, 26, 37, 43, 47, 63–64, 65, 67, 69–80, 91, 149, 153, 154–55, 156, 157–60, 229n85, 229n89, 242–43n10; role in reducing economic precarity, 9–10, 16, 20, 137–40; banks refusing loans for, 10–11; growth trends in, 12, 220n21; research on, 12–13; and multiplier effect, 13, 221n25; impact on governance and economy, 18, 195, 196–97; physical spaces of, 21–22, 32; practices of, 21–22, 27, 28, 29, 44, 197; structural boundaries of, 35, 45, 82; and multigenerational ownership, 45; and heritage tourism, 49–50, 75–76, 78, 229n89; and citizenship, 101–2; and brain drain, 105–6, 143, 144; and economic redistribution efforts, 140; and job creation, 143–44; unpaid family labor in, 167, 219n3, 245n45; and local community needs, 183, 184–85

American Indian small-business owners: challenges of, 2–3, 153–54; community-focused attitude of, 2, 42, 75, 76, 77–78, 144–46, 182; and markets, 2, 18, 22, 24, 31, 34, 37–44, 183, 184, 195; and Great Recession, 3, 10–12, 137, 156, 165; local, national, and international contexts of, 4; collective actions of, 5, 12–13; and representations, 19, 80, 112; citizenship of, 20, 101–7, 112; contributions of, 20, 150–51; and "dying breed" stories, 22–31; and tourism industry, 48–49, 70, 79–80; as authority on authenticity, 59–61, 77–78; and internet access, 90, 231n33; protections of business secrets, 110–11; bureaucratic requirements for, 152–53, 160, 162–64; financial and structural help for, 156–60, 197; and employee regulation and management, 160–67, 244nn36–37, 245n39; training and promotion for, 167–80, 181, 197, 245n44; and health problems, 179–80; and debt accumulation, 193–94

American Indian studies, 121

Analenisgi Recovery Center, 124

Analenisgi Substance Abuse and Mental Health Center, 166

Anderson, Benedict, 228n48

Anthony Edward Lossiah Justice Center, 124

anthropology, and authenticity, 52–53, 226n17

Appalachian Access, 136

Appalachian Mountains, 10

Arch, Davy, 138

Arch, Sabrina (Eastern Band citizen), 170

Artisan Studio Fund, 200

Asheville, North Carolina, 50, 56, 81

assimilation, 25, 26, 29, 30, 148

Atse Kituwah Academy (Cherokee-language-immersion academy), 1, 37, 73, 121, 124, 130

Australia, 195
Australian aboriginals, 95–96, 195
"Authentically Cherokee" brand,
78–79
authenticity: of American Indians as
entrepreneurs, 17, 23, 24, 29; of representations of American Indians, 49,
51–55, 57–63, 64, 67, 78, 94, 112,
232n47; and tourism industry, 49,
51–55, 57–64, 76–79, 95–96;
constructions of, 52, 53, 63; and
nationalist ideologies, 52–53, 59; and
settler-colonial society, 53, 55, 88;
staged authenticity, 53; and Eastern
band agency, 62–64, 65, 79; and
Native-styled art, 78, 107–11, 229n93;
and land status, 94, 95, 232n47
autonomy, 3, 19

Baker, Fred A., 87
Baker Roll (1924), 87, 88, 104
BalsamWest FiberNet, 90, 136, 239n93
Bank of America, 11
Barker, Joanne, 84, 117
Baxter, Cinda, 42
Begay, Manley A., Jr., 122
Benson, David, 158
Beyond Buckskin, 27, 222–23n26
Bigmeat pottery, 7
Bill Taylor Scholarship, 169
Biolsi, Thomas, 115
Bizarre Foods (television show), 23
Black Power movement, 56
Blankenship, Cory, 244n25
Blankenship, Lynn, 243n10
Blankenship, Ron: and Talking Leaves,
32–33; and family-based businesses,
34; and authenticity questions, 59,
72; and representation of American
Indian identity, 62, 183; and
citizenship, 104; and employment, 143;
and community support, 145; and
finances, 156; and entrepreneurship,
168; and success, 174
Blattman, Christopher, 131

blood-quantum measures, 52, 86,
87–88, 101–3, 106, 112
Blue Ridge law, 219n8
Blue Ridge National Heritage Area and
Smoky Mountain Host, 185
Blue Ridge Parkway, 50
Blythe, Larry, 154
Boome, Peter (Upper Skagit citizen),
171
border theory, 17, 19
Bourdieu, Pierre, 94
brain drain, 105–6, 143, 144
Britton, Steve, 95
Brown, Wendy, 31, 45
Bruner, Edward, 53, 57
Bruyneel, Kevin, 116
Bryson City, North Carolina, 37, 38,
91, 184
Buffalo Bill's Wild West show, 49
buffering and privacy, 38–41, 40, 51
Bureau of Indian Affairs (BIA), 85, 89,
91, 92, 109, 147, 157, 187, 190, 193
Bush, George W., 127
Business Enterprise Fund, 199–200
Business Opportunity Fair, 169
Butler, Elizur, 83
"Buy Local" movement, 41–43, 44, 45,
225n70
BWB Solutions, 188

California Native Nations, 223–24n39
California v. Cabazon Band of Mission
Indians (1987), 125
Canada, 194
capital building, 20, 34, 36, 45, 156–57
capitalism: and economic identity, 18;
concepts of, 27–31; heterogeneous
practices of, 29, 44–45; family
capitalism, 33, 34; racial capitalism,
228n46
Capital Projects Fund, 200
Catawba Indian Tribe of South Carolina
Land Claims Settlement Act, 187
Catawba Nation, 135, 187
Cattelino, Jessica, 15, 20, 26, 119

Cherokee Nation Indians distinguished from, 84; citizenship qualifications, 88, 106–7, 109, 112, 231nn28–29

Cherokee Nation Indians, 82–83, 230n9

Cherokee Nation v. Georgia (1831), 82

Cherokee Nation West, 83

Cherokee One Feather: on Small Business Saturday, 43–44; on chiefing, 61; on authenticity, 65; on tourism industry, 67, 71, 228n68; on representations, 69, 228n66; on Native American identity, 88; on Duke Energy, 97; on citizenship, 109; on gaming enterprises, 134; on Eastern Band citizen–owned alcoholic beverage distributorship, 139; on community support, 146; on funeral home, 150; on Valley River Casino, 185–86; on Walmart, 191, 192; on price gouging, 233n61; on disenrollment, 233n68; on alcohol sales, 238n80, 238n82; on Cherokee Preservation Foundation, 240n100; on taxation, 244n25

Cherokee Pottery Revitalization Project, 138

Cherokee Preservation Foundation (CPF), 36, 69, 137–38, 155, 175, 188–89, 215–16, 240nn99–100

Cherokee Pride, 175

Cherokee-specific courses, 63

Cherokee syllabary, 1, 5, 8–9, 32, 229n75

Cherokee Transit Service, 139

Cherokee Tribal Community Services program, 243n25

Cherokee Tribal Food Distribution Program, 124

Cherokee Tri-Council, 109

Cherokee War Dance and Eagle Tail Dance, 234n1

chiefing, 51, 55, 61, 79, 159

Churchill Roll (1908), 87

civil rights movement, 56

Clapsaddle, Annette, 154

Cobell v. Salazar (2009), 14, 148

Colloredo-Mansfeld, Rudi, 23–24

community support activities, and American Indian small businesses, 2, 42, 75, 76, 77–78, 144–46, 182

Cooper, Jim, 34

Cornell, Stephen, 15, 20, 142

Corporation for Enterprise Development (CFED), 223n33, 245n54. *See also* Prosperity Now

corporations: corporate dividends compared to Native Nation dividend payments, 127–28; cooperative corporations, 128; U.S. government-owned corporations, 128; alternative corporate ownership models, 129; private ownership of, 129; U.S. financial system's support for, 155

Costello, E. Jane, 132, 166

Council Roll (1907), 87

Cracker Barrel, 190

Credit Builder Fund, 199

Crowe, Charla, 5–9, 7, 34

cultural capital, 94–96, 232n47

cultural reclamation efforts, 2, 120–21, 137

cultural revitalization actions, 3, 120. *See also* cultural reclamation efforts

cultural tourism, 49, 58, 76

dark tourism, 49

Davis, Carmen, 222n6

Davis, Gary "Litefoot," 23, 222n6

Davis-Bacon Act, 162, 244n33

Dawes Commission Rolls (1906), 88, 231n28

Deloria, Philip, 23

Deloria, Vine, Jr., 52, 234n11

Dennison, Jean, 116, 119

development theory, debates in, 195

Diné Nation, 31

Disneyland, 94

dividend payments: and gaming enterprises, 126, 127–33, 237n59; corporate dividends compared to Native Nation dividend payments, 127–28; for Eastern Band citizens, 127, 128, 131–33; and lump-sum payments for minors at age eighteen, 129–32, 137, 158–59, 193, 237n67; and American Indian small-business owners, 158, 181, 193; and seasonal employees, 166, 181

DNA testing for paternity, 104

Dollywood, 94, 227n41

Dombrowski, Kirk, 15, 54

Downtown Revitalization Fund, 199

Drake Enterprises, 136

Duke Energy, 97–101, 99, 133

EARTH University, 240n99

Eastern Band citizens: and youth, 1, 129–32, 137, 144–45, 158–59, 166, 176–79, 193, 195–96, 237n67, 237n73, 246n72, 247n77; innovative expressions of self-determination, 3; and Cherokee by Design's popularity, 8–9; individual entrepreneurship practices of, 16, 24, 28; and tourism industry, 19, 39, 41, 45, 49, 50, 55, 58, 61–62, 71–75, 78; and history of American Indian small-business owners, 26; and family-based businesses, 34; employment of, 35–36, 42; homes and living spaces on Qualla Boundary, 39–40; and chiefing, 51; average income of, 58; representations of, 62–64, 65; and citizenship of American Indian small-business owners, 106, 109, 110, 112; dividend payments for, 127, 128, 131–33; as shareholders of EBCI as corporation, 127; financial education of, 130, 237n73; and hiring practices, 161–62

Eastern Band of Cherokee Indian Heritage Development Initiative, 225n3

EBCI (Eastern Band Cherokee Indian) government: gaming enterprises of, 3, 5, 18, 20, 47, 65, 79, 92–93, 112, 117, 119, 122–40, 185–88, 189, 248n8; tourism industry of, 3, 5, 19, 26, 38, 39, 41, 45, 47, 48–49, 51, 53–54, 57, 58, 61, 62–67, 69, 76, 79, 81, 110–11, 119, 136, 140, 142, 186–87, 190–91, 192, 193, 225n3; and private small businesses, 7, 9, 179, 219n4; Sequoyah Fund, 7, 43, 75, 78, 130, 138, 155, 157, 159, 169–70, 173, 176, 199–200, 215, 229n85, 242–43n10; economic successes achieved by, 9; and mitigation of economic precarity, 9, 133–40; small-business development efforts of, 9, 18, 26, 37, 43, 47, 63–64, 65, 67, 69–80, 91, 149, 153, 154–55, 156, 157–60, 182, 186, 188, 195, 197, 229n85, 229n89, 242–43n10; American Indian small-business owners' collective actions for, 12; and Ramah Navajo Chapter Settlement, 14; business history of, 19; cooperative shop hosted by, 19, 61; economic sovereignty of, 19, 21, 82, 88, 92–93, 115, 122–23, 124, 157, 182, 185, 186–87, 188; museum hosted by, 19; and representations, 19, 62–66, 67, 68, 69–80, 76, 78, 79–80, 139, 183, 228n66; sovereignty of, 19, 85, 86, 113–15, 114; theater hosted by, 19; Office of Budget and Finance's Revenue Office, 21; history of, 26, 116; American Indian small-business owners support for, 31; enterprises of, 43, 123, 136, 138, 148, 186, 240n112; and authenticity, 62–64, 78; Downtown Business Master Plan, 67; "Artisan and Craftsman" District, 69; Cultural District Streetscape, 69; citizenship qualifications, 81, 84, 85–88, 101–7, 112, 230n2; federal recognition of, 81, 219–20n9; land boundaries of, 82–85, 86, 87, 88, 89, 96–97, 111, 112; incorporation of, 84,

86, 117, 127; agency of, 85; Tribal Council, 85, 86, 87, 90, 91, 104, 109, 124, 128, 130, 137, 154–55, 158, 185, 186, 240n106, 242n7; censuses of, 86–87, 244n36; and land scarcity, 88–101, 106–7, 112; land purchased in Cherokee County, 89, 92–93; fiber-optic network of, 90; and land leasing, 91–93, 94, 232n41; Housing Summit, 92; Enrollment Committee, 104; and passports, 113–14, 213, 234n5; Travel and Promotion tourism campaign, 113; campaign contributions of, 119, 235n22; and economic development, 120, 137, 154, 155, 157, 180–81, 182, 189, 192, 242n9; Governing Documents Review Committee, 122; and dividend payments, 127–33; Minors' Trust Fund, 129, 137, 237n67; debt fund, 136–37, 193; Emergency Management, 146; and land management, 155; Office of Planning and Development, 155, 190, 215; loan programs of, 157; and employee regulation and management, 160–67; Tribal Employment Rights Commission, 161–62; and training and promotion, 167–80, 181; Enterprise Development, 170; and knowledge industry, 186, 187; and chain stores and restaurants, 190–92; and individual possessory holdings, 190; and real estate management, 190; enrollment facts, 205–6; disenrollment policies, 207–9; enrollment qualifications, 211–12; Small Business Assistance Offices, 215–16; and Blue Ridge law, 219n8; Kituwah Economic Development board, 240n112. See also Eastern Band citizens; Qualla Boundary

Ecological Indian stereotype, 28

economic bases: economic sovereignty protecting, 13; historic destruction of Native Nations' economic bases, 120, 148; concept of, 221n27

economic change, and assimilation, 25, 26

economic development: choices in, 3; and Native Nation economic sovereignty, 13, 16, 48, 100, 118, 119, 121, 125–27, 236n54; conceptions of, 15–16, 197; merits of globalized and local projects, 17–18; and social entre-preneurship, 25; and neoliberalism, 30; and EBCI, 120, 137, 154, 155, 157, 180–81, 182, 189, 192, 242n9; and gaming enterprises, 125

economic hegemony: defining of, 14; and forced acculturation and assimilation, 26; and sacred lands, 100; and land boundaries, 111–12; and Native American political sovereignty, 116, 126, 141, 187, 194; and EBCI's gaming enterprises, 125–27

economic identity, measures of, 3. See also American Indian economic identity

economic modernization, 25

economic precarity: EBCI's mitigation of, 9, 133–40; and role of American Indian small businesses, 9–10, 16, 20, 137–40; and one-industry dominant economies, 15, 20, 186, 188; and debt accumulation, 193

Economic Security Project, 131

economic self-determination, 3, 13, 122, 148

economic sovereignty: and strengthen-ing of overall sovereignty, 3, 5; defining of, 13; and economic self-determination, 13; goals of, 13–14; economic power distinguished from, 14–15; and Native Nation political sovereignty, 14, 116, 117, 118–19, 187; protections and practices for, 17–18, 197; of EBCI, 19, 21, 82, 88, 92–93, 115, 122–23, 124, 157, 182, 185, 186–87, 188. See also Native Nation economic sovereignty economic stability: of Native Nation governments, 4–5, 13, 15, 20, 119–20, 149, 194; sustainability of, 5, 9–10, 188, 194–97; small-business sector providing, 15, 17, 18–20, 115; for indigenous peoples, 16–17; and tourism industry, 51

economic syncretism, 25

economic violence: defining of, 14; and forced acculturation and assimilation, 26; and sacred lands, 100; and Native American political sovereignty, 116, 141, 187, 194

economy management, 13–14

education: and support for American Indian small-business owners, 20, 167–80, 181, 197, 245n44; and children and youth's financial training, 130, 144–45, 176–79, 237n73, 247n77

entrepreneurship: of American Indian people, 4, 12, 16, 17, 18, 22, 23, 24, 28, 29, 30, 45, 141–49, 194; conceptions of, 4, 12, 22, 23, 24, 28–29, 44, 189, 220–21n24, 223n33; statistics on, 12, 220n23; and cultural-mismatch fallacy, 23–24, 26, 31, 44–45, 189, 195; social entrepreneurship, 24, 25–26, 27, 28, 31, 222n13, 223n29, 223n33; historical American Indian entrepreneurship, 25–27; and capitalism, 27–31; contextual distinctiveness of, 28, 115, 121–22; and children and youth's financial training, 130, 144–45, 176–79, 237n73, 247n77; and Cherokee Preservation Foundation, 138; economic impacts of, 142–44; and multiplier effect, 142–43; community impacts of, 144–46; sovereignty impacts of, 146–47; and nation building, 149; and neoliberalism, 155, 179; culture of, 189; in Australia, 195. See also American Indian small-business owners; Indianpreneurship

environmental justice movements, 3

environmental preservation projects, 137, 240n99

Esarey, Duane, 24

Expo Center, 90

Fall Festival, 159, 244n26

familial mythology, 59, 79, 227–28n45

Fiala, Nathan, 131

fictional tourism, 50–51

Finger, John R., 26, 55

Finger-Smith, Anita, 230n11

First Citizens Bank, 130

Fletcher v. Peck (1810), 84

Florida State University, Osceola mascot, 55

The Flower Bug florist shop, 9

Forget, Evelyn, 131, 132

Foucault, Michel, 221n28

1491s (comedy troupe), 27, 223n26, 226n24

Fourteenth Amendment, 230n11

Fraser, James Earle, *The End of the Trail,* 49

Friedman, Milton, 131

Frontier Land, 53, 58

gadugi concept, 128, 146, 182

gaming enterprises: of EBCI, 3, 5, 18, 20, 47, 65, 79, 92–93, 112, 117, 119, 122–40, 185–88, 189, 248n8; research on, 16; and economic change, 26; and class designations of, 125–26; and economic hegemony, 125–27; and state governments, 125–26, 134, 236n52, 236n54, 239n90, 243n22; and dividend payments, 126, 127–33, 237n59; and market saturation, 133, 137, 238–39n84; and mitigating economic precarity of, 133–40; political debates on, 134–35; geographical restrictions on, 135, *135,* 248n8; and tourism industry, 140, 239n88; of Catawba Nation, 187

reservation lands: and neoliberalism, 30; leasing and possessory landholding laws, 35; checkerboarding of, 89; and land scarcity, 95; and American Indian small-business owners, 173; low-cost leasing to cattle ranchers, 223n37; and Google Maps, 231n32

Revitalization of Traditional Cherokee Artisan Resources (RTCAR) initiative, 138

Richards, Greg, 94

Riggs, Brett, 138

River's Edge Outfitters, 146

River Walk, 39

Road to Soco basket-weave pattern, 8, 177

Rogers, James, 97

Roubideaux, Yvette, 247n79

Sampson, Will (Muscogee [Creek] Nation), 57

Samuelson, Paul A., 130–31

Santa Fe Southwestern Association for Indian Arts, 160

Santa's Land theme park, 150

Sault Ste. Marie Tribe of Chippewa Indians (SSMTC), 117–18, 133

Saunooke Village, 90

Schwarzenegger, Arnold, 223–24n39

scratch test, 52, 226n17

Seagle, Russ (EBCI Sequoyah Fund, non-Native), 42, 157, 170–71, 173, 178–79, 183, 242n10

self-advocacy, 178

self-determination, 3, 13, 122, 148

Seminole Tribe of Florida, 26, 55, 125, 187, 188

Seminole Tribe of Florida v. Butterworth (1981), 125

Seneca Nation, 119

Sequoyah, as creator of Cherokee syllabary, 5

settler-colonial society: indigenous relationships with, 3, 4, 88–89, 195; economic subjugations of, 4, 14;

economic attacks leveled by, 14, 15, 120; and land procurement, 23, 84–85, 106–7; American Indian entrepreneurs operating within, 28, 30, 45; and authenticity, 53, 55, 88; and reservations, 95; and American Indian citizenship, 106–7, 231n29; and Native Nation political sovereignty, 115, 116–17; and resource acquisition, 194

Seven Clans beer, 139, 240n106

Sherman, Ben, 188

Sider, Gerald, 54

Simpson, Audra, 85

The Simpsons (television show), 29

Sitting Bull, 49

Sleeper-Smith, Susan, 24

Small Business Administration (SBA), 12, 152, 220n21, 246n59

small businesses: impact in global indigenous context, 3, 17–18; entrepreneurship compared to, 12, 220–21n24; minority-owned small businesses, 12; private-sector employment created by, 12; private ownership of, 219n4; individualism associated with, 222n12. *See also* American Indian small businesses; American Indian small-business owners

Small Business Saturday, 41, 43–44

Smith, Abe, 102–3, 105, 143, 165, 167, 174

Smith, Adam, 30

Smith, Dean Howard, 141

Smith, Natalie, 1, 36–37, 40, 75–76, 78, 96–98, 105, 143, 157, 165

Snowbird, 89, 231n32

social capital, 121

social entrepreneurship, 24, 25–26, 27, 28, 31, 222n13, 223n29, 223n33

South, 26

South Carolina, 82, 187

Southeast Tribes Festival, 64

South Park (television show), 29

CPSIA information can be obtained
at www.ICGtesting.com
Printed in the USA
LVHW090956220821
695823LV00001B/4